Visual QuickStart Guide

Microsoft Office 2000

for Windows

Steve Sagman

Revised for
this edition by
Gail Taylor

 **Peachpit Press**

Visual QuickStart Guide
Microsoft Office 2000 for Windows
Steve Sagman

Peachpit Press
1249 Eighth Street
Berkeley, CA 94710
(510) 524-2178
(510) 524-2221 (fax)

Find us on the World Wide Web at: http://www.peachpit.com

Peachpit Press is a division of Addison Wesley Longman

Project Editor: Lisa Theobald
Production Coordinator: Amy Changar
Editor: Jennifer Harris
Cover design: The Visual Group

ISBN: 0-201-35440-3

0 9 8 7 6 5 4 3 2 1

Printed and bound in the United States of America

 Printed on recycled paper

About the Authors

More than a million readers worldwide know Steve Sagman's books on PC software, including his international best-sellers on Harvard Graphics and PowerPoint. In 1995, his book *Traveling The Microsoft Network* was given the Award of Achievement for Design from the Society of Technical Communication.

His company, Studioserv (www.studioserv.com), provides book packaging and development, courseware, user documentation, and user interface consulting.

He welcomes comments, questions, and suggestions and can be reached at steves@studioserv.com.

Gail Taylor has written guide books for software and hardware since the mid 1980s. In addition to writing, she has a background in teaching and drafting, which helps her add illustrative graphics to the publications she designs.

After many years as an in-house writer and editor, during which she received accolades for a number of her publications, she moved to a tiny community on Vancouver Island where she now conducts most of her writing business over the Internet.

Gail welcomes e-mail at gtaylor@islandnet.com

Other Books by Steve Sagman

Running Microsoft PowerPoint 2000

Microsoft PhotoDraw 2000 At a Glance

Windows 98: Visual QuickStart Guide**

The Official Microsoft Image Composer Book

Running PowerPoint 97

Windows 95: Visual QuickStart Guide**

Running PowerPoint for Windows 95

Traveling The Microsoft Network

Running Windows 95*

Microsoft Office for Macintosh: Visual QuickStart Guide

Microsoft Office for Windows: Visual QuickStart Guide**

Harvard Graphics for Windows 2: Visual QuickStart Guide**

Running PowerPoint 4

The PC Bible* **

Mastering CorelDraw 4* **

Using 1-2-3 for Windows Release 4*

Using Freelance Graphics 2

Mastering CorelDraw 3* **

Using Windows Draw

Getting Your Start in Hollywood**

1-2-3 Graphics Techniques

Using Harvard Graphics

*　　Contributor

**　　Also published by Peachpit Press

Acknowledgments

I'd like to thank the fine writer Gail Taylor for her superb work in revising my earlier Microsoft Office book for this new edition.

I'd also like to thank Jennifer Harris for her fine copy editing and both Lisa Theobald and Amy Changar at Peachpit Press for their extraordinary efforts on my behalf.

TABLE OF CONTENTS

TABLE OF CONTENTS

Part 1
Common Office Techniques

Part 1
Common Office
Techniques

Introducing Windows

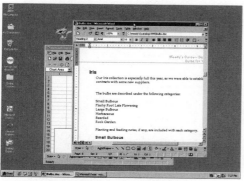

Figure 1.1 The Windows graphical working environment.

Microsoft Windows creates a graphical working environment on your PC screen that enables you to operate your computer using visual controls rather than typed commands (**Figure 1.1**). The Windows desktop includes icons, menus, and buttons that you can click with the mouse to perform various tasks, such as organize your folders and files, run programs, control your printer, and browse the Web.

Because all programs that run in Windows, like Word and Excel, run in on-screen windows that have similar menus, buttons, and other controls, they all work alike. This similarity makes it easy to learn and use Windows programs like those in Microsoft Office—you can simply transfer your knowledge of one program to all the others.

Windows provides other benefits too. You can open more than one window at a time and run programs side by side, and you can view your work on screen as it will look when it is printed or published on the Web.

The Windows Desktop

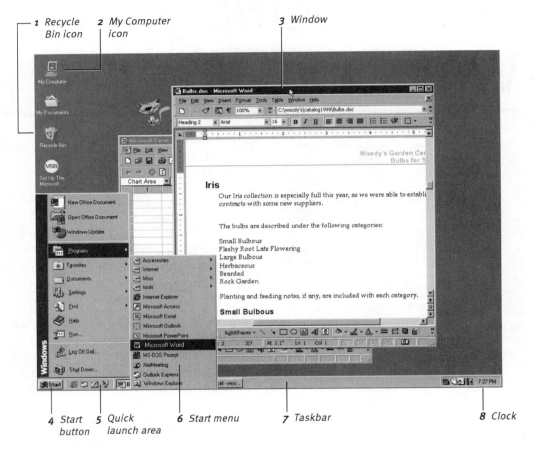

1 Recycle Bin icon   **2** My Computer icon   **3** Window

4 Start button   **5** Quick launch area   **6** Start menu   **7** Taskbar   **8** Clock

Figure 1.3 The Windows desktop.

Key to the Windows Desktop

1 Recycle Bin icon

Temporary storage space for deleted files. Drag a file or folder to the Recycle Bin to delete it. To permanently delete items, double-click the Recycle Bin to open it and then choose Empty Recycle Bin from the File menu.

2 My Computer icon

Access to various resources available on your computer. Double-click to open.

3 Window

The title bar of a window identifies the window and usually tells you the name of the open document. The window in which you are working is the active window, and its title bar is vividly colored. The title bars of inactive windows are a different, usually muted, color. Drag the title bar to move a window.

4 Start button

Click the Start button to open a menu of programs, view documents you've recently worked in, change system settings, find items on your computer, and initiate the shutting down of your computer.

5 Quick launch area

Click these icons to quickly open programs such as Internet Explorer.

6 Start menu

Click an item on the Start menu to start a program or perform a task.

7 Taskbar

Shows all currently running programs. Click a button on the taskbar to open the window it represents. Click the button again to hide the window.

8 Clock

Position the mouse pointer on the time without clicking to display the date.

THE WINDOWS DESKTOP

Using the Mouse

Although you can control Windows with the keyboard, it's much easier to use the mouse.

To click:

◆ Position the pointer on a menu, a button, or an icon and click the left mouse button once (**Figures 1.3** and **1.4**).

To double-click:

◆ Position the pointer on an item and click the left mouse button twice in quick succession (**Figure 1.5**).

To select:

1. Position the pointer on the first item to select.

2. Click and hold down the mouse button.

3. Move the mouse pointer across the items to select (**Figure 1.6**).

4. Release the mouse button.

To drag:

1. Position the pointer on an item.

2. Click and hold down the left mouse button.

3. Move the mouse.

4. Release the mouse button.

To scroll:

1. Drag the scroll button in the scroll bar up or down (**Figure 1.7**).

   or

2. Click a scroll arrow at either end of the scroll bar.

Figure 1.3 Click a toolbar button.

Figure 1.4 Click a menu item to select it.

Figure 1.5 Double-click an icon to open a document.

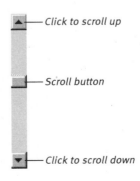

Figure 1.6 Selecting a range of dates in a calendar.

Click to scroll up

Scroll button

Click to scroll down

Figure 1.7 Drag the scroll button or click the scroll arrows.

Figure 1.8 Click a menu name to open the menu.

Figure 1.9 A menu item with a submenu.

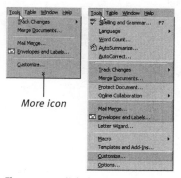

More icon

Figure 1.10 Click the More icon to expand a collapsed menu.

Figure 1.11 Pause on a toolbar button to view a description.

Choosing from Menus and Toolbars

The menu bar is located directly below the title bar at the top of every program window. You can click the names on the menu bar to open menus of commands or options. A menu item followed by an arrow accesses a submenu with more options. The submenu opens when you position the mouse pointer on the menu item.

To choose from a menu:

1. Click a menu name (**Figure 1.8**).

2. Click an item on a menu.

or

If the item is followed by an arrow, position the mouse pointer on the item to open the submenu and then click an item on the submenu (**Figure 1.9**).

To choose from a toolbar:

◆ Click a toolbar button.

✔ Tips

■ Menus in Office programs might be collapsed to show only frequently used items. To view the complete menu, click the More icon at the bottom of the menu (**Figure 1.10**) or pause with the pointer on any menu option.

■ Menu items that are grayed out are not currently available.

■ To display a tooltip, which is a description of a toolbar button, position the pointer on the button and pause for a moment without clicking (**Figure 1.11**).

Making Selections in Dialog Boxes

Dialog boxes offer a group of related options. You can change one or more settings in a dialog box and then click OK to implement the changes.

To make selections in a dialog box:

◆ Click a check box or an option button (**Figure 1.12**).

or

Click the arrows next to a numeric entry to increase or decrease the value (**Figure 1.12**).

or

Click the arrow button next to a drop-down list entry to open the list and then click an item in the list (**Figure 1.13**).

or

Type an entry in a text box or double-click an entry and type replacement text (**Figure 1.13**).

✔ Tips

■ To bring a different set of options to the front within the dialog box, you can click a tab (**Figure 1.13**).

■ You can press the Tab key to move to the next entry in the dialog box or press Shift+Tab to move to the previous entry.

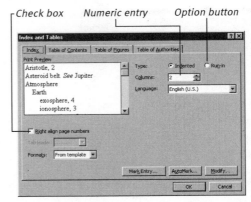

Figure 1.12 A dialog box with check boxes, option buttons, and numeric entries.

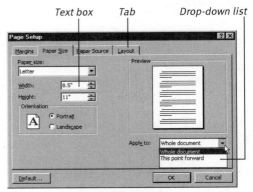

Figure 1.13 A dialog box with drop-down lists and text boxes.

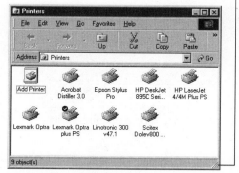

Figure 1.14 Drag a window's title bar to move the window.

Drag the window corner

Figure 1.15 Drag the corner of a window to resize the window.

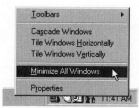

Figure 1.16 To switch to a window, click its icon on the taskbar.

Figure 1.17 Choose Minimize All Windows from the taskbar shortcut menu.

Managing Windows

As you work in a program, you can move or resize its window. You can also maximize a window to fill the screen or minimize it to temporarily set it aside as an item on the taskbar but leave it running.

To move a window:

◆ Position the pointer on the window's title bar and press and hold the mouse button as you drag the window (**Figure 1.14**).

To resize a window:

◆ Position the pointer on the window's corner and, when you see the diagonal pointer, drag to resize the window (**Figure 1.15**).

To minimize a window:

◆ Click the Minimize button (**Figure 1.15**).

To restore a minimized window:

◆ Click the button for the window on the taskbar (**Figure 1.16**).

To maximize a window:

◆ Click the Maximize button.

✔ Tip

■ To minimize all windows, you can right-click the taskbar and then click Minimize All Windows from the shortcut menu (**Figure 1.17**).

Switching and Closing Windows

You can work in only one window at a time, even though you might have several windows open on the screen. To close a program or document, you can close its window. If the document is not yet saved, the program will ask whether you want to save your changes.

To switch windows:

◆ Click any visible part of the window.

or

Click the button for the window on the taskbar (**Figure 1.18**).

To close a window:

◆ Click the Close button on the window (**Figure 1.19**).

or

Right-click the button for the window on the taskbar and choose Close from the shortcut menu. (**Figure 1.20**).

✔ Tip

■ If one window fills the screen, you might have to click its Restore button to return it to a partial-screen window (**Figure 1.19**). You will then be able to see and click other windows.

Figure 1.18 Click the button for a window on the taskbar to switch to that window.

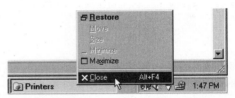

Figure 1.19 The Close and Restore buttons.

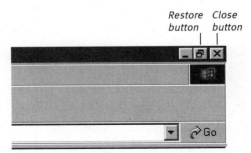

Figure 1.20 Choose Close from the taskbar's shortcut menu.

OFFICE TECHNIQUES

Figure 2.1 Menus and toolbars in the Office applications.

One advantage of working in the Microsoft Office applications is the body of procedures, menus, and toolbars that the applications share (**Figure 2.1**). If a procedure, menu, or toolbar works a certain way in one application, it almost always works identically in all the other applications.

Become acquainted with the common techniques in this chapter early and try them in any application. They always work, and you'll be using them constantly.

Undoing a Change

Remember Undo! You can undo just about any error.

To undo a change:

◆ Click the Undo button on the Standard toolbar (**Figure 2.2**).

or

Press Ctrl+Z.

or

From the Edit menu, choose the Undo option (**Figure 2.3**). This option changes depending on the last action.

✔ Tips

■ Click the arrow button next to the Undo button to display a list of recent actions that you can undo (**Figure 2.4**). You can select any or all of these actions.

■ To redo something you've undone, click the Redo button (**Figure 2.5**). You can also choose Redo from the Edit menu or press Ctrl+Y. Redo undoes an Undo. (Redo is not available in Access or Outlook.)

Figure 2.2 The Undo button.

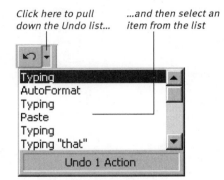

Figure 2.3 Choose the Undo command from the Edit menu.

Click here to pull down the Undo list...   *...and then select an item from the list*

Figure 2.4 Select from the Undo list.

Redo button

Figure 2.5 Click the Redo button to reverse an undo.

Figure 2.6 Choose Open Office Document from the Start menu.

Figure 2.7 The Open Office Document dialog box.

Table 2.1

Places Bar Buttons	
BUTTON	**DESCRIPTION**
History	Shortcuts to the files and folders you most recently accessed. You can sort the files and folders in a number of ways.
My Documents	The default folder in which all the documents you create are stored.
Desktop	Files and folders available on the Windows desktop.
Favorites	Shortcuts to files and folders you've added through the Tools button on the toolbar.
Web Folders	Shortcuts to Web documents on a corporate intranet or on the Internet.

Opening an Office Document

You can double-click any Office document in a folder to launch its application. You can use Windows Explorer to view the files on your system, or you can choose Open Office Document from the Start menu.

To open an Office document:

1. Click Open Office Document on the Start menu (**Figure 2.6**).

2. Click a document in the Open Office Document dialog box (**Figure 2.7**).

3. Click Open.

✔ Tips

- In the Open Office Document dialog box, you can click a button on the Places bar to view folders in popular locations. **Table 2.1** describes these buttons.

- Click the Views button on the toolbar to toggle through different views of the files and folders.

- Click the Tools button on the toolbar to add a shortcut to a file or folder to the Favorites folder.

- Click the arrow button next to the Look In drop-down list to display the hierarchy of disk drives and folders in your system.

Creating a New Document

Whenever you create a new document in an Office application by choosing New Office Document on the Start menu, you start with a template. The templates available on the General tab of the dialog box are generic. The templates on the other tabs contain more extensive formatting and placeholder text to aid you in customizing the type of document you select.

To create a new document:

1. Click New Office Document on the Start menu (**Figure 2.8**).

2. Double-click an icon on one of the tabs of the New Office Document dialog box (**Figure 2.9**).

✔ Tip

■ Some of the icons on the tabs in the New Office Document dialog box represent wizards that lead you through the various processes involved in creating your new document.

Figure 2.8 Choose New Office Document from the Start menu.

Figure 2.9 Click an icon in the New Office Document dialog box.

Figure 2.10 Type a question for the Office Assistant and click the Search button.

Figure 2.11 Right-click the Office Assistant to display the shortcut menu.

Figure 2.12 Choose Show the Office Assistant from the Help menu.

Getting Help from the Office Assistant

When you start your first Office application, Clippit, the Office Assistant, appears. This same assistant will appear in every other Office application unless you change or hide it.

To use the Office Assistant:

1. Click the Office Assistant.

2. Type your question (**Figure 2.10**).

3. Click Search to search the help database.

4. Click one of the topics displayed.

✔ Tips

- Move the Office Assistant to a convenient place on your desktop by dragging it, or right-click to display a shortcut menu that lets you choose another Assistant or hide the current Assistant (**Figure 2.11**).

- If you've hidden the Office Assistant, you can show it again by choosing Show the Office Assistant from the Help menu (**Figure 2.12**).

THE OFFICE ASSISTANT

Entering Text

Whenever an application is ready for you to type text, a blinking insertion point appears. The text you type appears at the insertion point. To revise or add to existing text, move the insertion point to where you want to make revisions.

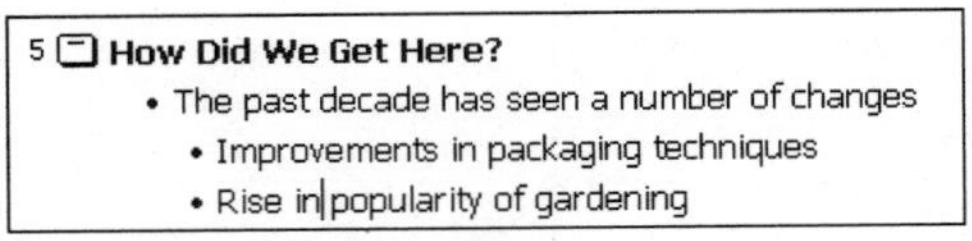
5 How Did We Get Here?
• The past decade has seen a number of changes
• Improvements in packaging techniques
• Rise in popularity of gardening

Figure 2.13 Anything you type is inserted at the insertion point.

To enter text:

◆ Click once in the existing text where you'd like to add or edit text (**Figure 2.13**).

or

Press the arrow keys on the keyboard to move the insertion point.

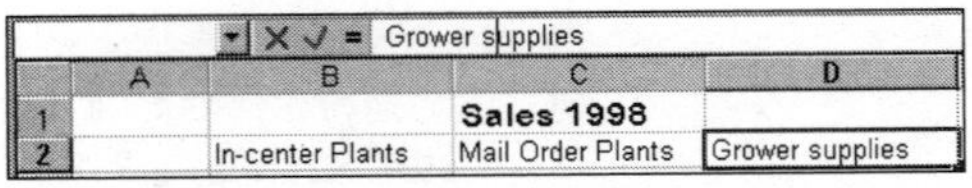
Grower supplies
A
B
C
D
1
2
Sales 1998
In-center Plants
Mail Order Plants
Grower supplies

Figure 2.14 The insertion point on the Excel edit line.

✔ Tips

- You can hold down the Ctrl key while pressing the right or left arrow key to move the insertion point a whole word to the right or left.
- Hold down the Ctrl key while pressing the up or down arrow key to move paragraph by paragraph.
- In Excel: The insertion point appears on the edit line (**Figure 2.14**).
- **Table 2.2** lists other keyboard shortcuts you can use to move the insertion point.

Table 2.2

Other Keyboard Shortcuts

Shortcut	Result
Home	Moves to beginning of a line
End	Moves to end of a line
Ctrl+Home	Moves to top of document
Ctrl+End	Moves to bottom of document

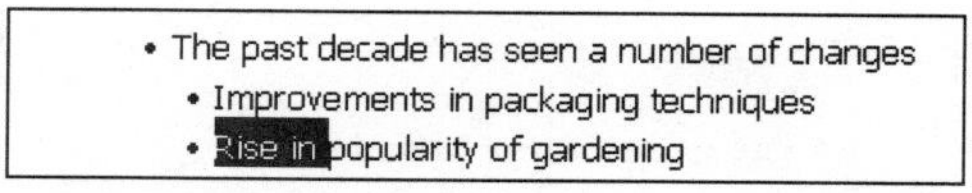

- The past decade has seen a number of changes
  - Improvements in packaging techniques
  - Rise in popularity of gardening

Figure 2.15 Drag across the text you want to select.

Dear Mr. Gardener,

Thank you very much for your inquiry last month about our hardy viburnums. Although we are able to offer many varieties, we are a little concerned about their ability to survive the severe winters in your area of the country.

Figure 2.16 Drag down to select several lines.

Selecting Text Using the Mouse

Knowing how to select text is important because you must always select text before you can format, copy, move, or delete it.

To select text with the mouse:

1. Position the pointer at one end of the text you want to select.

2. Hold down the mouse button and drag to the other end of the text you want to select (**Figure 2.15**).

   or

   To select text on multiple lines, hold down the mouse button and drag down through the document to highlight multiple lines.

3. Release the mouse button.

✔ Tips

- The Automatic Word Selection option guarantees that the entire first and last word of the selection are highlighted.

- To select a word, double-click the word.

- To select a paragraph, triple-click the paragraph.

- In Excel: You must select text on the edit line.

- In Word: To select an entire line of text, click the left margin next to the line.

- In Word: To select multiple entire lines, click to the left of a line and then drag down through the left margin (**Figure 2.16**).

Selecting and Replacing Text Using the Keyboard

To select text for formatting or editing, you can use a combination of keys. To replace text in a document or in a text box in a dialog box, you can always select the text and simply type over it. The characters that are selected will be replaced when you begin typing.

To select text using the keyboard:

1. Use the arrow keys to position the insertion point in front of the first character.

2. Press and hold the Shift key and use the arrow keys to move the insertion point to the end of the last word in the text you want to select.

✔ Tips

- Press and hold Shift and press the down arrow key to select multiple lines of text.

- Press the Ctrl and Shift keys along with the left or right arrow keys to select a word at a time.

To replace text:

1. Select the text you want to replace (**Figure 2.17**).

2. Type your replacement text (**Figure 2.18**).

✔ Tip

- To quickly replace an entry in a text box, click the entry and then type a replacement (**Figures 2.19** and **2.20**).

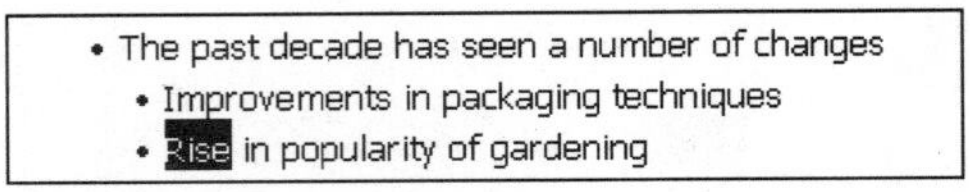

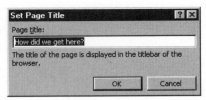

- The past decade has seen a number of changes
  - Improvements in packaging techniques
  - Rise in popularity of gardening

Figure 2.17 The selected text.

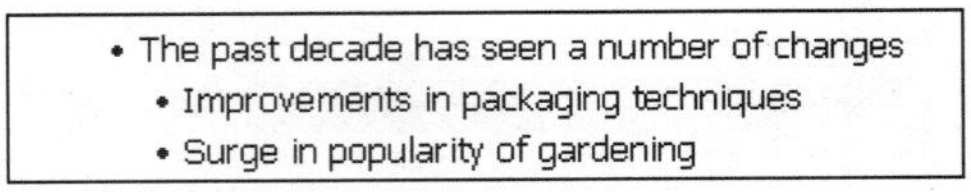

- The past decade has seen a number of changes
  - Improvements in packaging techniques
  - Surge in popularity of gardening

Figure 2.18 The typed text replaces the selected text.

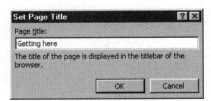

Figure 2.19 Click to select a text box entry.

Figure 2.20 A new typed entry replaces the selected entry.

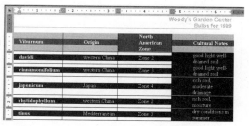

Figure 2.21 Select the text you want to move.

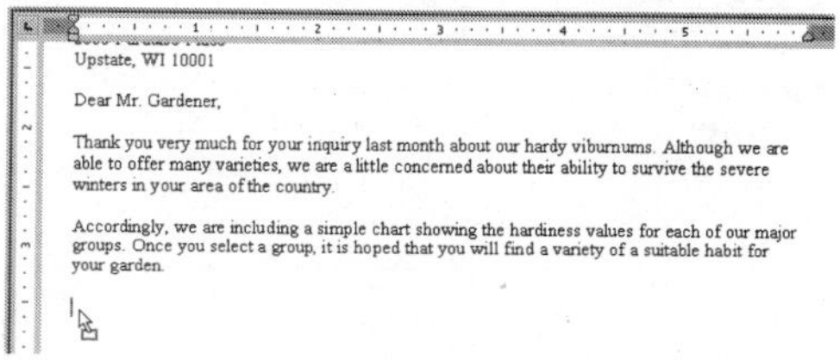

Figure 2.22 Drag the insertion point to the destination.

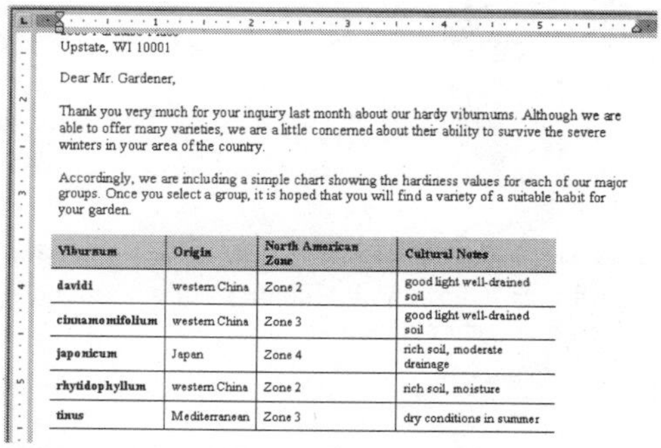

Figure 2.23 Release the mouse button to drop the text.

Figure 2.24 The scroll buttons represent the position of the visible text in relation to the entire document.

Dragging and Dropping Text

To move text in a document, you can always select the text and then drag it to a new location. You can even drag text from one document to another or from one application window to another.

To drag and drop text:

1. Select the text you want to move (**Figure 2.21**).

2. Position the mouse pointer on the selected text.

   The mouse pointer becomes an arrow.

3. Press and hold the mouse button and drag the pointer to the destination for the text.

   A gray insertion point indicates the exact spot at which the text will reappear (**Figure 2.22**).

4. Release the mouse button to drop the text at the new location (**Figure 2.23**).

✔ Tips

■ To copy rather than move the text (leaving the original intact), press and hold the Ctrl key while you drag.

■ Using these techniques, you can copy and move other kinds of objects (charts, graphics, and so on) as well.

■ Use the scroll bars at the right side and bottom of the window to jump to a position along the length or width of a document (**Figure 2.24**).

Selecting and Formatting Objects

Passages of text, drawings, charts, scanned images, and other items you can select are called objects. You can format objects and drag objects to reposition them on the page within an application, and you can usually drag them to other applications too.

◆ In Word: Select text to create an object that you can drag or format (**Figure 2.25**).

◆ In Excel: Drag diagonally from one corner of a range of cells to the opposite corner to create a selected range (**Figure 2.26**). The selected range, now enclosed in a box, is an object that you can drag or format.

◆ In PowerPoint: Each item on a page is an object. For example, a set of bulleted text items is an object that you can drag or format (**Figure 2.27**).

◆ In Access: Select a cell, and then drag down a column or across a row to create a selected group (**Figure 2.28**).

You must always first select an object and then choose a formatting command, not the other way around.

Figure 2.25 IN Word, select text to create an object.

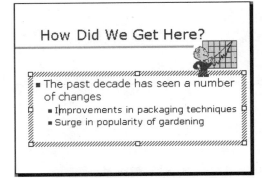

Figure 2.26 In Excel, drag from one corner to the opposite corner to select a range of cells.

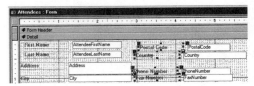

Figure 2.27 In PowerPoint handles appear around a selected object on a slide.

Figure 2.28 In Access, drag down a column or across a row to create a selected group.

Figure 2.29 Choose Paragraph from the Format menu.

To select and format an object:

1. Select the object you want to format.

2. Choose a formatting option from the Format menu (**Figure 2.29**).

or

Click the button for the formatting command on the Formatting toolbar.

or

Use the keyboard shortcut for the formatting command you want. **Table 2.3** shows some common keyboard shortcuts for text.

✔ Tip

■ The most popular formatting commands appear as buttons on the Formatting toolbar.

Table 2.3

Common Keyboard Shortcuts for Formatting Text	
KEYBOARD SHORTCUT	**FORMATTING EFFECT**
Ctrl+B	Bold
Ctrl+I	Italic
Ctrl+U	Underline

SELECTING/FORMATTING OBJECTS

Copying Formatting Using the Format Painter

The Format Painter transfers formatting from one object to another.

To copy formatting:

1. Select an object that has the formatting you want to copy (**Figure 2.30**).

2. Click the Format Painter button on the Standard toolbar to pick up the object's formatting (**Figure 2.31**).

3. Select the object to receive the formatting. If the object is a passage of text, drag across the text you want to format (**Figure 2.32**).

✔ Tips

- To apply formatting to an entire sentence, press and hold the Ctrl key and then click any word in the sentence.

- To apply the same formatting to other objects, double-click the Format Painter button instead of single-clicking it. Click the Format Painter button again when you have finished applying the formatting to other objects.

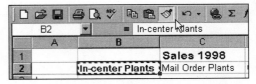

Figure 2.30 Select the formatted object.

Format Painter button

Figure 2.31 Click the Format Painter button.

Figure 2.32 Drag across the text with the Format Painter pointer, which displays a small paint brush.

Figure 2.33 Choose a toolbar from the Toolbars submenu.

Figure 2.34 A floating toolbar.

Figure 2.35 The Add or Remove Buttons button.

Figure 2.36 Select from the Add or Remove Buttons list.

Selecting Toolbars to Display

A default group of toolbars appears in each application, but you can choose others to display in a program to gain access to buttons for special tasks.

To select a toolbar for display:

1. From the View menu, choose Toolbars.

2. From the Toolbars submenu, choose the toolbar you want (**Figure 2.33**).

✔ Tips

- You can also display a new toolbar by right-clicking any visible toolbar and then choosing the new toolbar from the shortcut menu.

- You can let a toolbar "float," or you can "dock" it (**Figure 2.34**). Change a docked toolbar to a floating one by holding down the mouse button on the toolbar (without selecting a button) and dragging the toolbar toward the center of the program window. Dock a floating toolbar by dragging its title bar back to the original toolbar position.

- To add new toolbar buttons or remove buttons, click the arrow at the end of the toolbar, choose Add or Remove Buttons, and then select buttons from the Add or Remove Buttons list (**Figures 2.35** and **2.36**).

SELECTING TOOLBARS

Zooming In and Out

To enlarge your work on the screen, choose one of the preset zoom percentages from the drop-down list on the toolbar or enter your own value in the Zoom Control box on the Standard toolbar. For example, the setting 200% makes everything on the screen twice as large.

To zoom in or out:

◆ Click the current zoom percentage number in the Zoom Control box on the Standard toolbar, type a new zoom percentage, and press Enter (**Figure 2.37**).

or

Click the arrow button next to the Zoom Control box and then choose a preset percentage from the list (**Figure 2.38**).

or

From the View menu, choose Zoom, and then choose a preset percentage or enter your own in the Zoom dialog box (**Figures 2.39** and **2.40**).

✔ Tips

■ In Word: Page Width zooms to a percentage that neatly fits the text across the screen.

■ In Excel: Fit Selection zooms to the percentage that neatly fits the selected range of cells to the screen.

■ In PowerPoint: In Slide view, Fit zooms the current slide to fit the window.

■ In Access: Fit to Window zooms to the percentage that neatly fits the selected report to the screen.

Zoom Control box

Figure 2.37 Type a new percentage in the Zoom Control box.

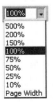

Figure 2.38 Select a new percentage from the list.

Figure 2.39 Choose Zoom from the View menu.

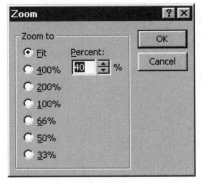

Figure 2.40 Select a percentage in the PowerPoint Zoom dialog box.

Figure 2.41 Choose Page Setup from the File menu.

Figure 2.42 The PowerPoint Page Setup dialog box.

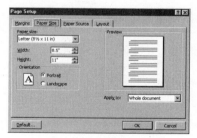

Figure 2.43 The Word Page Setup dialog box.

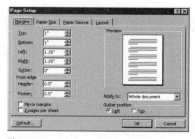

Figure 2.44 Adjust the margins on the Margins tab in Word.

Setting Up the Page

You set up the page by setting the size, orientation, and margins. The page margins give you white space at the top, bottom, left, and right sides of the page.

To set up the page:

1. From the File menu, choose Page Setup (**Figure 2.41**).

2. Select the paper size and print orientation (portrait or landscape) (**Figures 2.42** and **2.43**).

3. To adjust the margins, click the Margins tab (**Figure 2.44**).

4. Click OK when you have finished setting options.

✔ Tips

- To change margin settings, click and then type over the current margin settings, or click the arrow buttons next to each setting to incrementally increase or decrease the margins.

- The Page Setup settings are stored as part of the current document. The next new document you create will revert to the original, default page setup.

- In Word: You can click Default after changing the page setup to change the default for new documents that follow.

SETTING UP THE PAGE

Printing

You can print from any Office application and choose print options that fit the application.

To print:

1. From the File menu, choose Print (**Figure 2.45**).

   or

   Press Ctrl+P.

2. If necessary, choose different options in the Print dialog box (**Figure 2.46**).

3. Modify the number of copies, if you want.

4. Click All to print the entire document, or enter starting and ending page numbers.

5. Click OK to begin printing.

✔ Tips

- If you have more than one printer available, you can choose a printer other than the default printer. To change printers, click the arrow button next to the printer name and choose another printer from the list.

- In Word, you can enter a range of pages and individual pages at the same time. Entering *1-3,5* would print pages 1 through 3 and also page 5.

Figure 2.45 Choose Print from the File menu.

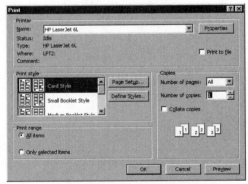

Figure 2.46 The Outlook Contacts Print dialog box.

Save button

Figure 2.47 Click the Save button.

Figure 2.48 Type a name in the Save As dialog box.

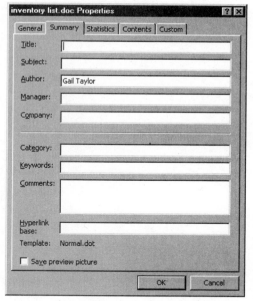

Figure 2.49 Type a title in the Properties dialog box.

Saving Your Work

To avoid losing changes to documents should the power suddenly fail or your system crash unexpectedly, you should save your work often.

To save your work:

1. From the File menu, choose Save.

   or

   Click the Save button (**Figure 2.47**).

   or

   Press Ctrl+S.

2. If the current document is new, in the File Name text box, type a filename over the temporary document name (**Figure 2.48**).

3. Specify where you want the document to be stored and then click Save or press Enter.

4. In the Properties dialog box, enter as much information in the text boxes as you want, pressing Tab to move from text box to text box (**Figure 2.49**).

5. Click OK.

✔ Tips

■ The information added in the Properties dialog box helps you find the file later.

■ You can turn off the Properties dialog box. Choose Options from the Tools menu, and click the Save tab in Word and PowerPoint or the General tab in Excel. The Properties dialog box does not appear in Access or Outlook.

■ Office saves all files in the default My Documents folder unless you select another location.

Reopening a Saved File

Once a file is saved and closed, reopen it to continue to work on it.

To reopen a saved file:

1. From the File menu, choose Open (**Figure 2.50**).

   or

   Click the Open button (**Figure 2.51**).

   or

   Press Ctrl+O.

2. In the Open dialog box, navigate to the location where the file you want is stored, and double-click the filename to open the file.

   or

   Click the filename and click OK.

✔ Tip

■ If the file you want to open is one you've used recently, it may appear in a list of recent documents at the bottom of the File menu. If so, just select it there to open it again.

Figure 2.50 Choose Open from the File menu...

Open button

Figure 2.51 ...or click the Open button.

Figure 2.52
Choose Exit from
the File menu.

Application
close button

File close button

Figure 2.53 Click a Close button.

Quitting an Office Application

Even if an Office application is minimized, it is still running. To quit an Office application, you must exit the application.

To quit an Office application:

◆ From the File menu, choose Exit. (**Figure 2.52**).

or

Click the Close button (**Figure 2.53**).

✔ Tips

■ Office will not let you quit an application without reminding you to save any open documents that have changed since you last saved them.

■ Word opens a window for each file you open. Clicking the Close button closes only the current file until you click Close in the last window and then it closes the application.

Part 2
Microsoft Word

Part 2
Microsoft Word

3. Introducing Word 2000

The Steps to Creating a Word Document

Starting Word

The Word Window

Key to the Word Window

4. Entering and Editing Text

Starting a New Document

Starting a Document Using a Wizard or Template

Entering Text

Turning On Paragraph Marks

Editing Text

Finding Text

Replacing Text

Using Print Layout View

Using Outline View

Using Web Layout View

5. Formatting Text

Changing the Font and Font Size

Boldfacing, Italicizing, and Underlining

Expanding and Condensing Character Spacing

Changing the Case of Text

Using Special Font Effects

Selecting Paragraphs

Using the Ruler to Indent Paragraphs

Setting a Different First Line Indent

Indenting Using the Paragraph Dialog Box

Double-Spacing Paragraphs

Centering and Justifying Paragraphs

Setting Tabs

Adding Bullets to Paragraphs

Numbering Paragraphs

Finding and Replacing Formatting

Using Styles

Choosing a Text Style

Creating a Paragraph Style

Modifying a Paragraph Style

Creating a Character Style

6. Formatting Pages

Changing the Page Size and Orientation

Changing the Margins

Setting Up Headers and Footers

Creating Multiple Sections

Paginating the Document

Numbering Pages

Setting Up Multiple Columns

AutoFormatting a Document

7. Creating Tables

Starting a Table

Drawing a Table

Drawing a More Complex Table

Entering Data in a Table

Aligning Data in a Table

Totaling Numeric Data

Deleting Data from a Table

Inserting Rows and Columns

Merging Cells

Turning On Borders and Shading

Converting Text to a Table

8. Special Word Techniques

Automatically Correcting Typos

Inserting Symbols from the Wingdings Font

Using AutoText

Printing Envelopes

Envelope Printing Options

Saving a Document as a Template

Using Automatic Saves

Creating Form Letters Using Mail Merge

9. Word and the Web

Inserting Hyperlinks

Editing a Hyperlink

Previewing a Document as a Web Page

Saving a Document as a Web Page

Using the Web Wizard to Create a Web Site

Formatting a Document with a Web Theme

INTRODUCING WORD 2000

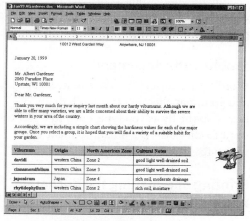

Figure 3.1 The Microsoft Word window.

With Word 2000, the word processing component of the Microsoft Office 2000 suite, you can create letters, memos, invoices, proposals, reports, forms, Web pages, and just about any other printed or electronically distributed documents.

You can type text into Word and insert drawings or scanned photos, formatting the text and graphics into sophisticated documents complete with running headers and footers, footnotes, cross-references, page numbers, tables of contents, and indexes. Or you can create simple text memos with Word's easy-to-use features.

Word's approach, like that of the other applications in the Office suite, is entirely visual. As you work in a document, you see all the text, graphics, and formatting exactly as they will appear when you print it.

Word can easily work in concert with the other Office applications too. It can display numbers from Excel or Access or slides from PowerPoint. It can use Outlook information to create labels and lists.

The Steps to Creating a Word Document

Entering and editing the text

Start a new document and type in your text. Don't worry about formatting. You'll take care of that later by using styles or by manually formatting the characters and paragraphs.

Formatting the characters

Select words or paragraphs whose characters require a special look (a different font or font size, boldfacing, italicizing, underlining, color, or other special font effect) and "font format" them. If you've created styles that contain font formatting, you can apply the styles to save time.

Formatting the paragraphs

Select paragraphs that need a different look and apply paragraph formats to them. You can change their indents, line spacing, centering, and tab settings. You can also add bullets and numbers. If you've created styles that contain preset combinations of paragraph formatting options, this is the time to use them.

Formatting the pages

Once the text is in shape, you can begin making overall adjustments to the pages. You can change the page size, page shape, and the margins; set up multiple columns of text; and repaginate the text to fit the pages. You can also set up the elements that appear on all pages, such as headers, footers, and page numbers.

Adding tables and graphics or objects from other applications

Word's table tools make creating tables of text or numbers quick and easy. If the table is a range of numbers from Excel, you can simply drag the range from Excel into your document. The range appears in Word with all the data and formatting you applied in Excel. You might want to augment the document with graphics created right in your document or brought in from other programs.

Proofing the document

Word's AutoCorrect feature and its spelling and grammar checkers can catch many errors on the fly as you type, but you'll still want to check the document to make sure you've fixed everything.

Printing or e-mailing the document and publishing to the Web

Before you print the document, you can preview its printed appearance on the screen to find obvious formatting errors. Or, you can skip the printing step and attach the document to an e-mail message or post it on a Web site.

Other features

Sometimes you'll need to perform a more specialized task, such as printing envelopes, creating form letters, and using templates to create virtually automatic documents.

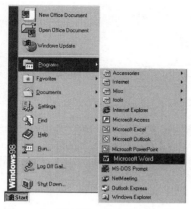

Figure 3.2 Click Microsoft Word on the Start menu to start Word.

Starting Word

The setup program for Microsoft Office creates an entry for Microsoft Word on the Windows Start menu, so it's easy to get Word up and running.

To start Word:

◆ From the Start menu, choose Programs, and then choose Microsoft Word (**Figure 3.2**).

or

From the Start menu, choose Open Office Document, and then double-click any Word document in the Open Office Document dialog box.

✔ Tip

■ If a button with a Microsoft Word icon is displayed on the taskbar, you can click it to open the Word window.

The Word Window

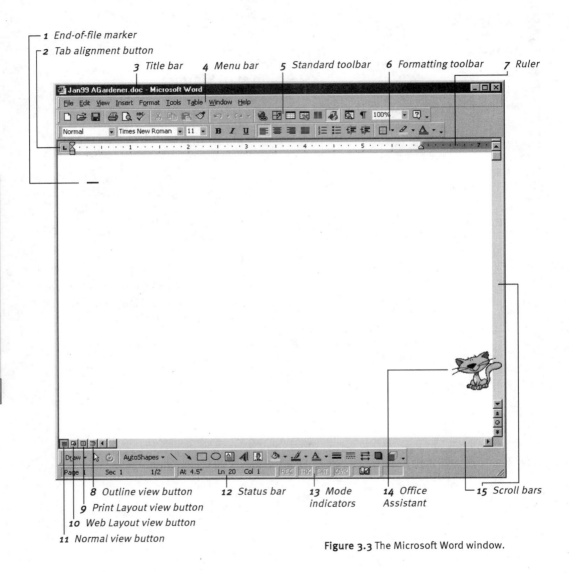

1 *End-of-file marker*

2 *Tab alignment button*

3 *Title bar* **4** *Menu bar* **5** *Standard toolbar* **6** *Formatting toolbar* **7** *Ruler*

8 *Outline view button* **12** *Status bar* **13** *Mode indicators* **14** *Office Assistant* **15** *Scroll bars*

9 *Print Layout view button*

10 *Web Layout view button*

11 *Normal view button*

Figure 3.3 The Microsoft Word window.

Key to the Word Window

1 End-of-file marker

Horizontal line showing the end of the current file. When you open a new document, the end-of-file marker appears at the top of the screen.

2 Tab alignment button

Click this button before setting a tab to select a tab type.

3 Title bar

Displays the document name. Drag the title bar to move the window.

4 Menu bar

Click on any name on the menu bar to pull down a menu.

5 Standard toolbar

Contains buttons that you can use for standard file management, text editing, and proofing commands.

6 Formatting toolbar

Contains buttons that you can use for formatting characters and paragraphs.

7 Ruler

Showing page width and position of tabs, indents, and columns.

8 Outline view button

Click this button to view the document outline so that you can develop the document's structure.

9 Print Layout view button

Click this button to switch to Print Layout view, which shows page borders, accurate margins, headers and footers, and other elements exactly as they'll appear when you print them.

10 Web Layout view button

If you're creating a Web page, click this button to see how the page will look online.

11 Normal view button

Click this button to switch to a normal view of the document.

12 Status bar

Shows the current page number and position of the insertion point in the document.

13 Mode indicators

These show special conditions that are in effect, such as recording a macro, tracking changes in the document, extending a selection, or overtyping.

14 Office Assistant

Click the Office Assistant for online help.

15 Scroll bars

Use these scroll bars to move the view of the document up or down or to quickly jump to a spot in the document. The length of the vertical scroll bar represents the length of the entire document. The position of the scroll position indicator represents the position in the document of the currently visible window.

THE WORD WINDOW

ENTERING AND EDITING TEXT

4

You can format your text as you type it, or you can leave all the formatting for a separate step. If you choose to postpone formatting, you can put substance before style and focus on what you're saying rather than on how it looks on the page.

In this chapter, you learn to enter text, make corrections, and search for and replace text. In subsequent chapters, you learn to format the fonts, paragraphs, and pages of your document.

Starting a New Document

When Word starts, *Document1* is open and ready for you to type text. Until you save them under new names, new documents are numbered sequentially (*Document2*, *Document3*, and so on).

To start a new document:

◆ On the Standard toolbar, click the New Blank Document button (**Figure 4.1**).

or

Press Ctrl+N.

or

1. From the File menu, choose New (**Figure 4.2**).

2. In the New dialog box, click the tab that corresponds to the type of document you want.

3. Click the template or wizard you want to use.

4. Click OK (**Figure 4.3**).

✔ Tips

■ If you select Web Page on the General tab of the New dialog box, Word will automatically save your document as an HTML page.

■ To switch from one open document to another, choose a document name from the list of open documents in the Window menu (**Figure 4.4**).

New Blank Document button

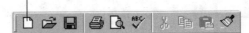

Figure 4.1 Click the New Blank Document button on the Standard toolbar.

Figure 4.2 From the File menu, choose New.

Figure 4.3 Choose a template or wizard.

Figure 4.4 Open documents appear on the Window menu.

Figure 4.5 The Memos tab of the New dialog box offers memo template and wizards for creating memos.

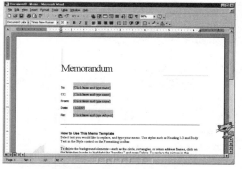

Figure 4.6 Follow the steps of the Memo Wizard.

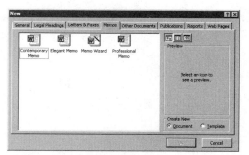

Figure 4.7 The Contemporary Memo template helps you create a memo in a contemporary style.

Starting a Document Using a Wizard or Template

When you start a new, blank document, you can choose a wizard or template from any tab other than the General tab in the New dialog box. A wizard guides you through a series of steps to help you create a document (**Figure 4.5**). A template starts a new document that has fields you can fill in and guidelines to help you create a file (**Figure 4.6**).

To start a document using a wizard or template:

1. From the File menu, choose New.

2. In the New dialog box, click a tab other than the General tab (**Figure 4.7**).

3. Double-click a wizard or template icon to open a new document.

✔ Tip

■ To have Word save the new document as a template, click the Template button in the Save As section of the New dialog box.

STARTING WITH A WIZARD

Entering Text

Typing in Word is just like typing on a typewriter except that you do *not* press Enter at the end of every line. When the insertion point reaches the right margin, it *wraps* automatically to the next line. You press Enter only to start a new paragraph.

✔ Tips

- Word uses a red wavy underline to indicate a possible misspelled word and a green wavy underline to indicate a possible grammar problem.

- Word automatically corrects many common typos—for example, when you forget to capitalize the first word in a sentence or typing "teh" instead of "the" (**Figure 4.8**).

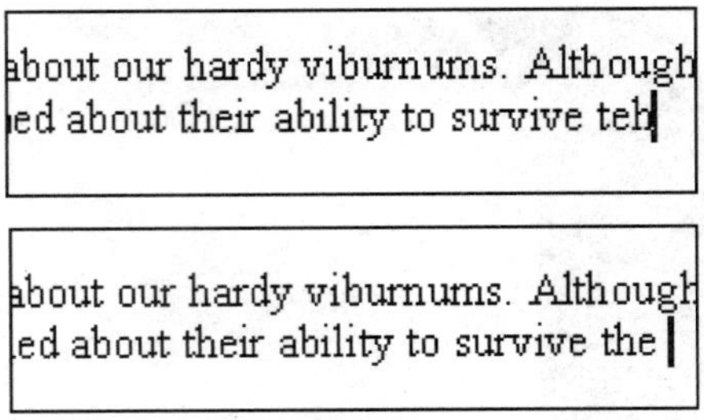

about our hardy viburnums. Although ed about their ability to survive teh

about our hardy viburnums. Although ed about their ability to survive the

Figure 4.8 Word automatically corrects a typo when you finish typing a word.

Spacebar   Enter   Tab

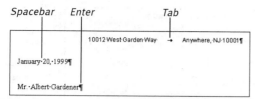

Figure 4.9 The nonprinting characters and their corresponding keys.

Show/Hide ¶ button

Figure 4.10 Click the Show/Hide ¶ button to turn paragraph marks on and off.

Table 4.1

Nonprinting Characters	
SYMBOL	**NONPRINTING CHARACTER (KEYSTROKE)**
¶	End of paragraph (Enter)
•	Space (Spacebar)
→	Tab (Tab)
↵	New line, same paragraph (Shift+Enter)

Turning On Paragraph Marks

If paragraph marks are turned on, you'll see a paragraph mark (¶) wherever you pressed Enter at the end of a paragraph, a dot wherever you pressed the Spacebar, and other symbols that indicate nonprinting characters in your document. These marks can help you understand the formatting in your document (**Figure 4.9**). **Table 4.1** lists these nonprinting characters.

To turn on paragraph marks:

◆ On the Standard toolbar, click the Show/Hide ¶ button (**Figure 4.10**).

✔ Tip

■ You can click the Show/Hide ¶ button again to turn off paragraph marks.

Editing Text

Using Word to prepare a document gives you the freedom to easily edit its text.

To insert new text:

1. Position the insertion point where you want the text to appear.

2. Start typing (**Figure 4.11**).

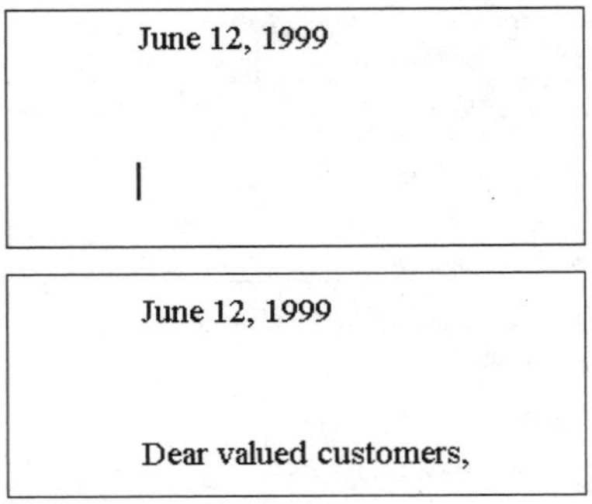

To delete text:

◆ Press Backspace to delete characters to the left of the insertion point (**Figure 4.12**).

   or

   Press Delete to delete characters to the right of the insertion point (**Figure 4.13**).

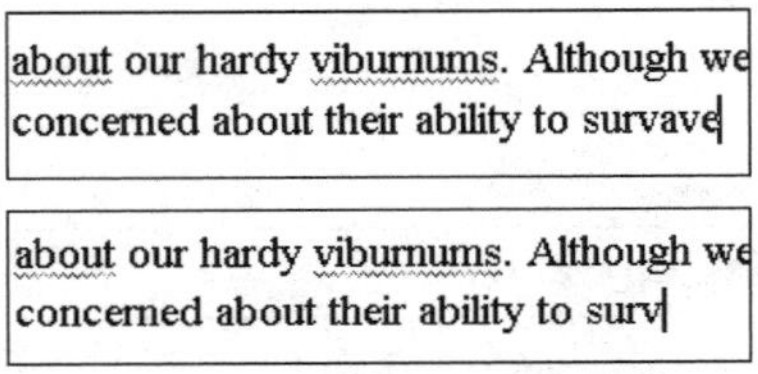

To replace existing text:

1. Select the text.

2. Type new text in its place (**Figure 4.14**).

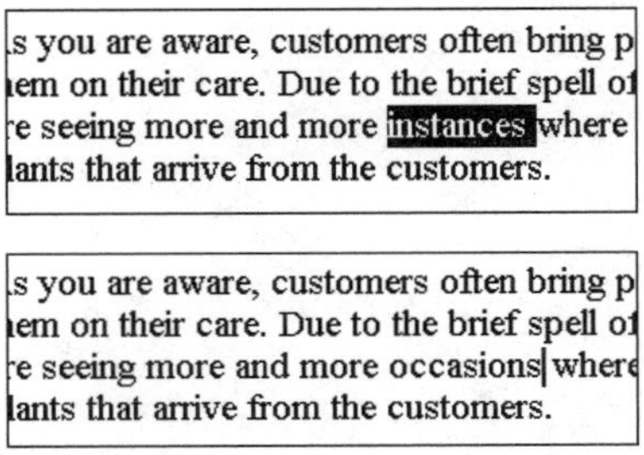

✔ Tips

■ To move or copy text, use the drag-and-drop method.

■ Double-click to select a word or triple-click to select an entire paragraph.

June 12, 1999

June 12, 1999

Dear valued customers,

Figure 4.11 To insert text, just start typing.

about our hardy viburnums. Although we concerned about their ability to survave

about our hardy viburnums. Although we concerned about their ability to surv

Figure 4.12 Press Backspace to delete characters to the *left* of the insertion point.

Thank you very much for your order. W to offer many types

Thank you very much for your order. W to offer many

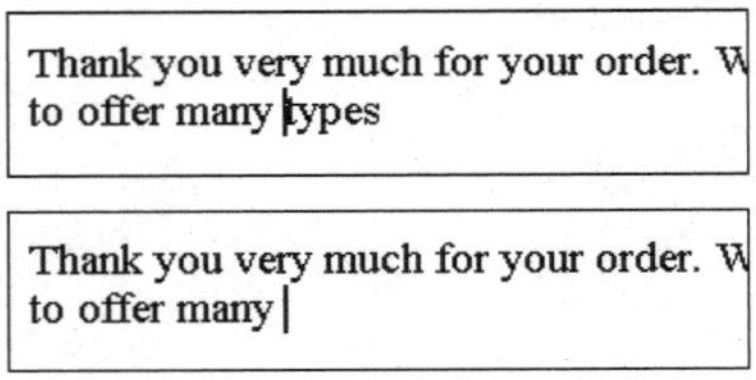

Figure 4.13 Press Delete to delete characters to the *right* of the insertion point.

s you are aware, customers often bring p em on their care. Due to the brief spell of e seeing more and more instances where ants that arrive from the customers.

s you are aware, customers often bring p em on their care. Due to the brief spell of e seeing more and more occasions where ants that arrive from the customers.

Figure 4.14 Anything you type while text is selected replaces the selected text.

EDITING TEXT

Figure 4.15 From the Edit menu, choose Find.

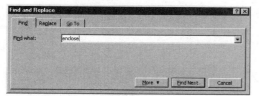

Figure 4.16 Type the text to find into the Find What text box.

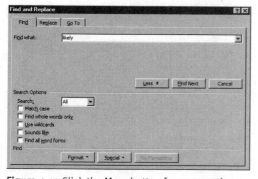

Figure 4.17 Click the More button for more options.

Finding Text

You can locate a spot in a document or a passage to edit by searching for a word or phrase.

To find text:

1. From the Edit menu, choose Find (**Figure 4.15**).

   or

   Press Ctrl+F.

2. In the Find and Replace dialog box, type text in the Find What text box (**Figure 4.16**).

3. Click Find Next. The text is found and highlighted on the screen.

4. To find the next occurrence, click Find Next again.

5. When you've found the text you want, close the Find and Replace dialog box.

✔ Tip

- For more search options, click the More button in the Find and Replace dialog box (**Figure 4.17**). **Table 4.2** lists these options.

FINDING TEXT

Table 4.2

More Find Options	
OPTION	**RESULT**
Match Case	Finds words that contain the same uppercase and lowercase characters
Find Whole Words Only	Finds text when not part of a larger word—for example, finds "art" but not "artistic"
Use Wildcards	Allows you to enter a code to specify a special character combination to find—for example, a "?" will match any single character
Sounds Like	Finds text that sounds like the Find What text
Find All Word Forms	Finds all variations of the chosen word—for example, "apple" and "apples," "sit" and "sat"

Replacing Text

You can use the Replace command to change all instances of one word or one phrase in a document to another word or phrase. For example, you can replace a recipient name throughout a letter or a project name in a proposal.

To replace text:

1. From the Edit menu, choose Replace (**Figure 4.18**).

    or

    Press Ctrl+H.

2. In the Find and Replace dialog box, type the text you want to find in the Find What text box (**Figure 4.19**).

3. In the Replace With text box, type the replacement text.

4. Click the Find Next button.

5. Click Replace to replace the found text, or click Find Next to skip to the next occurrence.

    or

    Click Replace All to replace all occurrences of the Find What text throughout the entire document.

✔ Tip

■ The Search pull-down list lets you direct your search Up from the insertion point, Down from the insertion point, or All (through the entire document) (**Figure 4.20**).

Figure 4.18 From the Edit menu, choose Replace.

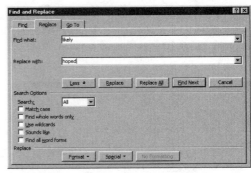

Figure 4.19 Type the text to find into the Find What text box.

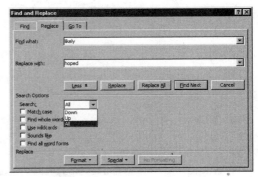

Figure 4.20 Choose a search direction from the Search pull-down list.

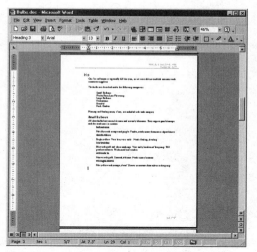

Figure 4.21 In Print Layout view, the document appears as it will print.

Print Layout View button

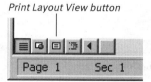

Figure 4.22 Click the Print Layout View button.

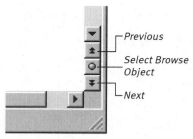

Previous

Select Browse Object

Next

Figure 4.23 Click the Next and Previous buttons to turn from page to page.

Using Print Layout View

If you switch to Print Layout view, you can work with the document while seeing it exactly as it will look when printed (**Figure 4.21**). In Print Layout view, you can see the accurate page borders, page margins, headers and footers, multiple columns, and frames that contain images.

To switch to Print Layout view:

◆ Click the Print Layout View button (**Figure 4.22**).

or

From the View menu, choose Print Layout.

✔ Tips

■ You can turn pages in Print Layout view by clicking the Next and Previous buttons (**Figure 4.23**). The Select Browse Object button, between the Next and Previous buttons, lets you set the Next and Previous buttons to take you to the next or previous table, graphic, or heading rather than to the next or previous page.

■ From Print Layout view, you can choose Whole Page from the Zoom Control list to view the entire page.

PRINT LAYOUT VIEW

Using Outline View

In Outline view, you can enter up to seven levels of headings, type text underneath the headings, and use drag and drop to easily rearrange both the headings and their corresponding text and revise the structure of a document (**Figure 4.24**). To get an overview of the document, you can also collapse subheadings and their accompanying text to leave only main headings visible.

To switch to Outline view:

◆ Click the Outline View button (**Figure 4.25**).

or

From the View menu, choose Outline.

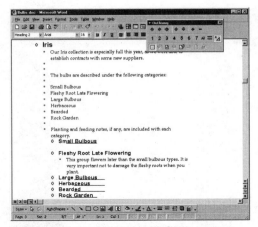

Figure 4.24 In Outline view, you can work with the document headings and subheadings.

Outline View button

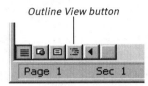

Figure 4.25 The Outline View button.

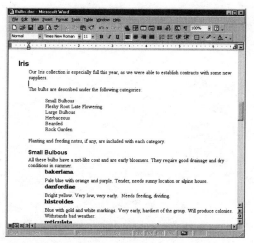

Figure 4.26 In Web Layout view, you can see a page as it will appear in a Web browser.

Web Layout View button

Figure 4.27 The Web Layout View button.

Using Web Layout View

In Web Layout view, you can preview a page as it will appear in a Web browser (**Figure 4.26**).

To switch to Web Layout view:

◆ Click the Web Layout View button (**Figure 4.27**).

or

From the View menu, choose Web Layout.

FORMATTING TEXT

Times New Roman 12 pt. *Italic*, *underlined*

Comic Sans MS 20 pt.

Arial 24 pt. **Bold**, *Italic*

SMALL CAPS

Superscript[1]

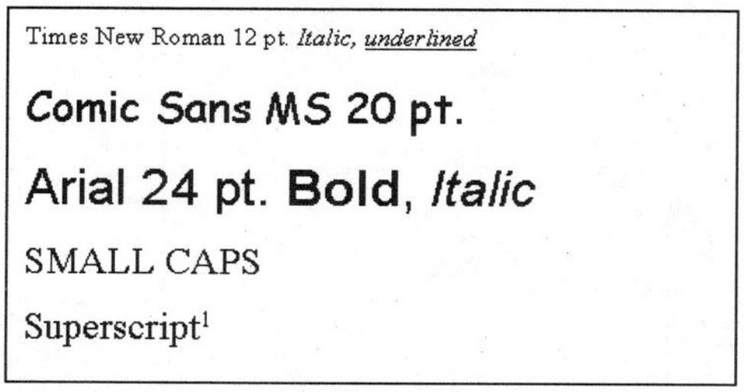

Figure 5.1 Font formatting changes the look of characters of text.

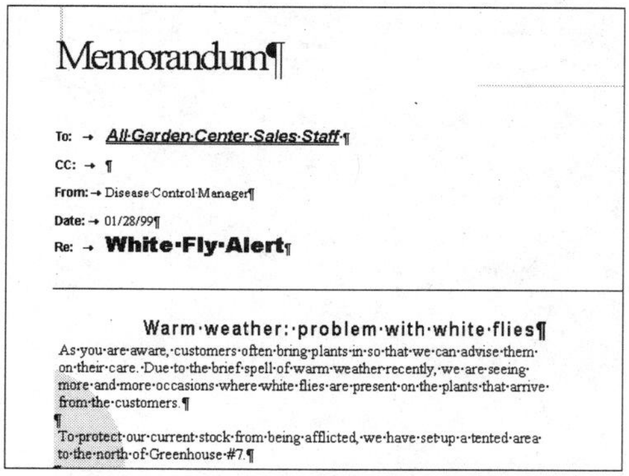

Memorandum¶

To: → *All·Garden·Center·Sales·Staff*·¶
CC: → ¶
From: → Disease·Control·Manager¶
Date: → 01/28/99¶
Re: → **White·Fly·Alert**¶

Warm·weather:·problem·with·white·flies¶
As·you·are·aware,·customers·often·bring·plants·in·so·that·we·can·advise·them·on·their·care.··Due·to·the·brief·spell·of·warm·weather·recently,·we·are·seeing·more·and·more·occasions·where·white·flies·are·present·on·the·plants·that·arrive·from·the·customers.¶
¶
To·protect·our·current·stock·from·being·afflicted,·we·have·set·up·a·tented·area·to·the·north·of·Greenhouse·#7.¶

Figure 5.2 Paragraph formatting changes the look of paragraphs.

In a Word document, you can change the appearance of both the text characters and the paragraphs. Changing the look of characters is font formatting. **Figure 5.1** shows several examples. Changing the appearance of paragraphs, on the other hand, is paragraph formatting. **Figure 5.2** shows a variety of paragraph formats. The most common paragraph formatting changes are indenting, double spacing, centering, justifying, numbering, and adding bullets to paragraphs.

As with any formatting change, you must first select the text to format (an individual character, a word or two, a paragraph, or the entire document) and then select either font or paragraph formatting from menus, dialog boxes, or Word's toolbars.

For speedy text formatting, font and paragraph formatting can be part of the information you record in a style. Applying a style that you've created to a paragraph automatically applies font and paragraph formatting to that paragraph.

Changing the Font and Font Size

In addition to the standard fonts that come with Windows, you can also use fonts that are installed by Microsoft Office 2000 and others that you buy or download.

To change the font and font size

1. Select the text to format (**Figure 5.3**).

2. Click the arrow button next to the Font list on the Formatting toolbar and select a font name from the drop-down list (**Figure 5.4**).

3. Click the arrow button next to the Font Size list on the Formatting toolbar and choose a different size.

   or

   Click the current font size on the Formatting toolbar and type a replacement (**Figure 5.5**).

   or

   From the Format menu, choose Font, and then, on the Font tab in the Font dialog box, select a font from the Font list and a font size from the Size list (**Figure 5.6**).

✔ Tips

■ To return selected text to the standard font and size for the paragraph, select the text and press Ctrl+Spacebar or Ctrl+Shift+Z.

■ To increase the font size of text you've selected, press Ctrl+Shift+>. To decrease the font size of text you've selected, press Ctrl+Shift+<.

Figure 5.3 Select the text to format.

Figure 5.4 Select a font name from the drop-down list.

Figure 5.5 The Font Size list.

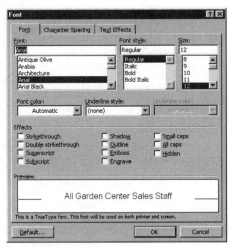

Figure 5.6 Select a font in the Font dialog box.

Figure 5.7 The Bold, Italic, and Underline buttons.

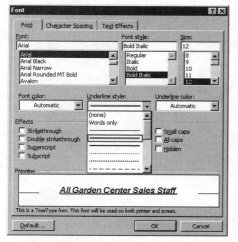

Figure 5.8 Choose options in the Font dialog box.

Single
Words Only
Double
Thick
Dotted
Thick Dotted
Dash
Thick Dash
Wide Dash
Thick Wide Dash
Dot Dash
Thick Dot Dash
Dot Dot Dash
Thick Dot Dot Dash
Wave
Thick Wave
Double Wave

Figure 5.9 Underline options.

Boldfacing, Italicizing, and Underlining

You can use the Font Style options to boldface, italicize, and underline characters, words, and paragraphs.

To boldface, italicize, or underline text:

1. Select the text to format.

2. On the Formatting toolbar, click the Bold, Italic, or Underline button (**Figure 5.7**).

   or

   From the Format menu, choose Font, and then, in the Font dialog box, select a style from the Font Style list. To change underlining, click the arrow button next to the Underline text box and then select an underline option from the list (**Figures 5.8** and **5.9**).

   or

   Use one of the keyboard shortcuts found in **Table 5.1**.

✔ Tip

- The Bold, Italic, and Underline buttons and keyboard shortcuts are toggles. Use them once to turn formatting on, again to turn formatting off.

BOLD, ITALIC, UNDERLINE

Table 5.1

Keyboard Shortcuts	
Keyboard Shortcut	**Effect**
Ctrl+B	Bold
Ctrl+I	Italic
Ctrl+U	Underline

Expanding and Condensing Character Spacing

Character spacing is the space between letters in words. You can uniformly increase or decrease this space to stretch or compress text.

To expand or condense character spacing:

1. Select the text to format (**Figure 5.10**).

2. From the Format menu, choose Font to open the Font dialog box.

3. On the Character Spacing tab of the Font dialog box, click the up or down arrow next to the By text box to expand or condense the character spacing (**Figure 5.11**).

✔ Tips

■ A sample in the Preview box at the bottom of the tab shows the character spacing you've chosen.

■ To quickly return expanded or condensed text to normal, select the text and then press Ctrl+Spacebar or Ctrl+Shift+Z.

Figure 5.10 Select the text to format.

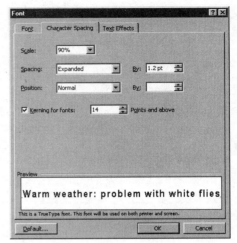

Figure 5.11 Change character spacing on the Character Spacing tab.

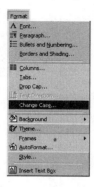

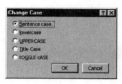

Figure 5.12 Choose Change Case from the Format menu.

Figure 5.13 Select an option in the Change Case dialog box.

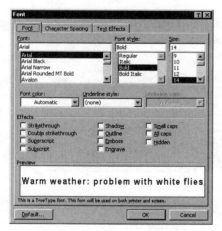

Figure 5.14 Change options on the Font tab.

Table 5.2

Keyboard Shortcuts	
KEYBOARD SHORTCUT	EFFECT
Shift+F3	Cycles through case options
Ctrl+Shift+K	Applies Small Caps
Ctrl+Shift+B	Applies All Caps
Ctrl+Spacebar	Removes Small Caps or All Caps applied using keyboard shortcut

Changing the Case of Text

Text case refers to whether the characters are all capital letters, all lowercase letters, or some combination of the two.

To change the case of text:

1. Select the text to format

2. Press Shift+F3 to toggle among the case options.

   or

   From the Format menu, choose Change Case (**Figure 5.12**). Select an option in the Change Case dialog box (**Figure 5.13**).

   or

   From the Format menu, choose Font. On the Font tab of the Font dialog box, check the Small Caps or All Caps check boxes. Click either one again to clear it (**Figure 5.14**).

✔ Tip

■ You can also select the text and use one of the keyboard shortcuts in **Table 5.2**.

Using Special Font Effects

You can use the check boxes on the Font tab of the Font dialog box to apply special effects to the text you've selected (**Figure 5.15**).

To apply special font effects:

1. Select the text to format.

2. From the Format menu, choose Font.

3. On the Font tab of the Font dialog box, select as many effects as you'd like to apply to the selected text (**Figure 5.16**).

✔ Tips

■ If you're preparing a document to be printed on a color printer or viewed in a Web browser, you can specify a color for selected text on the Font tab of the Font dialog box.

■ Click More Colors in the Color list to design a custom color (**Figure 5.17**).

Figure 5.15 The Font effects.

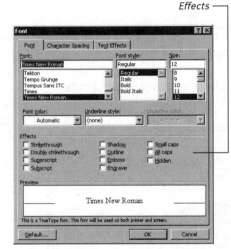

Figure 5.16 Select effects on the Font tab.

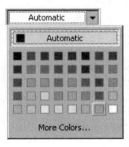

Figure 5.17 Click More Colors to design your own custom colors.

As you are aware, customers often bring plants in so that we c
brief spell of warm weather recently, we are seeing more and r
present on the plants that arrive from the customers.

To protect our current stock from being afflicted, we have set u
Greenhouse #7.

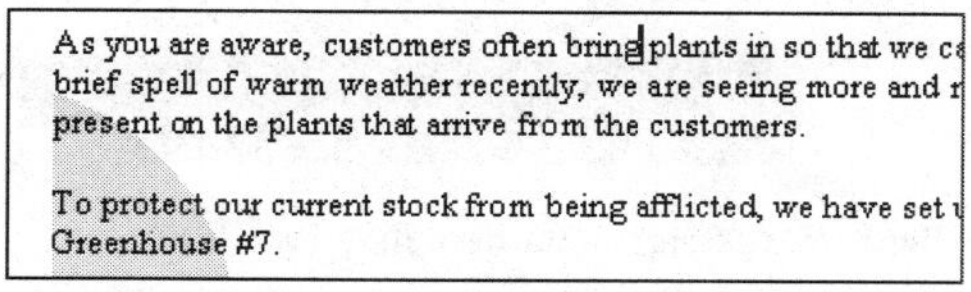

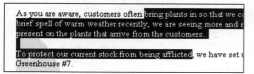

Figure 5.18 The paragraph containing the insertion point will be formatted.

As you are aware, customers often bring plants in so that we c
brief spell of warm weather recently, we are seeing more and r
present on the plants that arrive from the customers.

To protect our current stock from being afflicted, we have set u
Greenhouse #7.

Figure 5.19 Drag across multiple paragraphs that you want to format.

Selecting Paragraphs

To apply paragraph formatting, you must first select the paragraphs to be formatted.

To select a paragraph for paragraph formatting:

- Click anywhere in the paragraph to designate a paragraph to be formatted (**Figure 5.18**). You don't have to select the whole paragraph.

To select multiple paragraphs for formatting:

1. Click anywhere in the first paragraph to format.
2. Hold down the mouse button and drag into the last paragraph to format. You don't have to select all the text in both paragraphs. If the selection extends anywhere into a paragraph, that paragraph will be formatted (**Figure 5.19**).

✔ Tip

- To select multiple paragraphs quickly, hold down the mouse button and drag down through the margin to the left of the paragraphs.

Using the Ruler to Indent Paragraphs

The easiest and most direct way to change the indents of paragraphs is by dragging the indent markers on the ruler.

To indent paragraphs using the ruler:

1. Click in or select the paragraph or paragraphs to be formatted (**Figure 5.20**).

2. Drag the left indent marker to set the left indent of all of the lines in the paragraph except the first line (**Figure 5.21**).

   or

   Drag the rectangular button below the left indent marker to move the first line indent and the left indent markers simultaneously and maintain their relative positions (**Figure 5.22**).

3. Drag the right indent marker to set the right indent (**Figure 5.23**).

✔ Tips

- Click in a paragraph and then examine the indent markers on the ruler to check the indent settings for the paragraph.

- Click the Increase Indent button on the Formatting toolbar to increase the left indent one-half inch (**Figure 5.24**).

- Click the Decrease Indent button to decrease the left indent one-half inch.

Figure 5.20 Select a paragraph to format.

Figure 5.21 Drag the left indent marker to set the left indent.

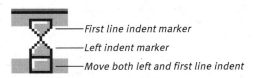

Figure 5.22 The indent markers.

Figure 5.23 Drag the right indent marker to set the right indent.

Figure 5.24 The Increase Indent and Decrease Indent buttons.

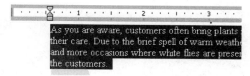

Figure 5.25 Select paragraphs to format.

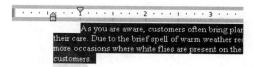

Figure 5.26 Drag the first line indent marker to create a first line indent.

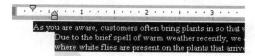

Figure 5.27 Drag the first line indent marker to the left to create a hanging indent.

Setting a Different First Line Indent

You can specify a special indent for the first line of a paragraph. This feature lets you create either an indented first line or a hanging indent, in which the first line begins to the left of the other lines in the paragraph.

To change the first line indent:

1. Click in or select the paragraph or paragraphs to be formatted (**Figure 5.25**).

2. Drag the first line indent marker to the right to change the indent of only the first line (**Figure 5.26**).

✔ Tip

■ Drag the first line indent marker to the left of the left indent marker to create a hanging indent (**Figure 5.27**).

FIRST LINE INDENT

Indenting Using the Paragraph Dialog Box

Instead of using the ruler to set indents, you can enter exact indent measurements in the Paragraph dialog box.

To specify indents using the Paragraph dialog box:

1. Select the paragraph or paragraphs to format.

2. From the Format menu, choose Paragraph (**Figure 5.28**).

3. On the Indents and Spacing tab of the Paragraph dialog box, change the Left and Right Indentation settings by clicking the arrows or by double-clicking the current setting and typing a replacement (**Figure 5.29**).

4. If you want a first line or hanging indent, select either First Line or Hanging from the Special drop-down list. You can then set the amount of the indent in the By text box.

5. Click OK.

✔ Tip

■ Indents are measured from the left and right margins.

Figure 5.28 Choose Paragraph from the Format menu.

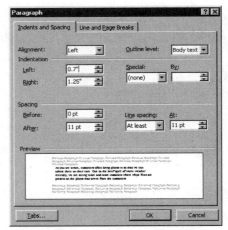

Figure 5.29 Change indentation on the Indents and Spacing tab of the Paragraph dialog box.

SETTING EXACT INDENTS

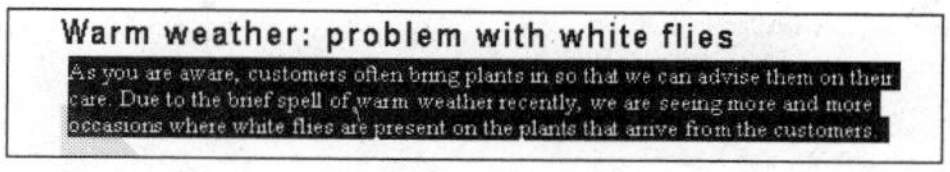

Warm weather: problem with white flies
As you are aware, customers often bring plants in so that we can advise them on their care. Due to the brief spell of warm weather recently, we are seeing more and more occasions where white flies are present on the plants that arrive from the customers.

Figure 5.30 Select paragraphs to format.

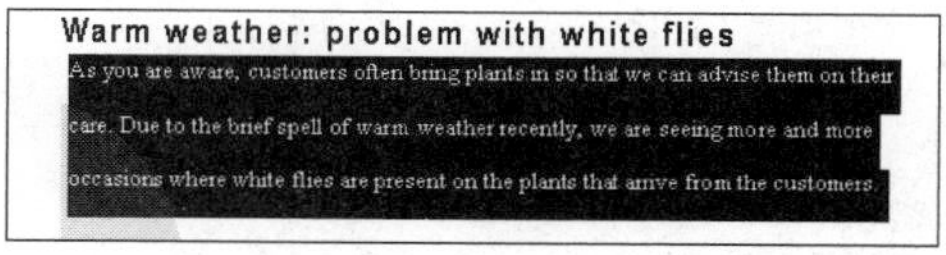

Warm weather: problem with white flies
As you are aware, customers often bring plants in so that we can advise them on their
care. Due to the brief spell of warm weather recently, we are seeing more and more
occasions where white flies are present on the plants that arrive from the customers.

Figure 5.31 Press Ctrl+2 to double-space a paragraph.

Paragraph
Indents and Spacing
Line and Page Breaks
Alignment:
Left
Outline level:
Body text
Indentation
Left:
0.63"
Right:
0.75"
Special:
By:
(none)
Spacing
Before:
0 pt
After:
0 pt
Line spacing:
At:
Single
Single
1.5 lines
Double
At least
Exactly
Multiple
Preview
Tabs...
OK
Cancel

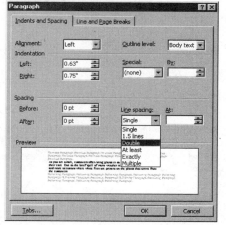

Figure 5.32 Choose Double from the Line Spacing drop-down list.

Double-Spacing Paragraphs

Paragraphs are single spaced by default; to spread the text out, you can specify double-spacing, which in effect inserts a blank line between each two lines of text.

To double-space paragraphs:

1. Select the paragraph or paragraphs to format (**Figure 5.30**).
2. Press Ctrl+2 (**Figure 5.31**).

   or

   From the Format menu, choose Paragraph, and then choose Double from the Line Spacing drop-down list and click OK (**Figure 5.32**).

✔ Tips

- Press Ctrl+1 to return a selected paragraph to single-spacing format.
- From the Line Spacing drop-down list in the Paragraph dialog box, you can also choose 1.5 lines, or set an exact line spacing in points by choosing Exactly. In the box labeled At, click the arrows to change the number of points of spacing, or type in a value.

Centering and Justifying Paragraphs

Centered paragraphs are horizontally centered between the left and right margins (**Figure 5.33**). The left and right sides of justified paragraphs are aligned with the left and right margins (**Figure 5.34**).

To center or justify paragraphs:

1. Select the paragraph or paragraphs to format.

2. Click the Center or Justify buttons on the Formatting toolbar (**Figure 5.35**).

   or

   Press Ctrl+E to center or Ctrl+J to justify the paragraphs.

✔ Tips

■ To return a paragraph to standard left alignment (aligned with the left margin and ragged right), click the Left button on the Formatting toolbar or press Ctrl+L.

■ You can also choose Paragraph from the Format menu to open the Paragraph dialog box and then select an option from the Alignment drop-down list (**Figure 5.36**).

■ Paragraphs that are indented will not be centered properly, so be sure to remove the indents before you try to center paragraphs.

■ To align paragraphs with the right margin, click the Align Right button or press Ctrl+R.

Figure 5.33 Centered paragraph.

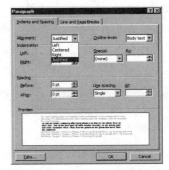

Figure 5.34 Select Justified.

Figure 5.35 The Align buttons on the Formatting toolbar.

Figure 5.36 Choose an option from the Alignment drop-down list.

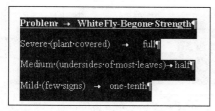

Figure 5.37 Select paragraphs to format.

Alignment marker

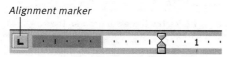

Figure 5.38 The alignment marker shows the tab type you can add by clicking on the ruler.

Figure 5.39 Click on the ruler to set a tab.

Table 5.3

Tab Alignment Settings	
SYMBOL	**ALIGNMENT**
L	Left-aligned tab
⊥	Center-aligned tab
⌐	Right-aligned tab
⊥	Decimal-aligned tab
I	Bar tab

Setting Tabs

You can use tabs to align text and numbers neatly in columns. Word 2000 offers standard tabs, plus a new type of tab, the bar tab, which places a vertical bar between columns. Bar tabs are ideal for dividing text buttons on Web page menu bars.

To set tabs:

1. Select the paragraph or paragraphs to which you want to add tabs (**Figure 5.37**).

2. Click the tab alignment button if you want to change the tab type (**Figure 5.38**). **Table 5.3** shows the tab alignment settings.

3. Click on the ruler to set a tab of the type shown on the tab alignment button (**Figure 5.39**).

4. Click again at a different spot on the ruler to set another tab of the same type.

   or

   Click the tab alignment button to select a different tab type before clicking on the ruler to set the tab.

✔ Tips

- The default tab is left-aligned.

- To delete a tab, drag it up and off the ruler.

- To change tab settings, select the relevant paragraphs and then drag the tab markers to the left or right along the ruler.

SETTING TABS

Adding Bullets to Paragraphs

You can emphasize statements or create a list of unordered items by adding bullets to paragraphs. To order emphasized items, you can instead give the paragraphs numbers.

To add default bullets to paragraphs:

1. Select the paragraph or paragraphs to be formatted (**Figure 5.40**).

2. Click the Bullets button on the Formatting toolbar to apply the default bullets to the paragraphs (**Figures 5.41** and **5.42**).

To select a different bullet shape:

1. Select the paragraph or paragraphs to format.

2. From the Format menu, choose Bullets and Numbering

3. On the Bulleted tab of the Bullets and Numbering dialog box, click on one of the large panes to select a bullet shape (**Figure 5.43**).

✔ Tips

■ To remove bullets, select the bulleted paragraphs and then click the Bullets button again.

■ To set the bullet size, distance from text, and other options, click Customize on the Bulleted tab of the Bullets and Numbering dialog box and enter the appropriate information.

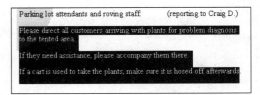

Figure 5.40 Select paragraphs to format.

Bullets button

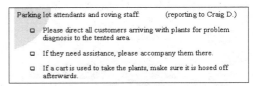

Figure 5.41 Click the Bullets button on the Formatting toolbar.

Figure 5.42. Paragraphs with bullets.

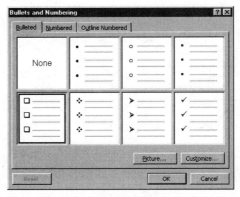

Figure 5.43 Select a bullet shape in the Bullets and Numbering dialog box.

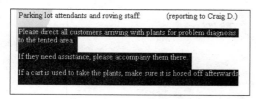

Figure 5.44 Select paragraphs to format.

Numbering button

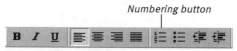

Figure 5.45 Click the Numbering button on the Formatting toolbar.

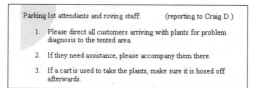

Figure 5.46 Paragraphs with numbers.

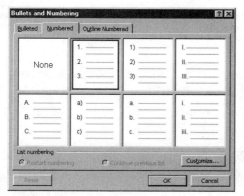

Figure 5.47 Select a numbering style in the Bullets and Numbering dialog box.

Numbering Paragraphs

To create an ordered list, you can give paragraphs numbers.

To number paragraphs:

1. Select the paragraph or paragraphs to format (**Figure 5.44**).

2. Click the Numbering button on the Formatting toolbar to number the paragraphs (**Figures 5.45** and **5.46**).

To specify a different numbering style:

1. Select the paragraph or paragraphs to format.

2. From the Format menu, choose Bullets and Numbering.

3. On the Numbered tab of the Bullets and Numbering dialog box, click one of the large panes to select a numbering style (**Figure 5.47**).

✔ Tips

■ To remove numbers, select the numbered paragraphs and click the Numbering button again or choose Bullets and Numbering from the Format menu and click the None pane on the Numbered tab of the Bullets and Numbering dialog box.

■ To set the numbering style, distance from text, and other options, click Customize on the Numbered tab of the Bullets and Numbering dialog box and change the appropriate settings.

NUMBERING PARAGRAPHS

Finding and Replacing Formatting

You can use this technique to make a stylistic change throughout a document.

To find and replace formatting

1. Press Ctrl+F to find or Ctrl+H to replace text.

   or

   From the Edit menu, choose either Find or Replace (**Figure 5.48**).

2. In the Find and Replace dialog box, click More for more options.

3. Click Format and choose Paragraph from the Format list (**Figure 5.49**).

4. Choose the formatting you want to find or replace in the Find Paragraph dialog box and click OK.

   The formatting you choose is described under the Find What text box (**Figure 5.50**).

5. Click Find Next to find the formatting.

   or

   If you are replacing formatting, click in the Replace With text box, click the Format button, choose Replacement Formatting, and then click Find Next.

✔ Tip

■ You can search for a style by clicking the Format button in the Find and Replace dialog box, selecting Style from the Format list, and then choosing a style.

Figure 5.48 Choose Find or Replace on the Edit menu.

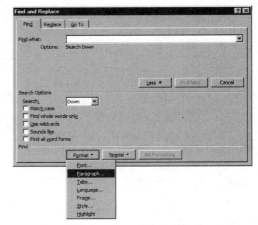

Figure 5.49 Choose Paragraph from the Format pull-down list.

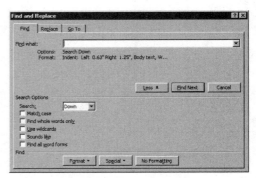

Figure 5.50 The Find tab on the Find and Replace dialog box.

FINDING FORMATTING

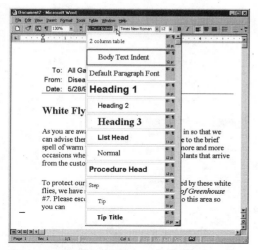

Figure 5.51 The list of styles available for the current document.

Text formatted using a character style

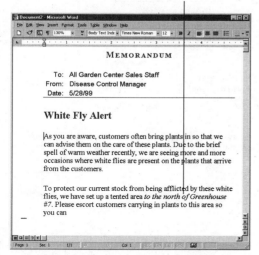

Figure 5.52 Formatting applied to selected text using a character style.

Using Styles

By creating a style, you can specify a preset combination of formatting options for text, such as the font, paragraph indents, and boldfacing. In a style named Heading, for example, you can specify the formatting information for paragraphs that you want to look like headings. To format a paragraph as a heading, you'd simply select the paragraph and choose the Heading style from the list of styles that you've created for the document (**Figure 5.51**).

Paragraph styles, which you assign to entire paragraphs, apply both font and paragraph formatting. Characters styles, a second type of style, assign just font formatting (font style, font size, boldfacing, underlining, italic, and so on) to selected characters or words within paragraphs without affecting the entire paragraphs (**Figure 5.52**).

Choosing a Text Style

By default, paragraphs are formatted using the settings in the Normal style, but you can apply to paragraphs any of the styles from the Style list. If the style you want is not available on this list, you can create a new style.

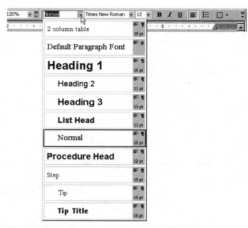

Figure 5.53 Select the characters or paragraphs to format.

To choose a style from the Style list:

1. Select the characters or paragraphs to format (**Figure 5.53**). You can either highlight the appropriate characters or simply click in the paragraph you want to format to position the insertion point in the paragraph.

2. On the Formatting toolbar, click the arrow button next to the Style box to pull down the list of styles (**Figure 5.54**).

3. Choose a style name from the list of styles.

   Your selection is automatically formatted according to the specified style (**Figure 5.55**).

Figure 5.54 Pull down the list of styles.

✔ Tip

- Paragraph styles are indicated by a paragraph mark in the pane to the right of the style name; character styles are indicated by an <u>a</u>.

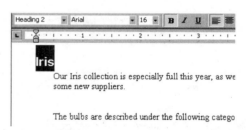

Figure 5.55 Selected paragraph has been formatted with a new paragraph style.

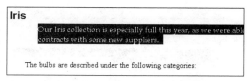

Figure 5.56 Apply formatting and leave the paragraph selected.

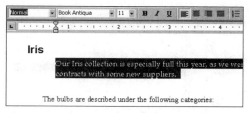

Figure 5.57 Click the current style name in the Style list.

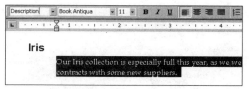

Figure 5.58 Replace the existing style name with a new one.

Creating a Paragraph Style

Each Word document starts with a basic set of styles. To give paragraphs other formats, you can create custom styles.

To create a paragraph style:

1. Apply font and paragraph formatting to a paragraph and then leave the paragraph selected (or leave the insertion point in the paragraph) (**Figure 5.56**).

2. In the Style list on the Formatting toolbar, click on the current style name to highlight it (**Figure 5.57**).

3. Type over the existing style name to replace it with a new style name and press Enter (**Figure 5.58**).

✔ Tips

■ You can also create a style by using the Style command on the Format menu.

■ The styles you create are stored in the document when you save the file.

CREATING A STYLE

Modifying a Paragraph Style

When you revise the formatting in a paragraph style, every paragraph to which the style has been applied takes on the modified formatting.

To modify a paragraph style:

1. Select a paragraph that has the paragraph style you want to modify. Make sure to select the entire paragraph.

2. Make changes to the font or paragraph formatting of the paragraph (**Figure 5.59**).

3. Click the down arrow next to the Style list, and choose the name of the style that was originally applied to the paragraph (**Figure 5.60**).

4. In the Modify Style dialog box, make sure Update the style to reflect recent changes? is selected (**Figure 5.61**).

5. In the Modify Style dialog box, check Automatically update the style from now on if you want the information in the style to update whenever you change the formatting of any paragraph that has been given that style (**Figure 5.62**).

6. Click OK.

✔ Tips

- You cannot use this technique to redefine the Normal style.

- You can also modify a style by using the Style command on the Format menu.

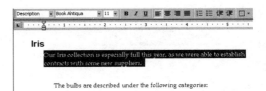

Figure 5.59 Apply font or paragraph formatting changes to the paragraph.

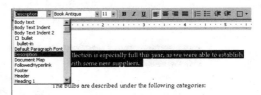

Figure 5.60 Choose the style originally applied to the paragraph.

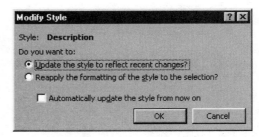

Figure 5.61 The Modify Style dialog box.

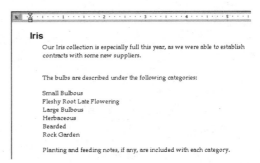

Figure 5.62 Other paragraphs controlled by the modified style get the new formatting, too.

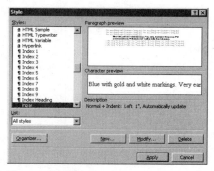

Figure 5.63 Click New to create a new style.

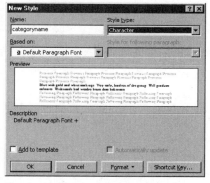

Figure 5.64 Type a style name to replace the current name.

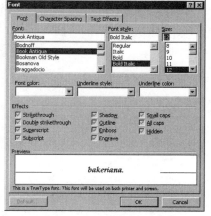

Figure 5.65 Choose Font from the Format drop-down list to open the Font dialog box.

Creating a Character Style

You can use character styles to apply font formatting to selected text characters and words within a paragraph without affecting the overall formatting of the paragraph.

To create a character style:

1. Select the first set of characters for which you want to define a new style.

2. From the Format menu, choose Style.

3. In the Style dialog box, click New to create a new style (**Figure 5.63**).

4. In the New Style dialog box, type a style name to replace the current, selected style name (**Figure 5.64**).

5. Choose Character from the drop-down Style Type list.

6. Click the Format button and choose Font from the Format drop-down list.

   The Font dialog box opens (**Figure 5.65**).

7. On the Font tab in the Font dialog box, specify the formatting you want and then click OK.

8. Click OK in the New Style dialog box to close the dialog box.

9. Click Apply in the Style dialog box. The text you selected in step 1 is formatted according to the new style, and the new style name appears in the style list.

✔ Tip

■ In the Style list on the Formatting toolbar, character styles are marked with an *a* in the panel to the right of the style name rather than with a paragraph mark.

CHARACTER STYLE

71

FORMATTING PAGES

6

Page formatting can be the first step in creating a new document or the last. Page formatting involves setting the size and shape of the page and the width of the margins. Word will adjust the text on the page to fit the new page size and margins.

If you always print portrait-orientation, 8½ x 11 pages with standard margins, you won't need to worry about page formatting. But if you want your pages to look a bit more unusual, try adjusting the page formatting.

Changing the Page Size and Orientation

You can choose from a number of common page sizes or set your own size, in either portrait (vertical) or landscape (horizontal) orientation.

To change the page size and shape:

1. From the File menu, choose Page Setup (**Figure 6.1**).

2. On the Paper Size tab of the Page Setup dialog box, choose one of the standard paper sizes from the Paper Size drop-down list (**Figure 6.2**).

   or

   Enter a custom page size in the Width and Height text boxes. The Preview area shows the new size.

3. Confirm that the Orientation setting you want for the page is selected: Portrait or Landscape.

4. Click OK.

✔ Tip

■ The selections you make for paper size and orientation apply to the current document only. New documents revert to the default settings.

Figure 6.1 Choose Page Setup.

Click to open the drop-down list

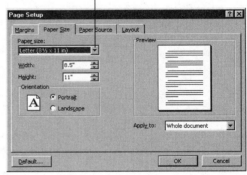

Figure 6.2 The Paper Size tab of the Page Setup dialog box.

*Additional margin for
binding or hole punching*

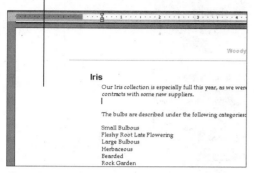

Figure 6.3 Increase the left margin to provide space for binding or hole punching.

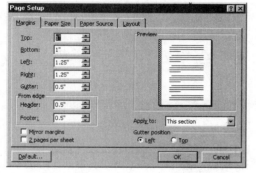

Figure 6.4 Change margins on the Margins tab of the Page Setup menu.

Changing the Margins

Margins are the blank spaces at the top, bottom, left, and right edges of a page. To provide extra space for binding or hole punching, for example, you might want to increase the left margin (**Figure 6.3**).

To change the margins:

1. From the File menu, choose Page Setup.

2. On the Margins tab of the Page Setup dialog box, change the Top, Bottom, Left, or Right settings (**Figure 6.4**).

3. Alter the Gutter setting if you want to change the space between multiple columns on the page.

4. Click OK.

✔ Tip

■ To print a book with text on both sides of the page, click the Mirror Margins check box on the Margins tab of the Page Setup dialog. The Left margin of a right-hand page becomes the Inside margin and the Right margin becomes the Outside margin. On left-hand pages, it's vice versa. To leave space for binding on the left side of the right page and the right side of the left page, for example, you'd increase the Inside margin setting.

Setting Up Headers and Footers

Headers are text that appears at the top of every page. Footers appear at the bottom of every page.

To set up a header and footer:

1. From the View menu, choose Header and Footer (**Figure 6.5**).

   Word switches to Print Layout view, positions the insertion point in the blank header space, and opens the Header and Footer toolbar (**Figure 6.6**).

2. To edit the footer instead of the header, click the Switch Between Header and Footer button on the Header and Footer toolbar.

3. Type text for the left side of the header or footer (**Figure 6.7**).

4. If you want text in the center of the header or footer, press Tab and type text.

5. If you want text at the right side of the header or footer, press Tab again and type text (**Figure 6.8**).

6. Click the Close button on the Header and Footer toolbar to finish editing the header or footer and return to the previous view.

✔ Tips

- You might want to change the Zoom setting to see the header or footer more clearly.

- Rather than type text, you can enter the page number, date, or time in the header or footer by clicking the appropriate buttons on the Header and Footer toolbar.

Figure 6.5 Choose Header and Footer from the View menu.

Page numbers · Date · Time · Switch Between Header and Footer

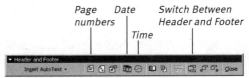

Figure 6.6 The Header and Footer toolbar.

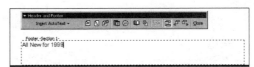

Figure 6.7 Type text at the left side of the header or footer.

Figure 6.8 Press Tab twice to skip to the right side of the header or footer.

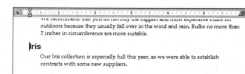

Figure 6.9 Place the insertion point at the location for a section break.

Figure 6.10 Break dialog box.

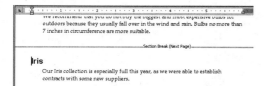

Figure 6.11 A section break.

Table 6.1

Section Breaks

BREAK	ACTION
Next Page	Starts a section at the top of the next page.
Continuous	Starts a section without moving following text to a new page.
Even Page	Starts a section on the next even-numbered page, leaving a blank odd page if necessary.
Odd Page	Starts a section on the next odd-numbered page, leaving a blank even page if necessary.

Creating Multiple Sections

A document can contain multiple sections, each of which can have different page setup attributes: different margins, page numbering, and headers and footers. A new document contains only one section until you insert a section break. Then you can apply page formatting to the new section independently.

To create a new section:

1. Position the insertion point where you want the new section to begin (**Figure 6.9**).

2. From the Insert menu, choose Break.

3. In the Break dialog box , choose one of the Section Breaks options (**Figure 6.10**).

4. Click OK.

   Word inserts a double dotted line labeled "Section Break" (**Figure 6.11**).

✔ Tips

■ Insert an Odd Page section break when you are printing left and right pages, you've started numbering on a right page (page 1), and you want each section to start on a new right page even if it means leaving an entire left page blank.

■ **Table 6.1** shows the section break options.

Paginating the Document

As you work in Normal view, Word enters an automatic page break (a dotted line across the page) whenever you fill a page. When you pause while typing, Word readjusts the automatic page breaks.

To start a new page before the automatic page break, enter a manual page break (**Figure 6.12**).

To insert a manual page break:

1. Position the insertion point in the line that you want to be the first line of the new page.

2. Press Ctrl+Enter.

    or

    From the Insert menu, choose Break.

3. Make sure Page Break is selected.

4. Click OK.

✔ Tips

- To delete a manual page break, select the page break and press the Delete key.

- You cannot delete an automatic page break or move it down. Your only option is to insert a manual page break above the automatic page break.

- By switching to Print Layout view or Print Preview, you can see how the text falls on pages with the current page breaks.

- To keep a heading from appearing at the bottom of one page and the following text at the top of the next page, select the heading, choose Paragraph from the Format menu, and specify Keep With Next.

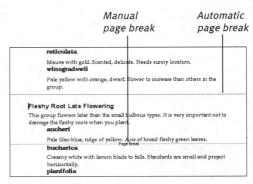

Figure 6.12 A manual page break vs. an automatic page break.

Figure 6.13 Choose Page Numbers from the Insert menu.

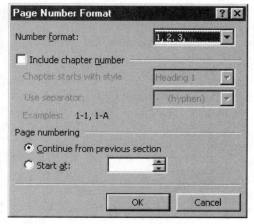

Figure 6.14 The Page Numbers dialog box.

Figure 6.15 The Page Number Format dialog box.

Numbering Pages

You can enter page numbering as you create a document's header or footer. But another approach that is more direct and gives you the option of choosing a number format and a starting number is to insert page numbers directly.

To insert page numbering:

1. From the Insert menu, choose Page Numbers (**Figure 6.13**).

2. In the Page Numbers dialog box, choose Top of Page or Bottom of Page from the Position drop-down list (**Figure 6.14**).

3. Choose an alignment from the Alignment drop-down list.

4. Click the Format button.

5. In the Page Number Format dialog box, choose a numbering style from the Number Format drop-down list (**Figure 6.15**).

6. Click OK to return to the Page Numbers dialog box.

7. Click OK.

✔ Tip

■ While the Page Number Format dialog box is open, you can also enter a number in the Start At text box to start numbering at a number other than 1.

NUMBERING PAGES

Setting Up Multiple Columns

You can set the number of columns for each section of your document and adjust the spacing between the columns.

To set the number of columns:

1. Click the Columns button on the Standard toolbar and then drag across the number of columns you want (**Figure 6.16**).

2. Adjust the column widths in the horizontal ruler.

or

1. From the Format menu, choose Columns (**Figure 6.17**).

2. In the Columns dialog box, click one of the Presets options or enter a number of columns in the Number of Columns text box (**Figure 6.18**).

3. To add a vertical line between the columns, click the Line Between check box.

4. Click OK.

✔ Tips

- To vary the widths of columns, clear the Equal Column Width check box in the Columns dialog box and then use the Width and Spacing controls to modify the width and spacing for each column.

- The maximum number of columns on a page is 12.

- The gutter width on the Margins tab of the Page Setup dialog box determines the spacing between equal columns.

The Columns button

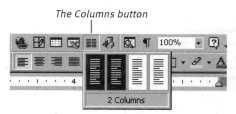

Figure 6.16 The Columns button.

Figure 6.17 Choose Columns on the Format menu.

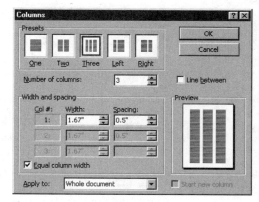

Figure 6.18 Click a Preset option on the Columns dialog box to set the number of columns.

Figure 6.19 Choose AutoFormat from the Format menu.

Figure 6.20 The AutoFormat dialog box.

AutoFormatting a Document

If you apply AutoFormatting to a document, Word analyzes the document and applies styles to the text. AutoFormatting also removes extra paragraph marks, replaces indents created using spaces or tabs with paragraph indents, replaces asterisks or hyphens in bulleted lists with real bullets, and replaces (C), (R), and (TM) with copyright, registered trademark, and trademark symbols.

To AutoFormat a document:

1. From the Format menu, choose AutoFormat (**Figure 6.19**).

2. In the AutoFormat dialog box, select a document type from the drop-down list (**Figure 6.20**).

3. Click OK.

✔ Tip

■ To change the way AutoFormat analyzes the document and to specify which of the standard actions it will carry out, click the Options button in the Auto-Format dialog box.

AUTOFORMATTING

CREATING TABLES

7

Viburnum	Origin	North American Zone	Cultural Notes
davidi	western China	Zone 2	good light well-drained soil
cinnamomifolium	western China	Zone 3	good light well-drained soil
japonicum	Japan	Zone 4	rich soil, moderate drainage
rhytidophyllum	western China	Zone 2	rich soil, moisture
tinus	Mediterranean	Zone 3	dry conditions in summer

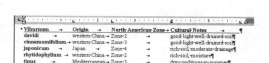

Figure 7.1 Tabs used to align text in columns.

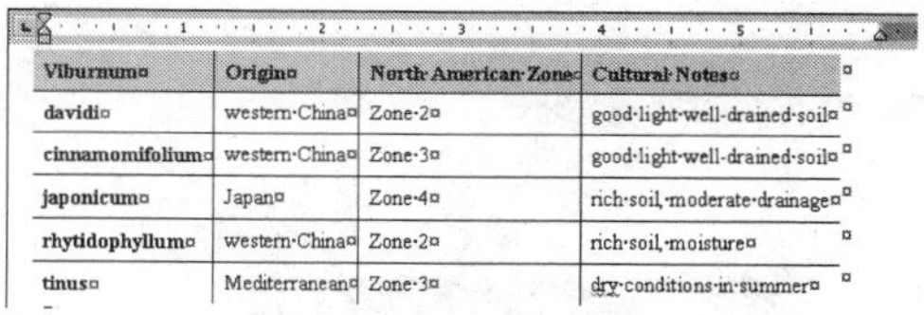

Viburnum	Origin	North American Zone	Cultural Notes
davidi	western China	Zone 2	good light well-drained soil
cinnamomifolium	western China	Zone 3	good light well-drained soil
japonicum	Japan	Zone 4	rich soil, moderate drainage
rhytidophyllum	western China	Zone 2	rich soil, moisture
tinus	Mediterranean	Zone 3	dry conditions in summer

Figure 7.2 A professional-looking Word table.

Typewriters and old-fashioned word processors used tabs to align text and numbers in columns (**Figure 7.1**). You can still use tabs in Word, but you're better off using Word's tables, which make it easy both to align data in columns and rows and to format the table so that it looks professional (**Figure 7.2**). Tables are so useful in Word that we're devoting an entire chapter to them.

Starting a Table

You can create the table structure before you enter any text, or you can convert text you've already created to a table. There's an easy way to create the structure for a simple table and a way to create a more complex table. We'll talk about both in the next two sections.

To create the structure for a simple table:

1. Position the insertion point at the location for the table.

2. Click the Insert Table button on the Standard toolbar (**Figure 7.3**).

3. Drag across the number of columns and down the number of rows you want (**Figure 7.4**).

   An unformatted table appears (**Figure 7.5**).

   or

1. Position the insertion point at the location for the table.

2. From the Table menu, choose Insert.

3. In the Insert Table dialog box, specify the columns and rows (**Figure 7.6**).

4. Click OK.

✔ Tip

- You can apply an AutoFormat to a table or change the AutoFormat applied at any time by clicking anywhere in the table and then choosing Table Auto-Format from the Table menu.

Insert Table button

Figure 7.3 The Insert Table button on the Standard toolbar.

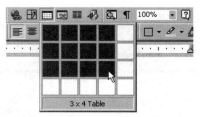

Figure 7.4 Drag across the grid to specify the table dimensions.

Figure 7.5 The new table.

Figure 7.6 The Insert Table dialog box.

STARTING A TABLE

Figure 7.7 The Tables and Borders toolbar.

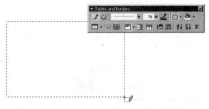

Figure 7.8 Drawing a table boundary.

Figure 7.9 Drawing a column boundary.

Figure 7.10 Erasing a boundary.

Drawing a Table

You can also draw a table to quickly create a more complex table structure

To draw a table:

1. From the Table menu, choose Draw Table.

   The Tables and Borders toolbar appears (**Figure 7.7**).

2. Click the Draw Table button on the toolbar, and drag the outline of a table in the document by clicking and holding where you want one corner, dragging diagonally to the other corner, and then releasing the mouse button (**Figure 7.8**).

3. Continue to use the Draw Table tool to draw the interior cell boundaries (**Figure 7.9**).

✔ Tips

■ To erase a boundary, click the Eraser tool and drag along the boundary you want to erase (**Figure 7.10**).

■ To draw colored lines, select a Border Color.

■ You can draw tables inside tables using the Draw Table tool.

DRAWING A TABLE

Drawing a More Complex Table

You can change different aspects of the structure to create a more complex table.

To move a line:

◆ Click the line and drag it to the new position (**Figure 7.11**).

Figure 7.11 Drag a boundary to move it.

To equalize cell heights or widths:

1. Click outside the table to clear the tool selection.

2. Click and drag through the cells you want to adjust.

3. Click either the Distribute Rows Evenly button or the Distribute Columns Evenly button on the Tables and Borders toolbar (**Figure 7.12**).

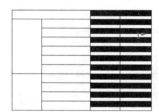

Figure 7.12 Distributing rows evenly.

To set row height or column width precisely:

1. Select the cells you want to modify (**Figure 7.13**).

2. From the Table menu, choose Table Properties.

3. In the Table Properties dialog box, enter the values you want to use in the text boxes on the Row, Column, or Cell tab, or use the arrows to choose predefined values (**Figure 7.14**).

4. Click OK.

Figure 7.13 Select the cells to adjust.

Figure 7.14 Enter a column width on the Column tab.

Entering Data in a Table

You can type data directly in table cells, and you can move or copy information to a cell.

To enter data in a table:

1. Click in a cell and then type to insert data in the cell

   As you type, the insertion point wraps within the cell and the entire row will become taller if it needs to accommodate multiple lines of text.

2. Press Tab to move to the cell to the right, and type text in the next cell (**Figure 7.15**).

3. Continue pressing Tab after you finish each cell.

4. When you finish entering text in the last cell of the table, press Tab to create a new row (**Figures 7.16** and **7.17**).

✔ Tips

- When you reach the rightmost cell, pressing Tab moves the insertion point to the next row.
- Press Shift+Tab to move back a cell.
- If a cell already contains text, pressing Tab to move to the cell also selects the text.

Iris		Purchased in 98	Sold in 98
Small Bulbous	I		

Figure 7.15 Entering data.

Iris		Purchased in 98	Sold in 98
Small Bulbous	bakeriana	1600	1488
	danfordiae	1200	1200
	histroides	2400	2250
	reticulata	1000	1000
	winogradowii	800	790
	Total		
Fleshy Root Late Flowering	aucheri	2400	1980
	bucharica	2400	2400
	planifolia	1600	1600
	Total		I

Figure 7.16 Insertion point in last cell.

Iris		Purchased in 98	Sold in 98
Small Bulbous	bakeriana	1600	1488
	danfordiae	1200	1200
	histroides	2400	2250
	reticulata	1000	1000
	winogradowii	800	790
	Total		
Fleshy Root Late Flowering	aucheri	2400	1980
	bucharica	2400	2400
	planifolia	1600	1600
	Total		
I			

Figure 7.17 The new row created.

Aligning Data in a Table

Once the data has been entered, you can align table elements.

To align data vertically or horizontally within cells:

1. Select the cells you want to align.

2. Click the appropriate alignment in the Alignment pull-down list on the Tables and Borders toolbar (**Figures 7.18** and **7.19**).

To change the orientation of data within cells:

1. Select the cells you want to orient.

2. Click the Change Text Direction tool on the Tables and Borders toolbar (**Figure 7.20**).

✔ Tip

■ To switch between the three possible text directions, click the Change Text Direction tool.

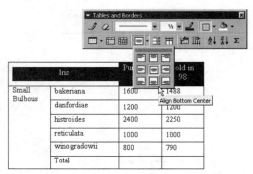

Figure 7.18 Using the Align Bottom Center button.

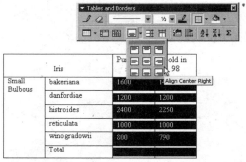

Figure 7.19 Using the Align Center Right button.

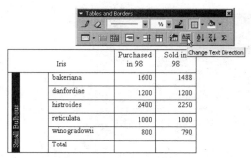

Figure 7.20 Using the Change Text Direction tool.

	Iris	Purchased in 98	Sold in 98
Small Bulbous	bakeriana	1600	1488
	danfordiae	1200	1200
	histroides	2400	2250
	reticulata	1000	1000
	winogradowii	800	790
	Total		
Fleshy Root Late Flowering	aucheri	2400	1980
	bucharica	2400	2400
	planifolia	1600	1600
	Total		

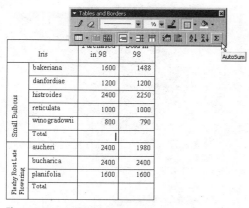

Figure 7.21 Using the AutoSum tool.

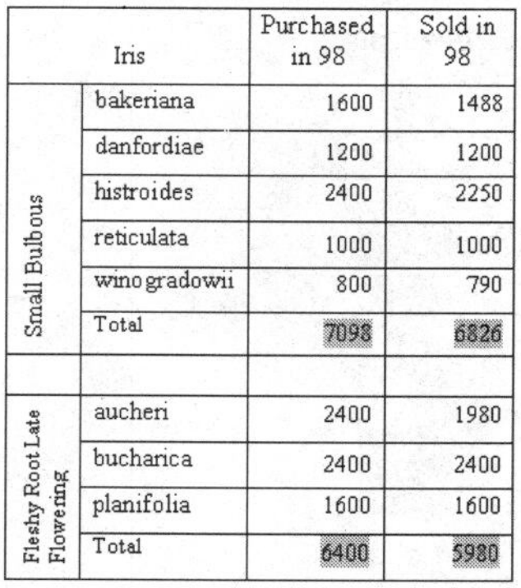

	Iris	Purchased in 98	Sold in 98
Small Bulbous	bakeriana	1600	1488
	danfordiae	1200	1200
	histroides	2400	2250
	reticulata	1000	1000
	winogradowii	800	790
	Total	7098	6826
Fleshy Root Late Flowering	aucheri	2400	1980
	bucharica	2400	2400
	planifolia	1600	1600
	Total	6400	5980

Figure 7.22 Columns of numbers added.

Totaling Numeric Data

You can sum the data in a column as well as perform more complex calculations.

To automatically total values in a column:

1. Click in the cell below the numbers to be added.
2. Click the AutoSum button on the Tables and Borders toolbar (**Figures 7.21** and **7.22**).

✔ Tips

- Word attempts to sum the whole column. Insert an extra blank row temporarily to arrive at a sum for only part of the column.
- To perform more complex calculations with values in a table, click in an empty cell and insert a formula by choosing Formula from the Table menu.

Deleting Data from a Table

To delete data from a table, you can clear the contents of a cell by selecting text and deleting it, but you can also delete cells, rows, and columns.

To delete cells from a table:

1. Select the cells you want to delete.

2. From the Table menu, choose Delete and then choose Cells from the Delete submenu (**Figure 7.23**).

3. In the Delete Cells dialog box, select an option to delete particular cells and move the remaining cells up or to the left or to delete entire rows or columns (**Figure 7.24**).

4. Click OK.

✔ Tip

■ To delete an entire table, choose Table from the pop-out menu (**Figure 7.25**) or drag the cursor over all the cells to select the whole table. Then click the Cut button on the Standard toolbar or choose Cut from the Edit menu.

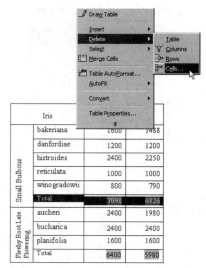

Figure 7.23 Choose Cells from the Delete submenu.

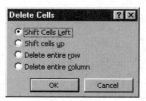

Figure 7.24 The Delete Cells dialog box.

Iris		Purchased in 98	Sold in 98
Small Bulbous	bakeriana	1600	1488
	danfordiae	1200	1200
	histroides	2400	2250
	reticulata	1000	1000
	winogradowii	800	790
Fleshy Root Late Flowering	aucheri	2400	1980
	bucharica	2400	2400
	planifolia	1600	1600
	Total	6400	5980

Figure 7.25 The chosen cells are deleted.

DELETING DATA FROM A TABLE

	Iris	Purchased in 98	Sold in 98
Small Bulbous	bakeriana	1600	1488
	danfordiae	1200	1200
	histroides	2400	2250
	reticulata	1000	1000
	winogradowii	800	790
Fleshy Root Late Flowering	aucheri	2400	1980
	bucharica	2400	2400
	planifolia	1600	1600
	Total	6400	5980

Figure 7.26 Place the insertion point to insert a row.

Figure 7.27 Choose Rows Below from the Insert submenu.

	Iris	Purchased in 98	Sold in 98
Small Bulbous	bakeriana	1600	1488
	danfordiae	1200	1200
	histroides	2400	2250
	reticulata	1000	1000
	winogradowii	800	790
Fleshy Root Late Flowering	aucheri	2400	1980
	bucharica	2400	2400
	planifolia	1600	1600
	Total	6400	5980

Figure 7.28 A blank row inserted in the table.

Inserting Rows and Columns

You can add rows and columns to any portion of your table.

To insert a row:

1. Click in a cell at the location for the new, blank row (**Figure 7.26**).

2. From the Table menu, choose Insert and then choose Rows Below from the Insert submenu (**Figures 7.27** and **7.28**).

To insert a column:

1. Position the mouse pointer at the top of the column at the location for the new column. A large down-arrow appears.

2. Click while the down-arrow is visible to select the column.

3. From the Table menu, choose Insert and then select one of the Columns options from the Insert submenu.

✔ Tip

■ To insert multiple columns or rows, select the number of existing columns or rows corresponding to the number that you want to insert before you choose an option from the Insert submenu. If there are not enough existing columns or rows where you want to do the insertion, do multiple Insert operations.

Merging Cells

You can merge two or more adjacent cells to create column or row headings.

To merge cells:

1. Select the adjacent cells to be merged.

2. Click the Merge Cells button on the Tables and Borders toolbar (**Figures 7.29** and **7.30**).

✔ Tip

■ To split merged cells back into their original individual cells, click the merged cell and click the Split Cells button on the Tables and Borders toolbar.

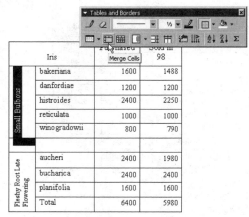

Figure 7.29 Click the Merge Cells tool on the Tables and Borders toolbar.

	Iris	Purchased in 98	Sold in 98
Small Bulbous	bakeriana	1600	1488
	danfordiae	1200	1200
	histroides	2400	2250
	reticulata	1000	1000
	winogradowii	800	790
Fleshy Root Late Flowering	aucheri	2400	1980
	bucharica	2400	2400
	planifolia	1600	1600
	Total	6400	5980

Figure 7.30 The selected cells are merged.

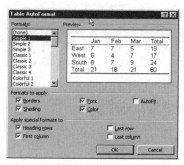

Figure 7.31 The Table AutoFormat
dialog box.

Figure 7.32 The Line Style and Line Weight
drop-down lists.

Figure 7.33 Choose borders on
the border drop-down palette.

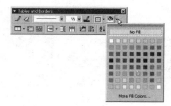

Figure 7.34
The Shading
drop-down list.

Turning On Borders and Shading

Borders are lines surrounding the cells.
Shading is fill within the cells.

To automatically format a table with a template:

1. Click anywhere in the table to select it.

2. From the Table menu, choose Table AutoFormat.

3. In the Table AutoFormat dialog box, select one of the available templates and look at the Preview window to see whether the template fits your needs (**Figure 7.31**).

4. Turn on or off any of the component options you want by clicking in the corresponding check boxes.

5. Click OK.

To manually set borders and shading:

1. Select the cells for which you want to modify the borders or add shading.

2. On the Tables and Borders toolbar, select line style and weight from the drop-down lists (**Figure 7.32**).

3. Click the Border tool, and use the options on the drop-down palette to apply borders to the top, bottom, left, right, inside, or outside of the selected cells (**Figure 7.33**).

4. To apply shading to the selected cells, select a shading option from the Shading drop-down list (**Figure 7.34**).

Converting Text to a Table

When someone else has created a table in a document using old-fashioned tabs, you can easily convert the tabbed text to a standard Word table that you can then modify and format.

To convert text to a table:

1. Select all the lines of the existing tabbed text (**Figure 7.35**).

2. Click the Insert Table button on the Standard toolbar.

   or

1. Select all the lines of the existing tabbed text.

2. From the Table menu, choose Convert and then choose Text to Table (**Figure 7.36**).

3. In the Convert Text to Table dialog box, select the number of columns, the AutoFit behavior, and the text separation (**Figure 7.37**).

4. Click AutoFormat if you want to select a format for the table.

5. Click OK to return to the Convert Text to Table dialog box.

6. Click OK (**Figure 7.38**).

✔ Tip

- To convert multiple paragraphs to a table, select those paragraphs, choose Convert from the Table menu and then choose Text to Table, and click Paragraphs in the Separate Text At box.

Figure 7.35 Select the tabbed table that you want to convert.

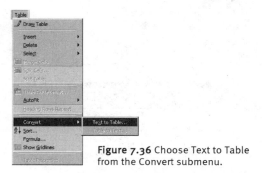

Figure 7.36 Choose Text to Table from the Convert submenu.

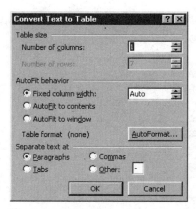

Figure 7.37 Set options in the Convert Text to Table dialog box.

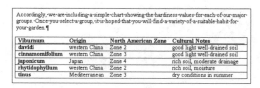

Figure 7.38 The converted table.

SPECIAL
WORD TECHNIQUES

8

To make working with and printing documents easy and efficient, Word provides a variety of special capabilities and tools. Features such as AutoCorrect, AutoText, automatic envelope printing, and mail merge take much of the drudgery out of ordinary tasks. Templates also help by providing stock formats for routine documents.

Automatically Correcting Typos

Word's AutoCorrect feature works quietly behind the scenes, automatically correcting many common typos as you type. It has its own short list of common misspellings and their corrections; you can add your own most frequent typos to this list.

AutoCorrect can also capitalize the first word in a sentence, remove instances of two capital letters at the beginning of a word, and capitalize the names of days.

Figure 8.1 Choose AutoCorrect from the Tools menu.

To add typos and corrections to the AutoCorrect list:

1. From the Tools menu, choose Auto-Correct (**Figure 8.1**).

2. Type the typo in the Replace text box (**Figure 8.2**).

3. Type the correction in the With text box.

4. Click the Add button.

5. Click OK when you have finished.

✔ Tips

■ To insert text with a special font formatting, type the correction and format it in a document and then copy the correction and paste it into the With text box in the AutoCorrect dialog box. Be sure to click Formatted Text before you click Add.

■ You can enter an abbreviation as the Replace term and the full technical, medical, or legal term as the With item and then have AutoCorrect enter long, complex terms for you whenever you type the abbreviation.

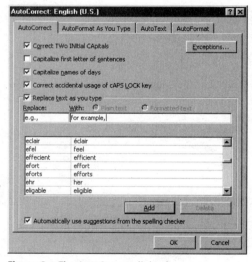

Figure 8.2 The AutoCorrect dialog box.

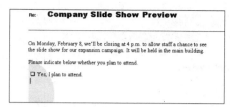

Figure 8.3 Position the insertion point.

Figure 8.4 Choose Symbol from the Insert menu.

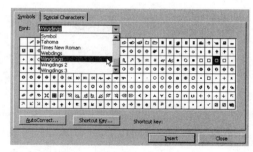

Figure 8.5 Choose Wingdings from the Font pull-down list.

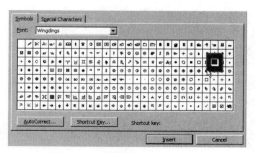

Figure 8.6 Enlarge a symbol by clicking it.

Inserting Symbols from the Wingdings Font

The Wingdings font contains dozens of useful and fun symbols that you can embed in a document. Word lets you insert symbols in a document automatically.

To insert a symbol:

1. Position the insertion point at the destination for the symbol (**Figure 8.3**).

2. From the Insert menu, choose Symbol (**Figure 8.4**).

3. On the Symbols tab of the Symbol dialog box, pull down the list of Fonts and choose Wingdings (**Figure 8.5**).

4. Click any symbol to enlarge it (**Figure 8.6**).

5. If this is the symbol, you want click Insert. Otherwise, select a different symbol and click Insert.

✔ Tips

- You can select symbols from other fonts by choosing the font from the Font list.

- On the Special Characters tab of the Symbol dialog box, you'll find frequently used characters that you can select and insert in any document.

Using AutoText

AutoText saves you from repetitively typing text that you need frequently. With Auto-Text, you can insert any amount of text in a document, from a single word to multiple paragraphs. Assembling boilerplate documents from standard passages, such as putting together contracts by combining standard clauses, is an ideal task for AutoText.

To use AutoText, type a passage of text once and then save it as an AutoText entry, giving it a name in the process—for example, Closing. To recall an AutoText entry, you type the name and press F3.

To create an AutoText entry:

1. Type the text you want to save and then select it (**Figure 8.7**).

2. From the Insert menu, choose AutoText, and then choose New from the submenu (**Figure 8.8**).

3. In the Create AutoText dialog box, replace the highlighted suggested name with a name of your own (**Figure 8.9**).

4. Click OK to add the text to the list of available AutoText entries.

✔ Tips

■ The name you choose for the AutoText entry must be at least four characters.

■ The AutoText entry must be at least two characters longer than the name you assign.

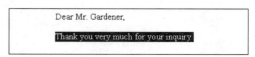

Figure 8.7 Select the text for an AutoText entry.

Figure 8.8 Select New from the AutoText submenu.

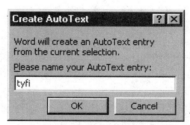

Figure 8.9 The Create AutoText dialog box.

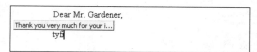

Figure 8.10 The AutoText entry appears in a small yellow box.

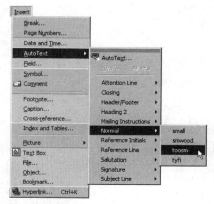

Figure 8.11 AutoText entries listed on the Normal submenu.

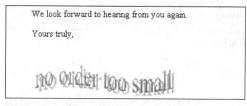

Figure 8.12 The AutoText picture inserted.

To insert an AutoText entry:

1. As you type, Word watches for the name of an AutoText entry. When it detects a name, a yellow box appears with the AutoText entry displayed (**Figure 8.10**).

2. To accept the AutoText replacement, press the Enter key while the yellow box is displayed.

✔ Tips

- You can include a picture in an Auto-Text entry to automatically insert a logo in a document. Type the name and press F3; orchoose AutoText from the Insert menu, choose Normal from the AutoText submenu, and then choose an AutoText entry that includes the picture on the Normal submenu (**Figures 8.11** and **8.12**).

- You can use AutoText to automatically enter long medical, legal, or technical terms.

- To save a formatted paragraph as an AutoText entry, include the paragraph mark at the end of the paragraph when you make a selection for AutoText.

USING AUTOTEXT

Printing Envelopes

Word can extract the mailing address from a letter and automatically format and print an envelope.

To print an envelope:

1. From the Tools menu, choose Envelopes and Labels (**Figure 8.13**).

   or

   If the document contains more than one address, select the appropriate address and then choose Envelopes and Labels from the Tools menu.

2. Make any necessary modifications to the address and return address (**Figure 8.14**).

3. Click Print.

✔ Tips

■ If your envelopes have a preprinted return address, be sure the Omit check box is checked to omit the return address before clicking the Print button.

■ To choose a different envelope size or change the font and location of the addresses on the envelopes, click the Options button in the Envelopes and Labels dialog box to display the Envelope Options dialog box.

■ To create a label, click the Labels tab to set options and then print the label (**Figure 8.15**).

Figure 8.13 Choose Envelopes and Labels from the Tools menu.

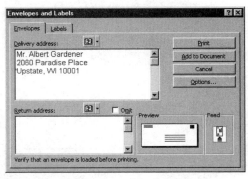

Figure 8.14 The Envelopes tab of the Envelopes and Labels dialog box.

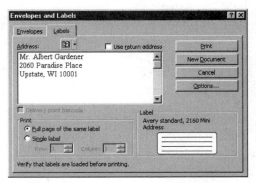

Figure 8.15 The Labels tab of the Envelopes and Labels dialog box.

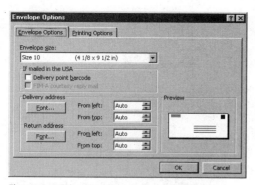

Figure 8.16 The Envelope Options dialog box.

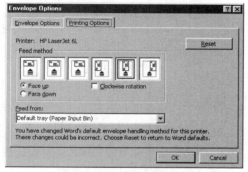

Figure 8.17 The Printing Options tab of the Envelope Options dialog box.

Envelope Printing Options

Before you print envelopes, you can review and set the envelope printing options.

To change the way envelopes are printed:

1. From the Tools menu, choose Envelopes and Labels.

2. In the Envelopes and Labels dialog box, click the Options button.

3. On the Envelope Options tab of the Envelope Options dialog box, change the envelope size, the font, and the positions of the addresses (**Figure 8.16**).

4. On the Printing Options tab of the Envelope Options dialog box, choose the envelope feed direction that matches the way your printer works (**Figure 8.17**).

5. If your printer has an envelope feeder, select the envelope tray from the Feed From drop-down list.

6. Click OK to return to the Envelopes and Labels dialog box.

7. Click OK when you have finished setting options.

✔ Tips

- The Delivery Point Bar Code option prints a machine-readable version of the zip code on the envelope, which assists the U.S. Postal Service in processing mail.

- If you are printing reply envelopes, you can also have Word print an FIM (Facing Identification Mark) code. FIMs are necessary only with business reply mail. Check with the U.S. Postal Service for more information about FIMs.

ENVELOPE PRINTING OPTIONS

Saving a Document as a Template

Templates contain entire document designs and can even include portions of text. When you start a new document, you can choose from among the many preformatted templates that come with Word, including templates for popular business and professional documents. If none of these templates suits your needs, you can modify an existing template or save your own document design as a new template and then use it to create new documents.

Figure 8.18 Choose Save As from the File menu.

To save a document as a template:

1. Create a sample document and format it by creating and applying a set of styles.

2. Delete any text that you do not want saved as part of the template. For example, to save only the styles and page formatting, delete all the text.

3. From the File menu, choose Save As (**Figure 8.18**).

4. From the Save File as Type pull-down list, choose Document Template (**Figure 8.19**).

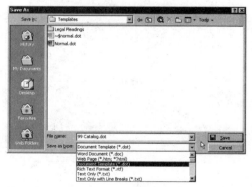

Figure 8.19 Choose Document Template from the Save As Type pull-down list.

5. Type a name for the template in the File Name text box and specify where you want to save the template.

6. Click Save.

✔ Tips

■ AutoText entries, macros, and custom toolbars are saved in the template.

■ If you save the template in Word's Template directory, you can easily use it as a base for a new document (**Figure 8.20**).

Figure 8.20 The New dialog box shows the new template.

Figure 8.21 Select Options from the Tools menu.

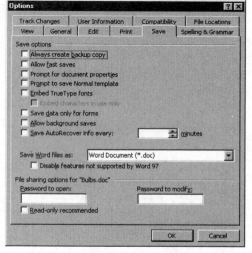

Figure 8.22 The Options dialog box.

Using Automatic Saves

You can have Word automatically save your document at preset intervals. It's a good idea to turn this feature on to protect your work in case of a power loss or other calamity. The saving process occurs very quickly and will not disturb your work.

To use automatic saves:

1. From the Tools menu, select Options (**Figure 8.21**).

2. Click the Save tab of the Options dialog box (**Figure 8.22**).

3. Make sure Save AutoRecover Info Every ___ Minutes is turned on.

4. Change the number of minutes if you want.

5. Click OK.

✔ Tips

■ Although Word can automatically save your work, you must still save your work in a file when you finish creating a document. Word's automatic saving simply creates a special file on disk so that Word can restore the file if your session is interrupted before you perform a normal save operation.

■ If the power fails or disaster strikes while you're working, Word will display a list of automatically saved documents when you next start the program. You can simply select the document you were working on when you were so rudely interrupted.

USING AUTOMATIC SAVES

Creating Form Letters Using Mail Merge

Word provides guided help for performing the three major steps in creating mail merged letters, labels, or envelopes that are personalized with names and addresses from a list. First, you create or open the data source (for example, a collection of names and addresses). Next, you create the merge document (with placeholders for the information that changes with each copy). Finally, you print the merged document.

To create a form letter using mail merge:

1. From the Tools menu, select Mail Merge.

2. In the Mail Merge Helper dialog box (**Figure 8.23**), click each numbered option in sequence and then follow the displayed instructions.

   Before Word helps you create the merge letter, it helps you create or open the data source for the database. It then returns to the merge document and displays the Mail Merge toolbar (**Figure 8.24**).

3. Type the text of the merge document, clicking the Insert Merge Field button whenever you want to include a placeholder for information from the data source.

4. Choose a field name from the Insert Merge Field list (**Figure 8.25**).

5. When the merge document is complete, click the Check for Errors button.

6. Click the Merge to Printer button or the Merge to New Document button to create a document that you can print later.

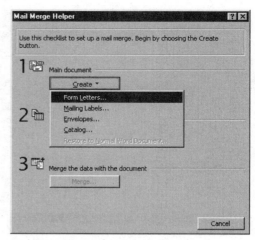

Figure 8.23 The Mail Merge Helper dialog box.

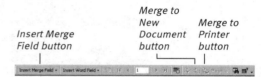

Figure 8.24 The Mail Merge toolbar.

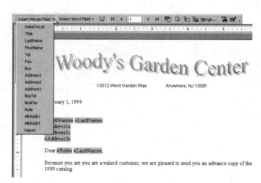

Figure 8.25 Choose field names from the Insert Merge Field list as you type the merge letter.

WORD AND THE WEB

With Word's Web-related capabilities, you can easily publish ordinary documents as pages on the Web or on an intranet (a private Web within an organization). You can also open existing Web pages, make changes to them in Word, and then resave them with the changes. And if you'd like to let Word take care of much of the work of creating Web pages or a Web site, you can let Word's Web Wizard work for you.

Inserting Hyperlinks

By inserting hyperlinks in a document, you can create hotspots in the text that people can click to go to a file, a location in a file, or a page on the Web.

To add a hyperlink:

1. Select the text you want to hyperlink (**Figure 9.1**).

2. From the Insert menu, choose Hyperlink.

   or

   Click the Insert Hyperlink button on the Standard toolbar (**Figure 9.2**).

3. In the Insert Hyperlink dialog box, type the Web page address (URL) of the destination to which you want to link (**Figure 9.3**).

   or

   Select from recent files, browsed pages, or links.

   or

   Click the File button to browse for a file in the Link to File dialog box for the file to which you want to link.

   or

   Click the Web Page button to use your Web browser to navigate to the Web page you want in the browser window. (You must be connected to the Web.)

4. Click OK.

   The text is now underlined and in a different color (**Figure 9.4**).

Figure 9.1 Select the text to hyperlink.

Insert Hyperlink button

Figure 9.2 The Insert Hyperlink button.

Figure 9.3 Enter a Web page name or address.

Figure 9.4 The hyperlink is underlined and in a different color.

INSERTING HYPERLINKS

Figure 9.5 Choose a heading in the current document in the Insert Hyperlink document.

To link to a place in the current document:

1. Select the text you want to hyperlink.

2. From the Insert menu, choose Hyperlink.

   or

   Click the Insert Hyperlink button on the Standard toolbar.

3. In the Insert Hyperlink dialog box, click Place in This Document in the Link To sidebar.

4. Click the plus sign box next to Headings to select a heading as the destination (**Figure 9.5**).

5. Click OK.

   The hyperlink text is colored and underlined.

✔ Tip

■ Use the Recent Files, Browsed Pages, and Inserted Links buttons as shortcuts to help you find recently used pages.

INSERTING HYPERLINKS

Editing a Hyperlink

You can edit the text that is displayed as well as the location of the link.

To edit a hyperlink:

1. Select the hyperlink by right-clicking when the hand pointer is on the hyperlink text (**Figure 9.6**).

2. Choose Hyperlink from the submenu, and then choose Edit Hyperlink (**Figure 9.7**).

3. Make the changes in the Edit Hyperlink dialog box (**Figure 9.8**).

4. Click OK.

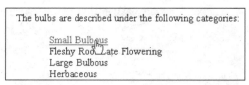

Figure 9.6 Place the pointer on a hyperlink and right-click.

Figure 9.7 Choose Edit Hyperlink.

Figure 9.8 Make changes in the Edit Hyperlink dialog box.

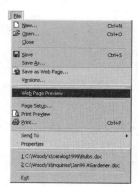

Figure 9.9 Choose Web Page Preview from the File menu.

Previewing a Document as a Web Page

You can test any document you create to see how it will be displayed in a browser.

To preview a document as a Web page:

◆ From the File menu, choose Web Page Preview (**Figure 9.9**).

Your default browser displays the document (**Figure 9.10**).

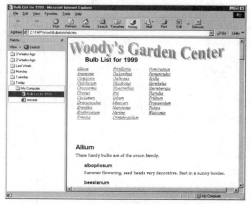

Figure 9.10 Your default browser displays the document.

Saving a Document as a Web Page

You can save any document in Word as a Web page. After the document has been saved, you can add it to your intranet or to a Web site on the Internet.

To save a document as a Web page:

1. From the File menu, choose Save As Web Page (**Figure 9.11**).

2. In the Save As dialog box, choose the name and location.

3. Click Change Title and type the text you want displayed as the title when the page is viewed in a browser (**Figure 9.12**).

4. In the Set Page Title dialog box, type the title (**Figure 9.13**).

5. Click OK to return to the Save As dialog box.

6. Click Save.

✔ Tips

- The extra files created are stored in a subdirectory. If you move the Web page you create, be sure to also move the subdirectory (**Figure 9.14**).

- If your system administrator or Internet service provider has set up a Web server that supports Web publishing, you can save the Web page in a Web folder.

Figure 9.11 Choose Save As Web Page from the File menu.

Figure 9.12 Enter a name and location for the Web page in the Save As dialog box.

Figure 9.13 Change the page title in the Set Page Title dialog box.

Supporting folder   Web page

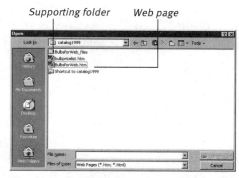

Figure 9.14 The Web page and supporting folder.

SAVING A WEB PAGE

Figure 9.15 Double-click the Web Page Wizard icon.

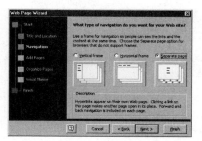

Figure 9.16 Select a navigation method.

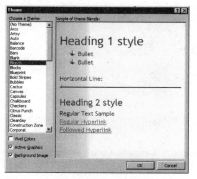

Figure 9.17 Select a theme.

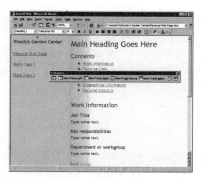

Figure 9.18 A Web page.

Using the Web Wizard to Create a Web Site

Word's Web Wizard lets you create a single Web page or an entire Web site. As you follow the steps of the Wizard, you can also choose a theme for the Web to give all the pages a consistent look.

To use the Web Wizard:

1. From the File menu, choose New.

2. Click the Web Pages tab of the New dialog box and double-click the Web Page Wizard icon (**Figure 9.15**).

3. In the Web Page Wizard dialog box, click Next to begin the wizard.

4. Fill in the Web site title and location and click Next.

5. Select a navigation method and click Next (**Figure 9.16**).

6. Add and organize pages, as necessary, pressing Next to advance.

7. Click Browse Themes to select a theme.

8. In the Theme dialog box, select a theme and click OK (**Figure 9.17**).

   You can select No Theme if you want to add your own background, link colors, and bullets later.

9. Click Finish to have the page or pages created and displayed (**Figure 9.18**).

✔ Tip

■ You can use the available Web templates to create individual Web pages.

Formatting a Document with a Web Theme

For any page you plan to save as a Web page, you can choose a theme.

To choose a Web theme:

1. From the Format menu, choose Theme (**Figure 9.19**).

2. Select a theme (**Figure 9.20**).

3. Click OK.

   The Web page takes on the design supplied by the theme (**Figure 9.21**).

✔ Tip

- The background is displayed only in Web Page view.

Figure 9.19 Choose Theme from the Format menu.

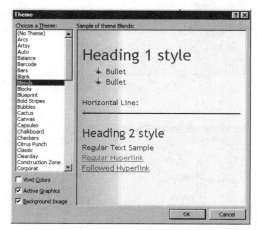

Figure 9.20 Choose a theme for the Web page.

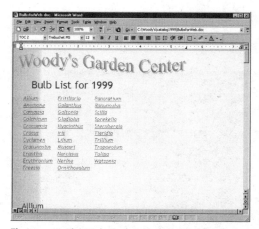

Figure 9.21 The Web page takes on the design of supplied by the theme.

Part 3
Microsoft Excel

Part 3
Microsoft Excel

INTRODUCING EXCEL 2000

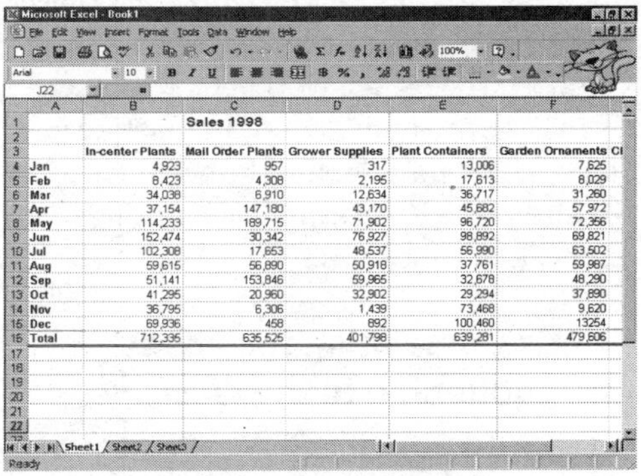

Figure 10.1 A Microsoft Excel worksheet.

With Excel 2000, the spreadsheet of the Microsoft Office suite, you can track, calculate, and analyze numbers and create charts to depict this information visually.

After you type numbers into a grid of cells on an Excel sheet (**Figure 10.1**), you can enter formulas in adjacent cells that total, subtract, multiply, or divide the numbers. You can also enter functions (special Excel formulas) that perform dozens of complex calculations, from simple averaging to sophisticated financial calculations such as Net Present Value. Excel can even calculate highly involved statistics, such as the inverse of the one-tailed probability of the chi-squared distribution.

Excel also offers simple database capabilities. You can accumulate records of information that are both textual and numeric and sort, search for, and extract data from a database.

To display numbers graphically, you can use Excel to create a chart. Excel uses the same charting program as PowerPoint, so its charts are both professional looking and readable. You can also create PivotTables and PivotCharts, which show alternative views of data.

The Steps to Creating an Excel Sheet

Filling the cells with row and column headings and data

In the worksheet grid of cells, enter the row and column headings and the relevant numbers. Use AutoFill, if you can, to enter sequences like month names.

Entering the calculations

In cells adjacent to the data, enter formulas to calculate the results you need. Summing a row or column is the most familiar formula, but Excel provides the dozens of special functions that can perform sophisticated calculations on your data.

Changing the sheet structure

With the numbers and calculations in place, you can structure the sheet to make it easy to interpret. You might widen a column, lock the headings so that they remain on the screen at all times, or split the sheet into panes you can use to view or edit different areas of the sheet simultaneously.

Formatting the sheet

AutoFormatting a sheet can enhance the sheet's appearance and make it more presentable or easier to understand. Excel's dozens of AutoFormat designs make designing the sheet a simple menu choice.

To refine the sheet, you can further format sheet elements. You can format the text or numbers, add borders and shading to cells, or use styles to apply formatting automatically. You can also use conditional formatting to highlight dynamic data you want to monitor.

Annotating and auditing the sheet

Add notes to cells to attach text messages or even voice annotations. You can also name the sheets in a workbook to make them easier to understand. And before you stake your reputation on the accuracy of the sheet, use Excel's built-in auditing tools to check the formulas.

Printing or mailing the sheet and publishing to the Web

Excel's Print Review and Web Page Preview give you a bird's-eye view of your work before you commit it to paper or the Internet. To send a sheet to a colleague, you can simply attach it to an e-mail message.

Other features

Excel includes sophisticated charting, graphics, and database capabilities that let you graphically represent numeric data or collect and store large quantities of information.

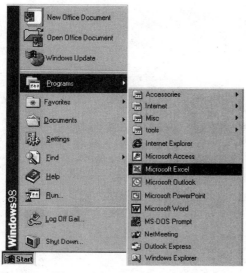

Figure 10.2 You can start Excel from the Start menu.

Starting Excel

You start Excel in the same way that you start every application in the Microsoft Office suite.

To start Excel:

◆ From the Start menu, choose Programs, and then choose Microsoft Excel (**Figure 10.2**).

or

Double-click any Excel workbook listed in the Open Office Document dialog box.

✔ Tip

■ If Microsoft Excel is already started, click its icon on the taskbar to restore the window.

STARTING EXCEL

The Excel Window

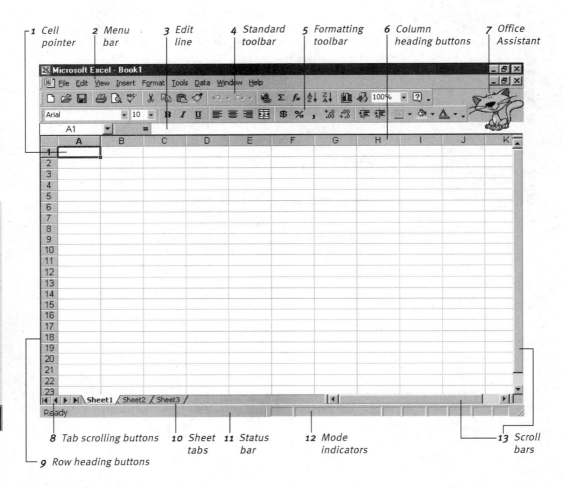

1 Cell pointer   **2** Menu bar   **3** Edit line   **4** Standard toolbar   **5** Formatting toolbar   **6** Column heading buttons   **7** Office Assistant

8 Tab scrolling buttons   **10** Sheet tabs   **11** Status bar   **12** Mode indicators   **13** Scroll bars

9 Row heading buttons

Figure 10.3 The Excel window.

Key to the Excel Window

1 Cell pointer

The cell pointer surrounds the currently selected cell. To move the cell pointer, click a different cell or press the arrow keys, Tab, Enter, Shift+Tab, or Shift+Enter.

2 Menu bar

Click any name on the menu bar to pull down a menu.

3 Edit line

Displays the contents of the selected cell. You can edit the contents here or within the cell.

4 Standard toolbar

Toolbar with buttons for standard file management and text editing and proofing commands.

5 Formatting toolbar

Toolbar with buttons for formatting cells and the contents of cells.

6 Column heading buttons

Column labels. Click a column heading button to select a column. Drag across column heading buttons to select multiple columns.

7 Office Assistant

Online help utility.

8 Tab scrolling buttons

Use these buttons to scroll forward or back a sheet or to jump to the first or last sheet.

9 Row heading buttons

Row labels. Click a row heading button to select a row. Drag across row heading buttons to select multiple rows.

10 Sheet tabs

Click these tabs to switch from sheet to sheet. Double-click a tab to rename a sheet.

11 Status bar

Provides information about the current sheet or the current operation.

12 Mode indicators

Show special conditions that are in effect, such as a pressed Caps Lock key.

13 Scroll bars

Used to move the view of the document up or down or to quickly jump to a spot in the document. The length of the vertical scroll bar represents the length of the entire document. The position of the scroll button represents the position of the insertion point in the document.

THE EXCEL WINDOW

Starting a New Workbook

When you start Excel, Book1 is open and ready for you to type data into cells. Workbooks are numbered sequentially and several can be open simultaneously.

To start a new workbook:

1. On the Standard toolbar, click the New button (**Figure 10.4**).

or

Press Ctrl+N.

or

From the File menu, choose New.

2. If you chose New from the File menu, click Workbook on the General tab in the New dialog box (**Figure 10.5**).

or

Click a template on the Spreadsheet Solutions tab of the New dialog box (**Figure 10.6**).

3. Click OK.

✔ Tip

■ To switch from one open workbook to another, choose a name from the list of open workbooks on the Window menu (**Figure 10.7**).

New button

Figure 10.4 The New button on the Standard toolbar.

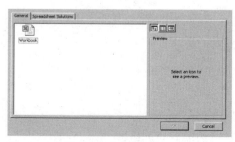

Figure 10.5 Click Workbook on the General tab in the New dialog box.

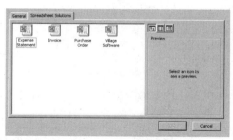

Figure 10.6 The Spreadsheet Solutions tab of the New dialog box.

Figure 10.7 You can switch to another open workbook in the Window menu.

ENTERING DATA AND FORMULAS

Figure 11.1 The most common worksheet structure.

A workbook consists of one or more worksheets, which usually conform to a standard design of rows and columns of data. Most worksheets have headings at the tops of columns and at the left ends of rows and calculations at the bottoms of columns and/or at the right ends of rows (**Figure 11.1**).

Because everyone is familiar with this basic structure, your worksheet will be generally understood. Excel is a blank slate, though, on which you can create any worksheet design. The 256 columns and 65,536 rows should give you ample space to be creative.

Starting with a Template

When you start with a template on the Spreadsheet Solutions tab of the New dialog box, you can customize a standard design to suit your needs.

To start with a template:

1. From the File menu, choose New.

2. Click a template on the Spreadsheet Solutions tab of the New dialog box (**Figure 11.2**).

3. Click OK.

4. In the open template, click the Customize tab or the Customize button to insert your own information (**Figures 11.3** and **11.4**).

✔ Tip

- Choose Save As from the File menu to save this template as a workbook.

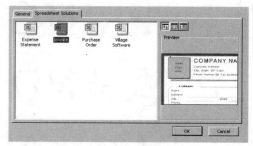

Figure 11.2 Select a template from the Spreadsheet Solutions tab of the New dialog box.

Figure 11.3 The Invoice template.

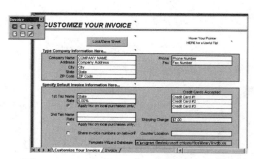

Figure 11.4 The Customize sheet for the Invoice template.

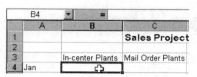

Figure 11.5 Move the cell pointer to the cell where you want to enter the date and then click.

Name box

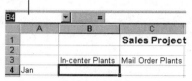

Figure 11.6 Replace the current cell address with a new address.

Table 11.1

Keyboard Shortcuts for Moving Within a Worksheet	
KEYBOARD SHORTCUT	**RESULT**
Arrow key	Moves to the adjacent cell (up, down, left, or right)
Ctrl+Arrow key	Moves to the edge of the current data region (up, down, left, or right)
Tab	Moves right one cell
Shift+Tab	Moves left one cell
Enter	Moves down one cell
Shift+Enter	Moves up one cell
Home	Moves to first cell of the row
Ctrl+Home	Moves to cell A1
Ctrl+End	Moves to last cell of last row with data
Page Down	Moves down one screen
Page Up	Moves up one screen
Alt+Page Down	Moves one screen to the right
Alt+Page Up	Moves one screen to the left
Ctrl+Page Down	Moves to the next sheet in the workbook
Ctrl+Page Up	Moves to the previous sheet in the workbook

Moving Within a Sheet

To enter data in a cell, you must first move to the cell.

To move to a cell:

◆ Click in the cell (**Figure 11.5**).

   or

   Press the arrow keys to move the cell pointer to the cell.

   or

   Select the current cell address in the Name box and replace it with the address of the cell to which you want to move (**Figure 11.6**).

✔ Tips

■ The cell surrounded by the cell pointer is called the active cell.

■ You can use the scroll bars to scroll through the document without changing the active cell.

■ To move within the worksheet, you can use the keyboard shortcuts listed in **Table 11.1**.

Typing Data into a Cell

You can enter text, a number, or a formula into each cell in a worksheet. You enter text to create a label, such as a column heading. You enter a number to provide something with which to calculate, and you enter a formula to carry out the calculation.

To type data in a cell:

1. Select the cell.

2. Type text, a number, or a formula (**Figure 11.7**).

3. Move to the next cell (**Figure 11.8**).

   The data is entered in the previous cell automatically.

✔ Tips

■ You don't have to press Enter after you type the contents of a cell. You can simply press an arrow key to move to the next cell.

■ If you want to add a new line in the current cell, press Alt+Enter.

■ Until you specify a different format, text is automatically left-aligned in cells and numbers are right-aligned.

■ If you need a series of consecutive dates or numbers for column or row headings (month names, for example), use AutoFill to enter them automatically.

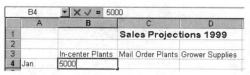

Figure 11.7 Type in the cell.

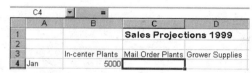

Figure 11.8 Move to the next cell.

TYPING DATA INTO A CELL

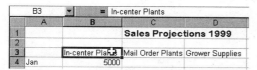

Figure 11.9 Select a cell and then type to replace the cell's contents.

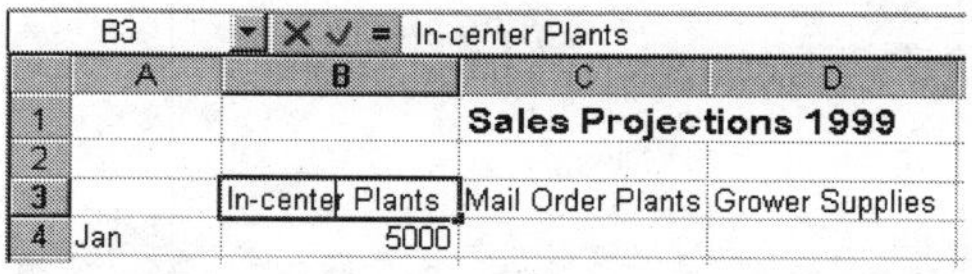

Figure 11.10 Double-click in the cell to place an insertion point in the contents.

Editing Cells

The easiest way to change the text or number in a cell is to click the cell and then type right over the contents. But if you have a formula or extensive text in the cell, you might prefer to edit the existing contents to avoid retyping the whole entry.

To edit data in a cell:

1. Click the cell and then type over its contents (**Figure 11.9**).

   or

   Double-click the cell to position an insertion point within the cell contents (**Figure 11.10**).

2. Edit the contents as though you were editing text in Word.

3. Press Enter to enter the revision in the cell.

✔ Tips

- When you click a cell, the cell contents also appear on the edit line. You can click on the edit line and edit the cell contents there.

- To abandon any revisions you've made, press Esc to leave the original contents of a cell intact and then press Enter to exit the cell.

- If you edit a formula, all cells affected by the change are recalculated when you press Enter.

EDITING CELLS

Adding a Hyperlink

A hyperlink is specially marked text or a graphic that you click to go to a file or an HTML page on the Web or on an intranet.

To add a hyperlink:

1. Select text in a cell to hyperlink or select an empty cell.

2. From the Insert menu, choose Hyperlink (**Figure 11.11**).

   or

   Press Ctrl+K.

3. In the Insert Hyperlink dialog box, type the destination link or browse for the file (**Figure 11.12**).

4. Add the text to display as a hyperlink if you picked an empty cell. The default is the filename or URL (Universal Resource Locator).

5. Click OK. The text is now colored and underlined (**Figure 11.13**).

✔ Tip

- To edit or remove the hyperlink, right-click the link, point to Hyperlink on the shortcut menu, and choose either Edit Hyperlink or Remove Hyperlink from the shortcut menu (**Figure 11.14**).

Figure 11.11 Choose Hyperlink from the Insert menu.

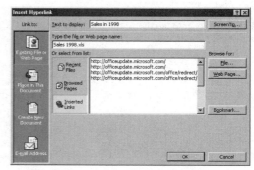

Figure 11.12 The Insert Hyperlink dialog box.

Figure 11.13 The cell is now hyperlinked.

Figure 11.14 Right-click the hyper-linked text to open the shortcut menu.

ADDING A HYPERLINK

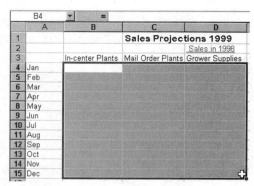

Figure 11.15 Drag to the last cell to create a range.

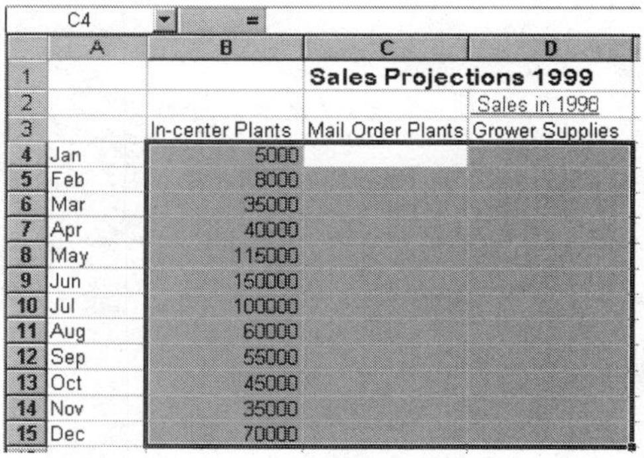

Figure 11.16 Press Enter at the bottom of a column to continue at the top of the next column.

Filling an Entry Range

To quickly enter data in a rectangular range of cells, create an entry range.

To create and fill an entry range:

1. Position the mouse pointer in the upper left corner cell of the range.

2. Click and drag to the lower right corner cell of the range (**Figure 11.15**).

   The active cell is the cell at the upper left corner of the entry range.

3. Type data into each cell and then press Enter.

   The cell pointer moves down each column from cell to cell automatically. When it reaches the bottom of a column, it jumps to the top of the next column within the entry range (**Figure 11.16**).

✔ Tips

- Press Ctrl+Enter to fill all cells in the range with the entry you type in the first cell.

- Press Shift+Enter to fill in the cells in reverse order, from the last cell to the first.

FILLING AN ENTRY RANGE

AutoFilling a Range

When you want to fill a range of cells with consecutive numbers, numbers that follow a specific pattern, dates, or dates that follow a specific pattern (such as every Monday), use AutoFill as a quick and convenient method of automatically entering the sequence.

To AutoFill a range:

1. In the first cell of the sequence, type the first number or date (**Figure 11.17**).

2. In an adjacent cell, type the next number or date.

3. Select the two cells and carefully position the mouse pointer on the Fill handle, the very small square at the lower right corner of the border surrounding the two cells.

4. Drag the Fill handle to extend the sequence (**Figure 11.18**).

5. Release the mouse button when the sequence is complete (**Figure 11.19**).

✔ Tip

■ As you drag to extend the sequence, the current value appears in a yellow ToolTip next to the cursor.

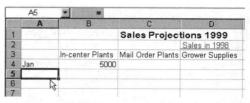

Figure 11.17 Enter the first number or date.

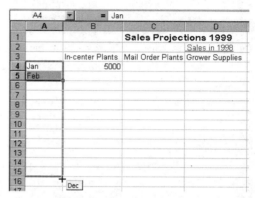

Figure 11.18 Select the first two cells and drag the Fill handle to extend the pattern established in the first two cells.

Figure 11.19 Release the mouse button to complete the sequence.

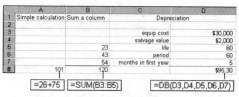

Figure 11.20 Some typical calculations.

Entering Simple Calculations

A calculation can be simple (the sum of a column of numbers) or complex (a financial, statistical, or scientific computation), but it is always entered as a formula that begins with an equal sign (=). If any numbers change in the cells that supply values to the formula, the result of the calculation changes immediately. This immediate recalculation lets you perform what-if analyses; you can see the change in the bottom line immediately when you change any of the contributing numbers.

To sum two numbers in a cell:

◆ Type *=number+number*—for example, *=26+75*.

To sum the contents of two cells:

◆ Type the cell addresses in the formula— for example, *=B3+B4*.

The cell in which you type the formula displays the result of the calculation (**Figure 11.20**).

✔ Tip

■ Use a comma to separate cell addresses and a colon to indicate a range of cell addresses. To include the cells C1, C3, and C4, you'd enter C1, C3, C4. To include all the cells between C1 and C4 (including C1 and C4), you'd enter C1:C4.

Building a Simple Formula

As you build a formula, you can type in values or select cell references from anywhere in a workbook.

To build a simple formula:

1. Click the destination cell for the formula and type an equal sign (**Figure 11.21**).

2. Click the first cell whose address you want in the formula (**Figure 11.22**).

3. Type an operator. **Table 11.2** lists the available operators and their functions.

4. Click the next cell whose address should appear in the formula (**Figure 11.23**).

5. Type another operator and continue building the formula.

   or

   Press Enter to enter the formula in the cell and display the result of the calculation (**Figure 11.24**).

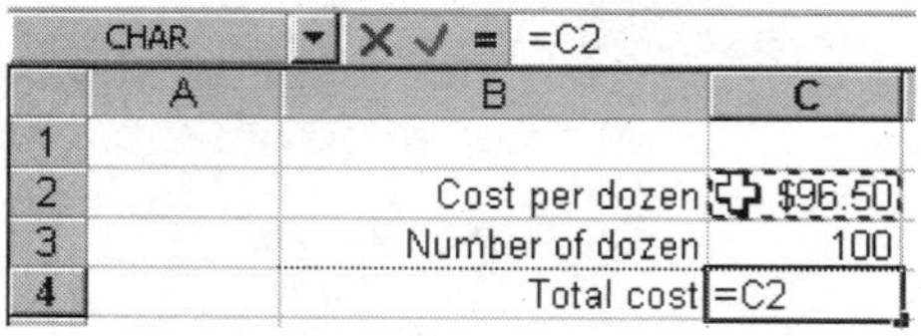

✔ Tips

- If adjacent cells require a similar formula, you can copy the formula from cell to cell.

- You can enter a combination of typed numbers and cell addresses in formulas, such as *=C2*2.5* (the contents of cell C2 multiplied by 2.5).

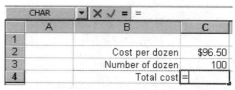

Figure 11.21 Click in the destination for a formula and press the equal sign key.

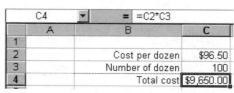

Figure 11.22 Click a cell.

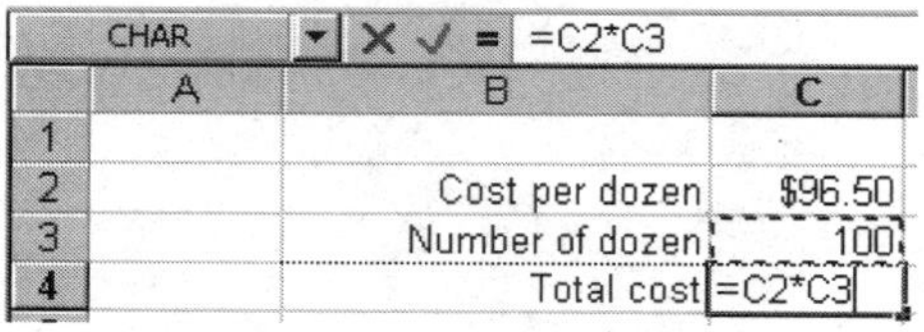

Figure 11.23 Type an operator and click a cell to add to the formula.

Figure 11.24 The result appears in the cell, while the edit line displays the formula.

Table 11.2

Operators	
OPERATOR	**FUNCTION**
+	Plus
−	Minus
*	Multiply (asterisk)
/	Divide

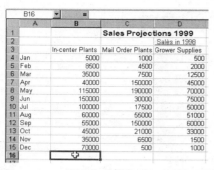

Figure 11.25 Click the cell for the total.

AutoSum button

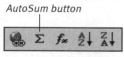

Figure 11.26 Click the AutoSum button.

	A	B	C	D
			Sales Projections 1999	
2				Sales in 1998
3		In-center Plants	Mail Order Plants	Grower Supplies
4	Jan	5000	1000	500
5	Feb	8500	4500	2000
6	Mar	35000	7500	12500
7	Apr	40000	150000	45000
8	May	115000	190000	70000
9	Jun	150000	30000	75000
10	Jul	100000	17500	50000
11	Aug	60000	55000	51000
12	Sep	55000	150000	60000
13	Oct	45000	21000	33000
14	Nov	35000	6500	1500
15	Dec	70000	500	1000
16		=SUM(B4:B15)		

Figure 11.27 Excel has created the formula.

	A	B	C	D
1			Sales Projections 1999	
2				Sales in 1998
3		In-center Plants	Mail Order Plants	Grower Supplies
4	Jan	5000	1000	500
5	Feb	8500	4500	2000
6	Mar	35000	7500	12500
7	Apr	40000	150000	45000
8	May	115000	190000	70000
9	Jun	150000	30000	75000
10	Jul	100000	17500	50000
11	Aug	60000	55000	51000
12	Sep	55000	150000	60000
13	Oct	45000	21000	33000
14	Nov	35000	6500	1500
15	Dec	70000	500	1000
16				

Figure 11.28 You can select the cells below any number of adjacent columns before clicking the AutoSum button.

Summing Columns and Rows

Excel includes special help for quickly summing a column or row.

To sum a column or row:

1. Click in the empty cell below the last entry in the column or to the right of the last entry in the row (**Figure 11.25**).

2. Click the AutoSum button on the Standard toolbar (**Figure 11.26**).

3. Press Enter to enter the formula that has automatically appeared in the cell (**Figure 11.27**).

✔ Tips

■ Excel looks for the range of numbers to sum above the cell you've selected for the total. If it does not find a range of numbers or if it finds text, it looks to the left for a range of numbers.

■ Excel will not skip over an empty cell when it is looking for a range of cells to sum.

■ To quickly enter sums below multiple adjacent columns, select the empty cells at the bottoms of all the columns before clicking the AutoSum button. Excel will insert a sum in each selected cell (**Figure 11.28**).

SUMMING COLUMNS, ROWS

Totaling a Column Using the Sum Function

The Sum function is perhaps the most commonly used of the Excel functions that carry out mathematical, statistical, financial, date, time, and other calculations.

To total a column using the Sum function:

1. Click the destination cell for the formula.

2. Type an equal sign to start the formula and then type the word *sum* and a left parenthesis (Shift+9) (**Figure 11.29**).

3. Drag down the column of numbers to sum (**Figure 11.30**).

4. Press Enter (**Figure 11.31**).

✔ Tips

- You don't need to type the close (right) parenthesis before you press Enter—Excel will do it for you.

- Use this technique instead of AutoSum to sum ranges of cells that contain blanks.

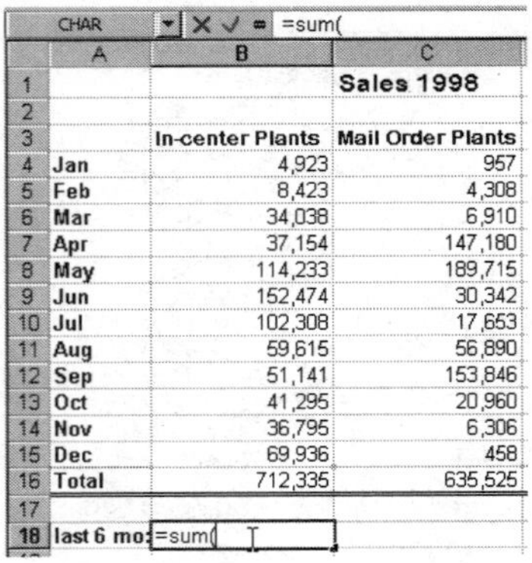

Figure 11.29 Type "=sum" followed by a left parenthesis in the destination cell.

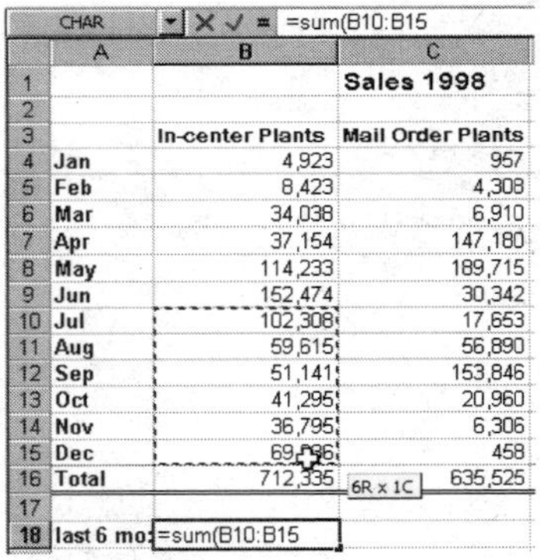

Figure 11.30 Drag down the column to sum, in this case, from B10 to B15.

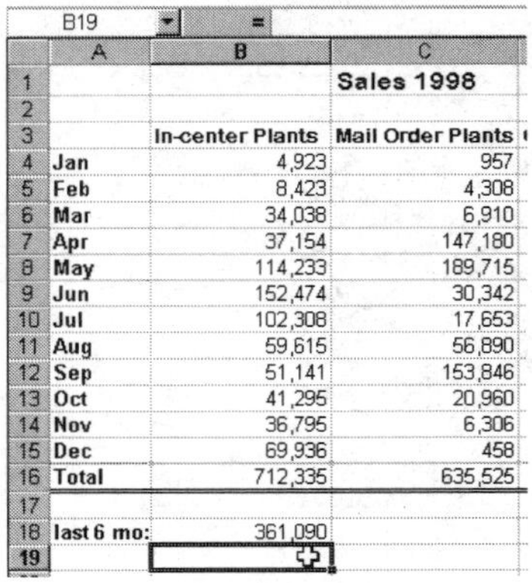

Figure 11.31 Press Enter to complete the formula.

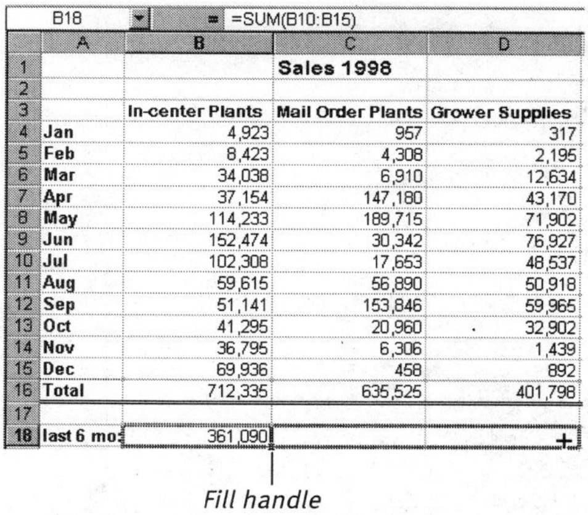

B18	▼	= =SUM(B10:B15)	
	A	B	C	D
1			Sales 1998	
2				
3		In-center Plants	Mail Order Plants	Grower Supplies
4	Jan	4,923	957	317
5	Feb	8,423	4,308	2,195
6	Mar	34,038	6,910	12,634
7	Apr	37,154	147,180	43,170
8	May	114,233	189,715	71,902
9	Jun	152,474	30,342	76,927
10	Jul	102,308	17,653	48,537
11	Aug	59,615	56,890	50,918
12	Sep	51,141	153,846	59,965
13	Oct	41,295	20,960	32,902
14	Nov	36,795	6,306	1,439
15	Dec	69,936	458	892
16	Total	712,335	635,525	401,798
17				
18	last 6 mo:	361,090		+

Fill handle

Figure 11.32 Click the cell with the formula and drag the Fill handle across adjacent cells.

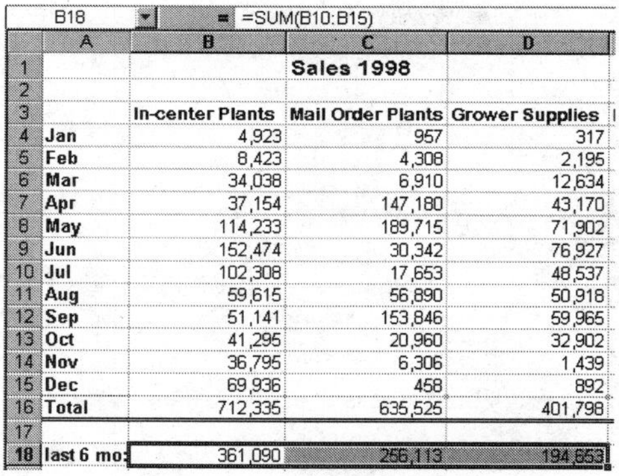

B18	▼	= =SUM(B10:B15)	
	A	B	C	D
1			Sales 1998	
2				
3		In-center Plants	Mail Order Plants	Grower Supplies
4	Jan	4,923	957	317
5	Feb	8,423	4,308	2,195
6	Mar	34,038	6,910	12,634
7	Apr	37,154	147,180	43,170
8	May	114,233	189,715	71,902
9	Jun	152,474	30,342	76,927
10	Jul	102,308	17,653	48,537
11	Aug	59,615	56,890	50,918
12	Sep	51,141	153,846	59,965
13	Oct	41,295	20,960	32,902
14	Nov	36,795	6,306	1,439
15	Dec	69,936	458	892
16	Total	712,335	635,525	401,798
17				
18	last 6 mo:	361,090	256,113	194,653

Figure 11.33 The formula copied to adjacent cells.

Copying Formulas to Adjacent Cells

Rather than retype a formula in adjacent cells, you can copy it automatically. Excel will adjust the formula as it copies it.

To copy a formula to adjacent cells:

1. Click the cell containing the formula.

2. Drag the Fill handle at the lower right corner of the cell across the adjacent cells to which you want to copy the formula (**Figures 11.32** and **11.33**).

✔ Tips

- When the mouse pointer is positioned properly on the Fill handle, the pointer becomes a small plus sign. Otherwise, the mouse pointer is a large, heavy plus sign.

- You can drag in any direction to copy formulas to the right, the left, up, or down.

COPYING FORMULAS

Averaging Numbers Using the Average Function

You can use the Average function to calculate the average of values in cells.

To average selected numbers:

1. Click the destination cell for the formula that will calculate the average.
2. Type an equal sign and then type the word *average* and a left parenthesis (Shift+9) (**Figure 11.34**).
3. Drag across the cells whose values you want to average (**Figure 11.35**).
4. Press Enter (**Figure 11.36**).

✔ Tip

- Blank cells in the range are not counted in the average. Cells that contain 0s are counted in the average.

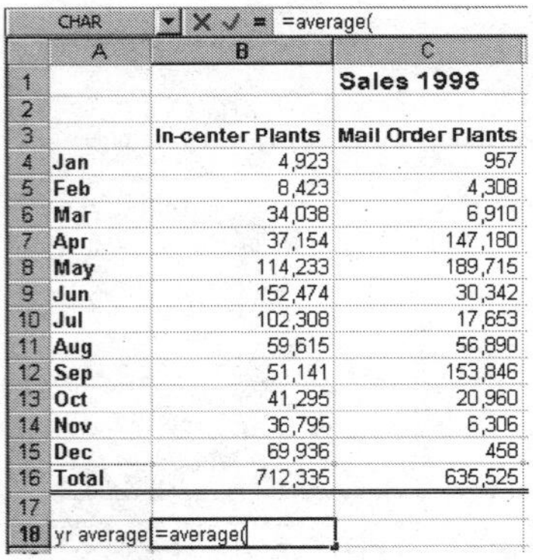

CHAR =average(

	A	B	C
1			Sales 1998
2			
3		In-center Plants	Mail Order Plants
4	Jan	4,923	957
5	Feb	8,423	4,308
6	Mar	34,038	6,910
7	Apr	37,154	147,180
8	May	114,233	189,715
9	Jun	152,474	30,342
10	Jul	102,308	17,653
11	Aug	59,615	56,890
12	Sep	51,141	153,846
13	Oct	41,295	20,960
14	Nov	36,795	6,306
15	Dec	69,936	458
16	Total	712,335	635,525
17			
18	yr average	=average(	

Figure 11.34 Click the destination for the formula and type the formula.

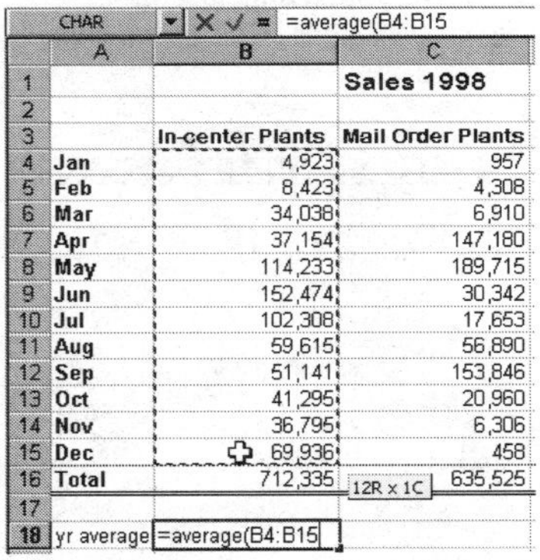

CHAR =average(B4:B15

	A	B	C
1			Sales 1998
2			
3		In-center Plants	Mail Order Plants
4	Jan	4,923	957
5	Feb	8,423	4,308
6	Mar	34,038	6,910
7	Apr	37,154	147,180
8	May	114,233	189,715
9	Jun	152,474	30,342
10	Jul	102,308	17,653
11	Aug	59,615	56,890
12	Sep	51,141	153,846
13	Oct	41,295	20,960
14	Nov	36,795	6,306
15	Dec	69,936	458
16	Total	712,335	12R x 1C 635,525
17			
18	yr average	=average(B4:B15	

Figure 11.35 Drag across the cells to average.

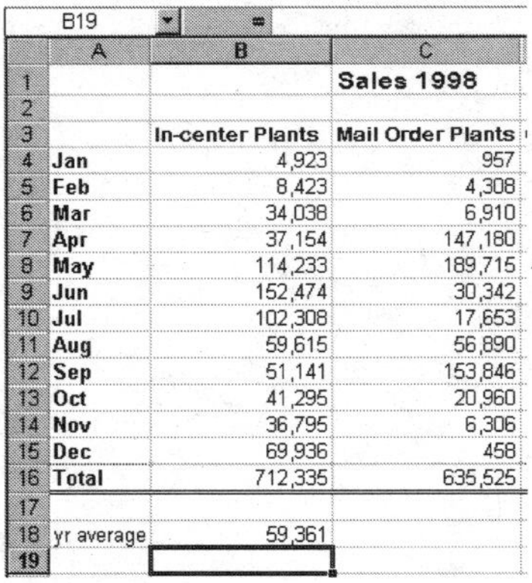

B19 =

	A	B	C
1			Sales 1998
2			
3		In-center Plants	Mail Order Plants
4	Jan	4,923	957
5	Feb	8,423	4,308
6	Mar	34,038	6,910
7	Apr	37,154	147,180
8	May	114,233	189,715
9	Jun	152,474	30,342
10	Jul	102,308	17,653
11	Aug	59,615	56,890
12	Sep	51,141	153,846
13	Oct	41,295	20,960
14	Nov	36,795	6,306
15	Dec	69,936	458
16	Total	712,335	635,525
17			
18	yr average	59,361	
19			

Figure 11.36 The cell displays the result of the formula.

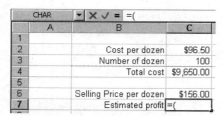

Figure 11.37 Click the destination for the formula and start with the equal sign and left parenthesis.

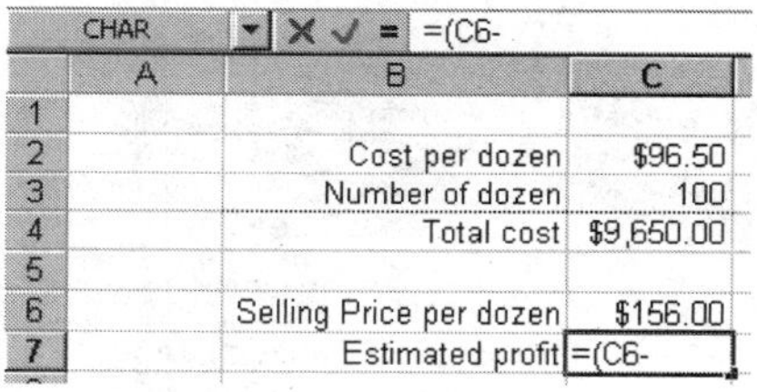

CHAR	▼	X ✓ =	=(C6-
	A	B	C
1			
2		Cost per dozen	$96.50
3		Number of dozen	100
4		Total cost	$9,650.00
5			
6		Selling Price per dozen	$156.00
7		Estimated profit	=(C6-

Figure 11.38 Click a cell and add an operator.

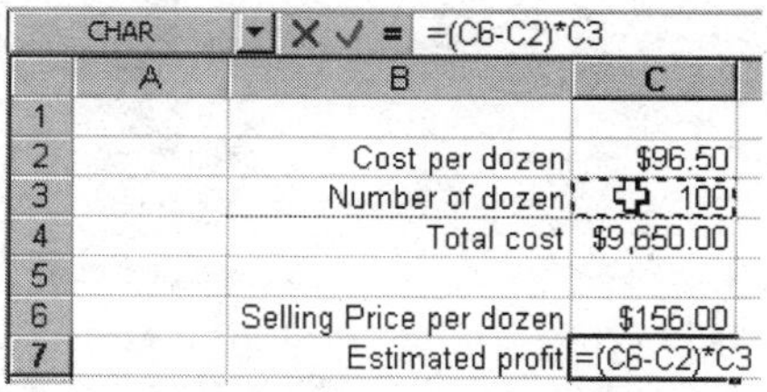

CHAR	▼	X ✓ =	=(C6-C2)*C3
	A	B	C
1			
2		Cost per dozen	$96.50
3		Number of dozen	100
4		Total cost	$9,650.00
5			
6		Selling Price per dozen	$156.00
7		Estimated profit	=(C6-C2)*C3

Figure 11.39 Continue clicking cells and adding operators until formula is complete.

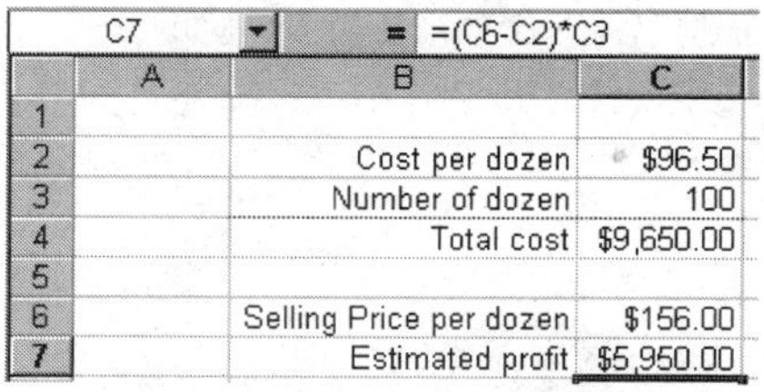

C7	▼	=	=(C6-C2)*C3
	A	B	C
1			
2		Cost per dozen	$96.50
3		Number of dozen	100
4		Total cost	$9,650.00
5			
6		Selling Price per dozen	$156.00
7		Estimated profit	$5,950.00

Figure 11.40 The cell displays the result of the formula.

Calculating Numbers in Nonadjacent Cells

When you build a formula, you can select cells from anywhere in your workbook.

To calculate numbers in nonadjacent cells:

1. Click the destination cell for the formula.

2. Start the formula as usual with an equal sign and type a function, if necessary, followed by a left parenthesis (**Figure 11.37**).

3. Click the first cell you want to include and add an operator (**Figure 11.38**).

4. Repeat step 3 until you have included as many cells as necessary (**Figure 11.39**).

5. Press Enter to enter the formula (**Figure 11.40**).

✔ Tip

- A formula can contain a combination of cells and ranges of cells, such as =SUM(B2,B4,B9:B11). This formula will total up the contents of cells B2, B4, and B9 through B11.

CALCULATING NUMBERS

Building Formulas Using the Paste Function Wizard

Sum and Average are just two of the dozens of functions that are included in Excel. To find others, click the Paste Function button on the Standard toolbar as you are building the formula. The Paste Function Wizard takes you through the steps of building a formula. **Table 11.3** lists many useful functions.

To build a formula using the Paste Function Wizard:

1. Click the destination cell for the formula.

2. Click the Paste Function button on the Standard toolbar (**Figure 11.41**).

3. In the Paste Function dialog box, select the category and then the function (**Figure 11.42**).

4. Click OK.

5. Use the Paste Function Wizard to guide you in completing the formula (**Figure 11.43**).

6. Click OK when you have finished (**Figure 11.44**).

Paste Function button

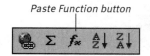

Figure 11.41 The Paste Function button.

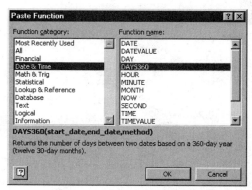

Figure 11.42 Select the function category and name.

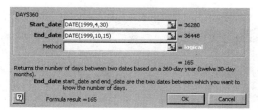

Figure 11.43 The wizard helps you fill in the fields. You can enter functions as arguments to other functions.

Figure 11.44 The completed functions.

Table 11.3

Some Useful Functions	
FUNCTION	DESCRIPTION
DATE(*year, month, day*)	Provides the serial number of a particular date
DAYS360(*start_date, end_date, method*)	Calculates the number of days between two dates based on a 360-day year, which is used in some accounting systems
TODAY( )	Provides the serial number of today's date
NOW( )	Provides the serial number of the current date and time
DDB(*cost, salvage, life, period, factor*)	Provides the depreciation of an asset for a specified period using the double-declining balance method or some other method you specify
FV(*rate, nper, pmt, pv, type*)	Calculates the future value of an investment
IRR(*values, guess*)	Provides the internal rate of return for a series of cash flows
NPV(*rate, value1, value2, ...*)	Calculates the net present value of an investment based on a series of periodic cash flows and a discount rate
PMT(*rate, nper, pv, fv, type*)	Calculates the periodic payment for an annuity or a loan
PV(*rate, nper, pmt, fv, type*)	Calculates the present value of an investment
ROUND(*number, num_digits*)	Rounds a number to a specified number of digits
SUM(*number1, number2, ...*)	Calculates the sum of all the numbers in the list of arguments*
AVERAGE(*number1, number2, ...*)	Calculates the average (arithmetic mean) of the arguments*
MAX(*number1, number2, ...*)	Calculates the maximum value in a list of arguments*
MEDIAN(*number1, number2, ...*)	Calculates the median of the given numbers*
MIN(*number1, number2, ...*)	Calculates the smallest number in the list of arguments*
VAR(*number1, number2, ...*)	Estimates variance based on a sample*
VALUE(*text*)	Converts text to a number

USEFUL FUNCTIONS

* (number1, number2, ...) *can also be specified as a range (for example, C25:C47) or as a comma-separated list of numbers and/or ranges.*

STRUCTURING THE SHEET

An Excel worksheet has no default structure. It's just a grid of blank cells. As you begin entering text labels and numeric information, you establish the structure of rows and columns.

The initial structure you establish is not fixed. You can add rows and columns to fit more information, and you can enlarge rows and columns to more easily see the information you've entered. You can shrink rows and columns to see more information in a single screen, and you can move information in the worksheet, freeze headings, and split worksheets to make it easier to work with your data.

Enlarging Columns and Rows

Although Excel does not automatically adjust cell height or width to accommodate a cell entry, you can easily change the width of a column or the height of a row.

To change the width of a column:

1. Position the mouse pointer on the right edge of the gray column heading button for the column you want to widen (**Figure 12.1**).

2. When the mouse pointer changes to a double arrow, drag right or left (**Figure 12.2**).

   While you're dragging, you'll see the new width of the column in a yellow ToolTip, measured in pixels.

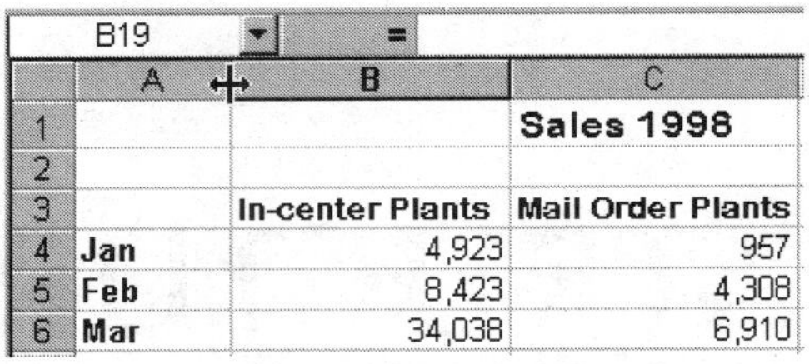

To change the height of a row:

1. Position the mouse pointer on the bottom edge of the gray row heading button for the row whose height you want to change.

2. When the mouse pointer changes to a double arrow, drag up or down. (**Figure 12.3**).

✔ Tip

- You can also select Column or Row from the Format menu and then choose Width or Height from the submenu to open the Column Width or Row Height dialog box. In these dialog boxes, you can specify an exact setting.

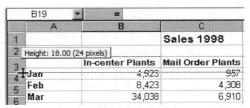

Figure 12.1 The mouse pointer changes to a double arrow.

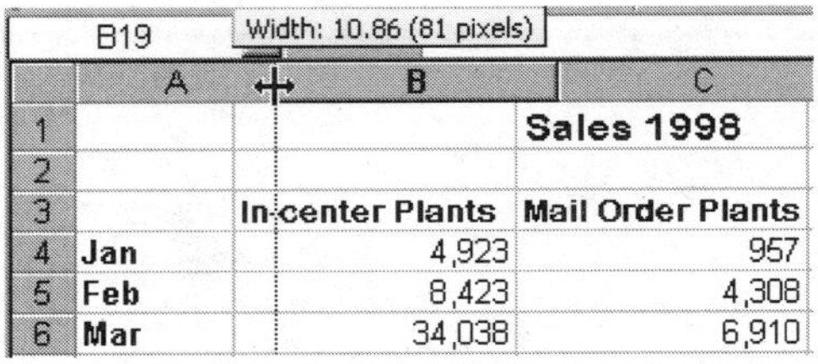

Figure 12.2 Drag left or right to widen or narrow the column below.

Figure 12.3 Drag the edge of a row heading button to change the height of the row.

10	Jul	102,500	17,055
11	Aug	59,615	56,890
12	Sep	51,141	153,846
13	Oct	41,295	20,960
14	Nov	36,795	6,306
15	Dec	69,936	458
16	Total	712,335	635,525
17	mo. Average	59,361	52,960

Figure 12.4 Click a cell in the row where you want to insert a new row.

Figure 12.5 Choose Rows or Columns from the Insert menu.

10	Jul	102,500	17,055
11	Aug	59,615	56,890
12	Sep	51,141	153,846
13	Oct	41,295	20,960
14	Nov	36,795	6,306
15	Dec	69,936	458
16	Total	712,335	635,525
17			
18	mo. Average	59,361	52,960

Figure 12.6 The new blank row appears.

10	Jul	102,500	17,055
11	Aug	59,615	56,890
12	Sep	51,141	153,846
13	Oct	41,295	20,960
14	Nov	36,795	6,306
15	Dec	69,936	458
16	Total	712,335	635,525
17	mo. Average	59,361	52,960
18			

Figure 12.7 Drag across two rows to specify two rows for insertion.

Inserting Rows and Columns

You can insert rows and columns at any time, and Excel adjusts all formulas to accommodate the new rows or columns. If you insert a row, it will appear above the selected cell; if you insert a column, it will appear to the left of the selected cell.

To insert a row or a column:

1. Click any cell of the row or column in which you'd like to insert the new blank row or column (**Figure 12.4**).

2. From the Insert menu, choose Rows to insert a row or choose Columns to insert a column (**Figures 12.5** and **12.6**).

✔ Tips

■ To insert multiple rows or columns, drag across to highlight the same number of cells as rows or columns you want to insert (**Figure 12.7**).

■ You can also right-click a column or row heading button and choose Insert from the shortcut menu.

INSERTING ROWS, COLUMNS

Inserting and Deleting Cells

When you tell Excel to insert or delete a cell within a range of data, Excel needs to know how to move the data that's in adjacent cells. You specify your preferences in the Insert or Delete dialog box.

To insert a cell:

1. Click the destination for the new, blank cell (**Figure 12.8**).

2. Choose Cells from the Insert menu.

   or

   Right-click the cell and choose Insert from the shortcut menu.

3. In the Insert dialog box, select either Shift Cells Right or Shift Cells Down (**Figure 12.9**).

   The new cell appears (**Figure 12.10**).

To delete a cell:

1. Click the cell you want to delete.

2. Choose Delete from the Edit menu.

   or

   Right-click the cell and choose Delete from the shortcut menu.

3. In the Delete dialog box, select either Shift Cells Left or Shift Cells Up (**Figure 12.11**).

✔ Tip

■ To delete an entire row or column, select at least one cell in the row or column, choose Delete from the Edit menu, and in the Delete dialog box, choose either Entire Row or Entire Column.

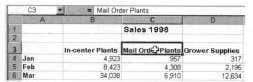

Figure 12.8 Click a cell.

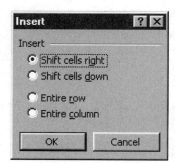

Figure 12.9 Shift cells right or down in the Insert dialog box.

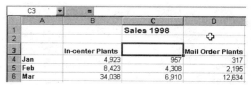

Figure 12.10 The inserted cell.

Figure 12.11 Shift cells left or up in the Delete dialog box.

INSERTING, DELETING CELLS

Figure 12.12 Select a range of cells.

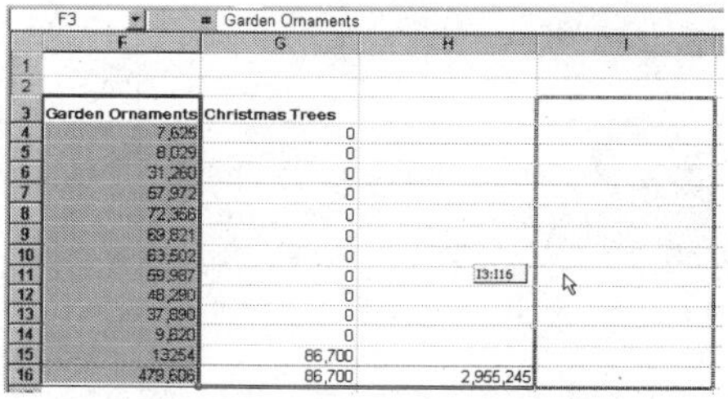

Moving and Copying Data

Excel's drag-and-drop technique makes moving and copying data especially easy.

To move or copy data:

1. Select the range of cells to move or copy (**Figure 12.12**).

2. Position the mouse pointer on the border of the range; the pointer becomes an arrow.

3. Drag the border of the range to move the range to a new location (**Figure 12.13**). A yellow ToolTip appears to indicate the destination.

   or

   To copy the cells, press and hold Ctrl while dragging the border of the range. A small plus sign appears next to the mouse pointer to indicate that you are copying rather than moving (**Figure 12.14**).

4. Release the mouse button to drop the range at the new location (**Figure 12.15**).

Figure 12.13 Drag the border of the range to move the range.

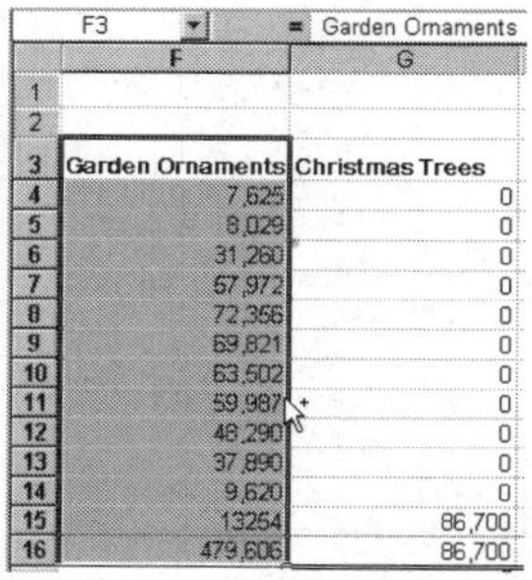

Figure 12.14 The small plus sign next to the mouse pointer shows that a copy is in progress.

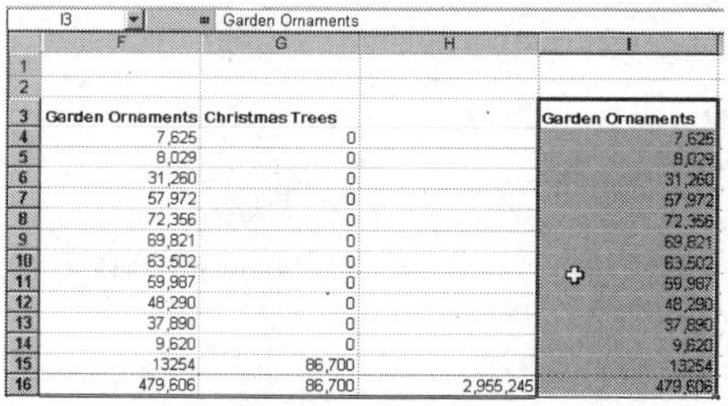

Figure 12.15 The range copied to its new location.

MOVING, COPYING DATA

Freezing the Headings

To keep the column and row headings from scrolling off the screen while you scroll through a large worksheet, you can freeze the headings.

To freeze the headings:

1. Click the cell at the upper left corner of the region that contains the data (**Figure 12.16**).

2. From the Window menu, choose Freeze Panes (**Figure 12.17**).

   Lines appear to indicate which areas of the sheet will stay frozen as you scroll through the data (**Figures 12.18** and **12.19**).

✔ Tips

- After you freeze panes, you can press Ctrl+ Home to move the cell pointer to the upper left corner of the data range instead of to cell A1.

- To unfreeze the panes, choose Unfreeze Panes from the Window menu.

	A	B	C
1			**Sales 1998**
2			
3		**In-center Plants**	**Mail Order Plants**
4	Jan	4,923	957
5	Feb	8,423	4,308
6	Mar	34,038	6,910
7	Apr	37,154	147,180
8	May	114,233	189,715

Figure 12.16 Click the upper left corner of the data range.

Figure 12.17 Choose Freeze Panes from the Window menu.

	A	B	C	D
1			**Sales 1998**	
2				
3		**In-center Plants**	**Mail Order Plants**	**Grower Supplies**
4	Jan	4,923	957	317
5	Feb	8,423	4,308	2,195
6	Mar	34,038	6,910	12,634
7	Apr	37,154	147,180	43,170
8	May	114,233	189,715	71,902
9	Jun	152,474	30,342	76,927
10	Jul	102,308	17,653	48,537
11	Aug	59,615	56,890	50,918
12	Sep	51,141	153,846	59,966

Figure 12.18 Lines appear to indicate which areas of the sheet are frozen.

	A	C	D	E
1		**Sales 1998**		
2				
3		**Mail Order Plants**	**Grower Supplies**	**Plant Containers**
4	Jan	957	317	13,006
5	Feb	4,308	2,195	17,613
6	Mar	6,910	12,634	36,717
7	Apr	147,180	43,170	45,682
8	May	189,715	71,902	96,720
9	Jun	30,342	76,927	98,892
10	Jul	17,653	48,537	56,990
11	Aug	56,890	50,918	37,761
12	Sep	153,846	59,966	39,679

Figure 12.19 The headings stay frozen when you scroll through the data.

FORMATTING THE SHEET

13

Although formatting a sheet might seem to be mostly a cosmetic affair, careful formatting can help you and others more readily understand the information in the sheet. By emphasizing heading text, adding borders and shading, and changing the format of numbers, you can give the information a visual organization in addition to its structural framework.

Choosing an AutoFormat

The fastest and easiest way to make a sheet presentable is to give it an AutoFormat. An AutoFormat supplies a complete look for a range of data by changing the font, text alignment, number formatting, borders, patterns, colors, column widths, and row heights. Excel provides a selection of AutoFormats, each with a unique look.

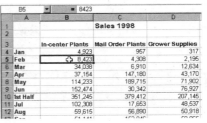

Figure 13.1 Click a cell in the range that you want to format.

To choose an AutoFormat:

1. Click any cell in the range to format (**Figure 13.1**).

   or

   Select the range to format.

2. From the Format menu, choose Auto-Format (**Figure 13.2**).

3. In the AutoFormat dialog box, select an AutoFormat from the display (**Figure 13.3**).

4. Click OK (**Figure 13.4**).

Figure 13.2 Choose AutoFormat from the Format menu.

✔ Tips

■ To remove an AutoFormat immediately after applying it, use Undo.

■ To remove an AutoFormat later, select the range, follow steps 2 and 3 above, and then choose None from the list of AutoFormats.

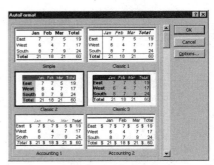

Figure 13.3 Select a format in the AutoFormat dialog box.

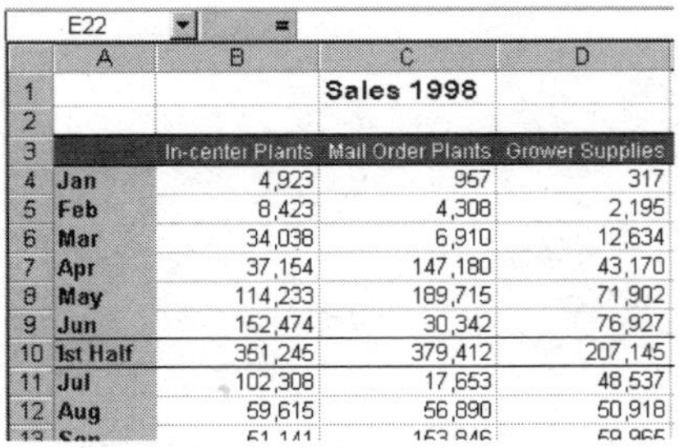

Figure 13.4 The AutoFormatted range.

CHOOSING AN AUTOFORMAT

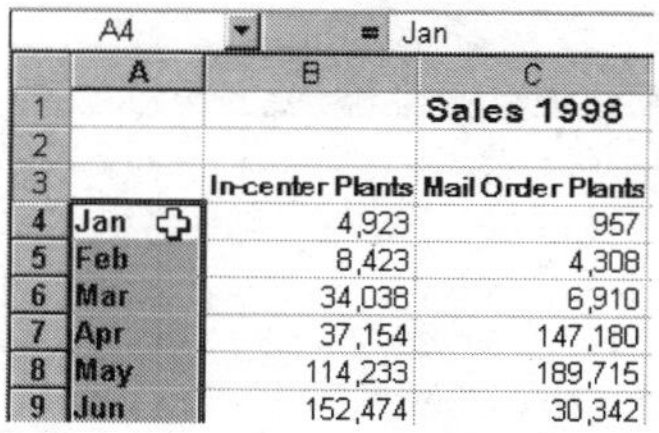

Figure 13.5 Select the cells with the text to format.

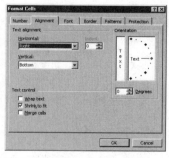

Figure 13.6 The Formatting toolbar.

Figure 13.7 Change alignment on the Alignment tab.

Figure 13.8 Change font, font style, and size on the Font tab.

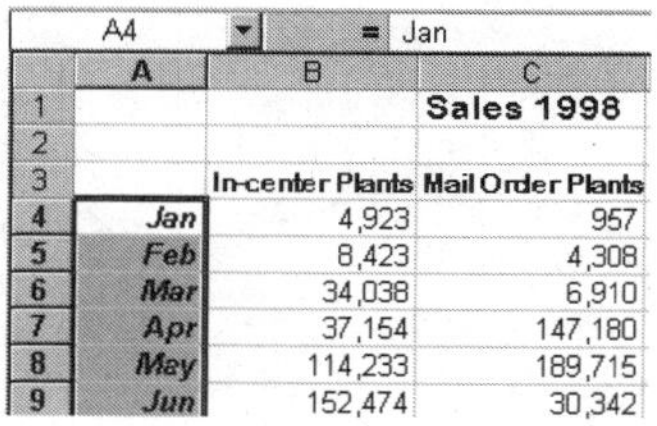

Figure 13.9 The formatted text.

Formatting Text

You can use formatting to improve the appearance of your worksheet and to make it easier to locate the information you need.

To format selected text:

1. Select the cell or cells containing the text to format (**Figure 13.5**).

2. Choose formatting options by clicking the text formatting buttons on the Formatting toolbar (**Figure 13.6**).

   or

1. Select the cell or cells containing the text to format.

2. From the Format menu, choose Cells, or right-click and choose Format Cells from the shortcut menu.

3. In the Format Cells dialog box, change the options on the Alignment and Font tabs (**Figures 13.7** and **13.8**).

4. Click OK (**Figure 13.9**).

FORMATTING TEXT

Centering a Title Above a Range

You can center the cell containing title text across several columns by merging cells.

To center a title above a range:

1. Type the title in a cell above the range.

2. Select the cells above the range (**Figure 13.10**).

3. Click the Merge and Center button (**Figure 13.11**).

or

1. Type the title in a cell above the range.

2. Select the cells above the range.

3. From the Format menu, choose Cells.

4. On the Alignment tab in the Format Cells dialog box, pull down the Horizontal list and choose Center, and in the Text Control box, click Merge Cells (**Figure 13.12**).

5. Click OK to see the centered title (**Figure 13.13**).

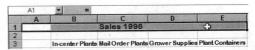

Figure 13.10 Select the cells above the range.

Merge and Center button

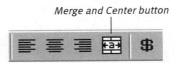

Figure 13.11 Click the Merge and Center button to center the text.

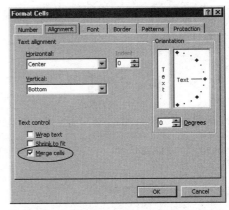

Figure 13.12 Choose options on the Alignment tab in the Format Cells dialog box.

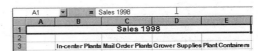

Figure 13.13 The Centered title.

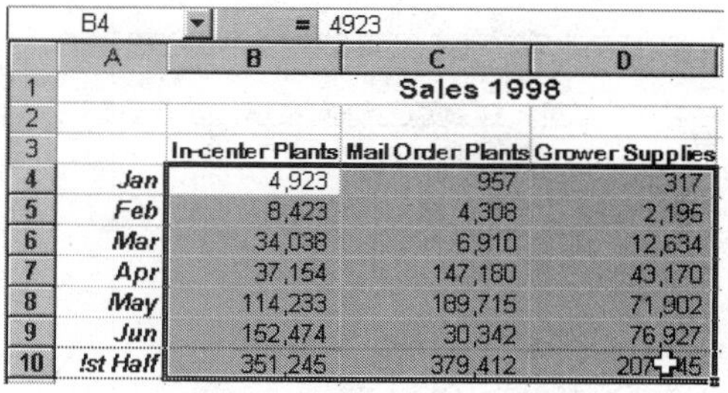

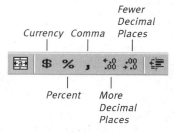

Figure 13.14 Select the numbers to format.

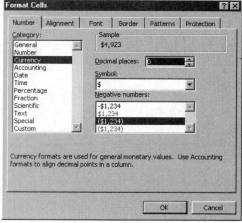

Fewer Decimal Places

Currency   Comma

Percent

More Decimal Places

Figure 13.15 Use the number formatting buttons on the Formatting toolbar.

Figure 13.16 Choose a category on the Number tab of the Format Cells dialog box.

Formatting Numbers

Excel makes available to you a variety of number formatting options, some from the Formatting toolbar and others from the Format Cells dialog box.

To format numbers:

1. Select the numbers to format (**Figure 13.14**).

2. Click the appropriate number formatting button on the Formatting toolbar (**Figure 13.15**).

   or

1. Select the numbers to format.

2. From the Format menu, choose Cells.

3. On the Number tab of the Format Cells dialog box, choose a category and other options (**Figure 13.16**).

4. Click OK.

✔ Tips

- Until you choose a special number format, numbers are formatted with the General number format (right-aligned, up to 11 decimal places).

- If you enter numbers preceded by a dollar sign, Excel automatically applies Currency formatting. If you enter numbers followed by a percent sign, Excel automatically applies Percentage formatting.

- You can save number formatting as a style.

Adding Borders to a Range

A border is a line at the edge of a cell. You can use borders to divide the information on the sheet into logical regions. Borders appear on the screen and will print when you print the sheet.

Figure 13.17 Select the range first.

To add a border to a cell or range of cells:

1. Select the range to which you want to apply a border (**Figure 13.17**).

2. Click the arrow button next to the Borders button to see the full range of border options (**Figure 13.18**).

3. Select the pane on the display of borders that matches the border you want for the range (**Figure 13.19**).

   or

1. Select the range to which you want to apply a border.

2. From the Format menu, choose Cells, or right-click and choose Format Cells from the shortcut menu.

3. On the Border tab of the Format Cells dialog box, choose a border, a border style, and a color (**Figure 13.20**).

4. Click OK and the broder is added to the range (**Figure 13.21**).

✔ Tips

■ To choose the most recently used border, you can click the Borders button on the toolbar.

■ To remove the borders around a range, select the range, pull down the display of borders, and choose the pane at the upper left corner, which displays a cell with no borders.

Click here

Figure 13.18 Click the down arrow to see the available borders.

Figure 13.19 Select one of these panes to choose the border it displays.

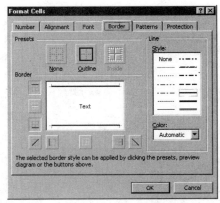

Figure 13.20 The Border tab of the Format Cells dialog box.

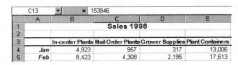

Figure 13.21 A border added to the range.

18R x 1C			
A	B	C	D
Sales 1998			
	In-center Plants	Mail Order Plants	Grower Supplies
Jan	4,923	957	317
Feb	8,423	4,308	2,195
Mar	34,038	6,910	12,634
Apr	37,154	147,180	43,170
May	114,233	189,715	71,902
Jun	152,474	30,342	76,927

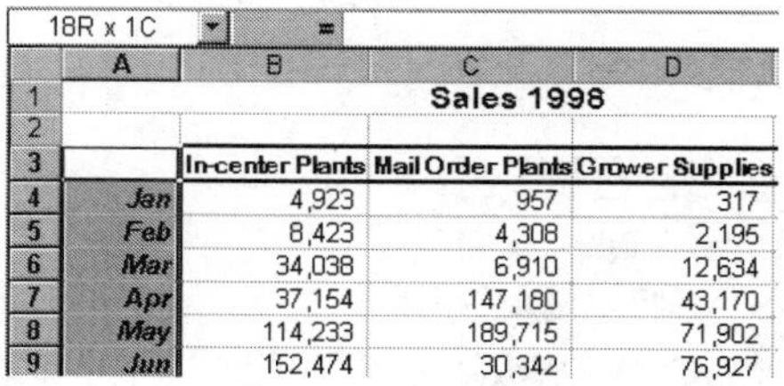

Figure 13.22 Select the range to shade.

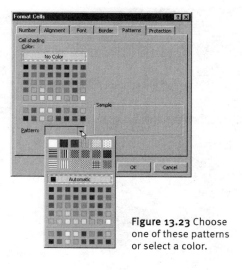

Figure 13.23 Choose one of these patterns or select a color.

C22			
A	B	C	D
Sales 1998			
	In-center Plants	Mail Order Plants	Grower Supplies
Jan	4,923	957	317
Feb	8,423	4,308	2,195
Mar	34,038	6,910	12,634
Apr	37,154	147,180	43,170
May	114,233	189,715	71,902
Jun	152,474	30,342	76,927

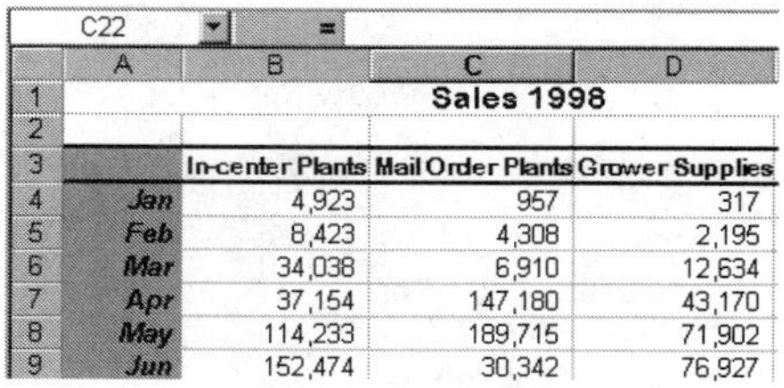

Figure 13.24 The range is shaded.

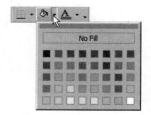

Figure 13.25 Choose one of these colors or No Fill.

Adding Shading to a Range

Shading can make your spreadsheet easier to understand.

To add shading to a cell or range of cells:

1. Select the range to which you want to add shading (**Figure 13.22**).
2. From the Format menu, choose Cells, or right-click and choose Format Cells from the shortcut menu.
3. On the Patterns tab of the Format Cells dialog box, choose a color or shade of gray.
4. To choose a monochrome pattern, pull down the list of patterns and choose one of the patterns at the top of the palette (**Figure 13.23**).
5. Click OK.

✔ Tips

- Shading is often applied automatically to parts of a range when you select an AutoFormat (**Figure 13.24**).
- To quickly fill a cell or range of cells with a color, click the Fill button on the Formatting toolbar and choose a color from the Fill menu (**Figure 13.25**).

Applying Conditional Formatting

If a cell or range of cells contains data that you want to highlight if certain conditions are met, you can use conditional formatting.

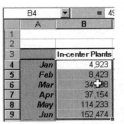

Figure 13.26 Select the cell or cells to format.

To apply conditional formatting to a cell or range of cells:

1. Select the cells to format (**Figure 13.26**).

2. From the Format menu, choose Conditional Formatting.

3. Use the pull-down lists and the edit box to set the first condition (**Figure 13.27**).

Figure 13.27 Set the condition in the Conditional Formatting dialog box.

4. Click the Format button to choose the formatting that will be applied if the condition is met (**Figure 13.28**).

5. Click OK when you have finished, or click the Add button to add another condition (**Figure 13.29**).

   The conditions are applied (**Figure 13.30**).

✔ Tips

- To find cells that have conditional formatting applied, choose Go To from the Edit menu. Click the Special button in the Go To dialog box, and then click Conditional Format (All or Same).

- You can use the Format Painter to copy conditional formatting to other cells.

- You can save conditional formatting as a style.

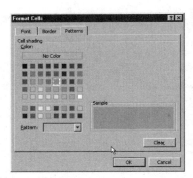

Figure 13.28 Choose the conditional formatting.

Figure 13.29 The first condition set.

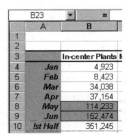

Figure 13.30 The first condition applied.

CONDITIONAL FORMATTING

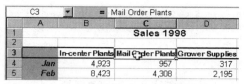

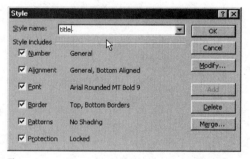

Figure 13.31 Format a sample cell.

Figure 13.32 Choose Style from the Format menu.

Figure 13.33 Type the name in the Style dialog box.

Creating a Style

A style is a preset combination of formatting. When none of the existing styles has the formatting you want, you can create your own style.

To create a style:

1. Format a cell with whatever formatting you want (**Figure 13.31**).

2. From the Format menu, choose Style (**Figure 13.32**).

3. Type a new style name in the Style Name text box (**Figure 13.33**).

4. Make sure the check boxes for the formatting options you want to apply are checked in the Style dialog box.

5. Click OK.

✔ Tip

■ By clicking the Merge button in the Style dialog box, you can copy the styles from another open workbook.

CREATING A STYLE

Selecting a Style

When an existing style has the formatting you want, you can select it.

To select a style:

1. Select the cells to format.

2. From the Format menu, choose Style.

3. In the Style dialog box, choose a style from the Style Name drop-down list (**Figure 13.34**).

4. Make sure the check boxes for the formatting options you want to apply are checked in the Style dialog box.

5. Click OK.

✔ Tips

■ Styles in the Style Name list that are followed by a *[0]* are formatted to zero decimal places.

■ Cells are given the Normal style by default. Therefore, to change the default cell formatting, you can modify the Normal style.

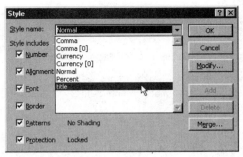

Figure 13.34 Choose the new style in the Style dialog box.

USING EXCEL CHARTS

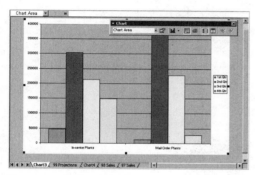

Figure 14.1 An Excel chart.

Numeric information is often easiest to understand when it is presented graphically in an Excel chart (**Figure 14.1**).

In Excel, you can create a default chart with a single click. Once Excel has created the chart, you can tailor it to your needs by clicking any element and using Excel's tools to edit that element. You can add, change, or delete titles, labels, legends, and gridlines. You can choose any of nearly two dozen chart styles, including bar, column, line, area, pie, scatter, bubble, and radar charts, and you can add 3-D effects to many of them. You can easily add, change, or remove color, patterns, and shading, and you can change the scale, labeling, and look of the axes. If you go back and edit the data used to create the chart, the chart changes to reflect the new values.

Creating a Default Chart

You can create a chart using the current default settings and then modify it, or you can use the Chart Wizard to guide you in making initial decisions.

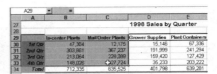

Figure 14.2 Select the data to chart.

To create a chart using the default settings:

1. Select the data to chart (**Figure 14.2**).

2. Press the F11 key to create a chart with all the default settings.

   A column chart of the selected data appears in a new worksheet (**Figure 14.3**).

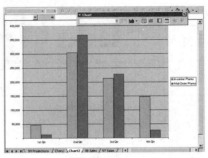

Figure 14.3 Default chart on a new sheet.

To order the data by rows rather than columns:

1. Choose Source Data from the Chart menu (**Figure 14.4**).

2. In the Source Data dialog box, click the Rows button (**Figure 14.5**).

3. Click OK.

   or

   Click the By Row button on the Chart toolbar (**Figure 14.6**).

Figure 14.4 Choose Source Data from the Chart menu.

✔ Tips

- To select nonadjacent data to chart, press Ctrl while dragging across groups of cells.

- You can change the default chart type from a column chart to any other type you use frequently. To do so, click a chart and choose Chart Type from the Chart menu. Then select a chart type to use, and click the Set as Default Chart button.

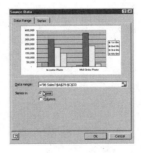

Figure 14.5 Click the Rows button in the Source Data dialog box.

By Row By Column

Figure 14.6 Click By Row on the Chart toolbar.

Chart Wizard button

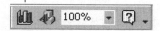

Figure 14.7 Click the Chart Wizard button on the Standard toolbar.

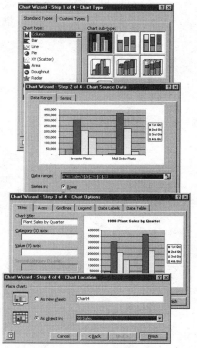

Figure 14.8 The four steps in the Chart Wizard.

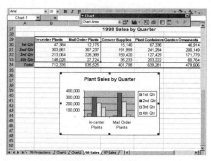

Figure 14.9 The completed chart, on the same sheet as the data.

Creating a Chart Using the Chart Wizard

The Chart Wizard helps you make some preliminary decisions while setting up your chart.

To create a chart using the Chart Wizard:

1. Select the data to chart.

2. Click the Chart Wizard button on the Standard toolbar (**Figure 14.7**).

3. Follow the four Chart Wizard steps (**Figure 14.8**) to select a chart type, confirm the source data, add a title, make changes to gridlines, and determine the placement of a legend and labels.

4. Specify whether the chart is embedded in an existing worksheet or created in a separate sheet.

5. Click Finish.

   The completed chart is displayed (**Figure 14.9**).

✔ Tip

■ After you use the wizard, you are free to make modifications as for any other chart.

Modifying a Chart

If you move the pointer slowly over areas of a chart, you can see ToolTips identifying the items that make up the chart. Each item can be formatted separately.

To modify a chart:

◆ Double-click a chart object to display the formatting dialog box appropriate for that object.

or

Right-click a chart object, and choose the appropriate formatting dialog box from the shortcut menu.

or

Click a chart object, and click the Chart toolbar's Format button to display the appropriate formatting dialog box (**Figure 14.10**).

or

Click a chart object, and choose Selected Chart Area from the Format menu to display the appropriate dialog box (**Figure 14.11**).

or

Choose the object you want to modify from the Chart Objects list on the Chart toolbar, and click the Chart toolbar's Format button to display the dialog box (**Figure 14.12**).

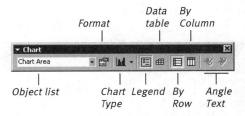

Figure 14.10 Choose Format on the Chart toolbar.

Figure 14.11 Choose Selected Chart Area from the Format menu.

Figure 14.12 Choose the object to modify from the Chart Object list.

MODIFYING A CHART

Figure 14.13 Choose Chart Options from the Chart menu.

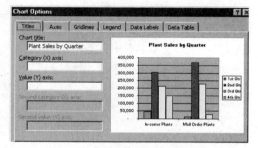

Figure 14.14 Click a tab in the Chart Options dialog box.

✔ Tips

- To modify several chart elements at the same time, choose Chart Options from the Chart menu and use the various tabs in the Chart Options dialog box (**Figures 14.13** and **14.14**).

- Drag the chart to move it on the sheet, or drag the handles of the chart window to resize the chart.

- Format the most general elements of the chart first (such as the chart area), and then format individual elements within that area (such as axis labels).

- Don't be afraid to experiment with options you don't completely understand; you can easily undo almost any change by using the Undo command on the Edit menu or the Undo button on the Standard toolbar.

MODIFYING A CHART

Modifying the Chart Type

Excel provides many chart types to help you display data in a way that will best communicate its meaning.

To modify the chart type:

1. Click the chart.

2. From the Chart menu choose Chart Type (**Figure 14.15**).

3. Select a type in the Chart Type dialog box (**Figure 14.16**).

4. Click OK.

    or

1. Click the chart.

2. Select a type from the Chart Type list on the Chart toolbar (**Figure 14.17**).

    The chart type changes (**Figure 14.18**).

✔ Tip

■ The Chart Type option on the Chart menu offers more options than the Chart Type list on the Chart toolbar.

Figure 14.15 Choose Chart Type from the Chart menu.

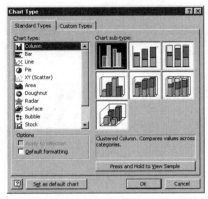

Figure 14.16 Select a type in the Chart Type dialog box.

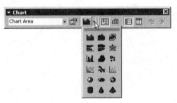

Figure 14.17 Pull down the Chart Type list on the Chart toolbar.

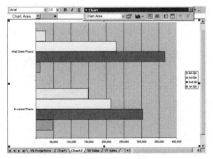

Figure 14.18 The chart type changed to bar from column.

Chart area   Plot area   Gridlines

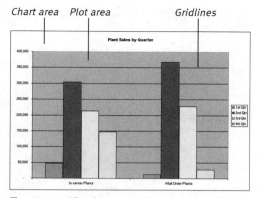

Figure 14.19 The chart area, plot area, and gridlines.

Modifying the Chart Area, Plot Area, and Gridlines

The chart area is the background of the sheet on which the chart is drawn. The plot area is the background of the chart itself, inside the axes. The gridlines are lines in the plot area denoting major values along the axes.

To modify the chart area:

1. Double-click the chart area (**Figure 14.19**).

2. In the Format Chart Area dialog box, click the Patterns tab and enter new settings to change the border surrounding the chart area, its color, and any fill effects, such as gradient, texture, or even using a picture for the chart area.

3. Click the Font tab and enter new settings to change the font characteristics of the axis labels, legend, and chart title.

4. Click OK.

To modify the plot area format:

1. Double-click the plot area.

2. In the Format Plot Area dialog box, change the border surrounding the plot area, its color, and any fill effects, such as using a gradient, texture, or even a picture for the plot area.

3. Click OK.

To modify a gridline format:

1. Double-click a gridline.

2. In the Format Gridlines dialog box, click the Patterns tab and enter new settings to change the style, color, and weight of the gridlines.

3. Click the Scale tab and enter new settings to change the scale of the axis connected to these gridlines and the crossing point of the other axis (**Figure 14.20**).

4. Click OK.

The gridline format changes (**Figure 14.21**).

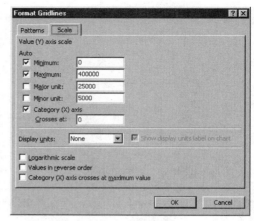

Figure 14.20 Change the scale on the Scale tab of the Format Gridlines dialog box.

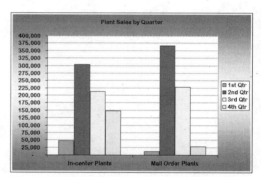

Figure 14.21 The chart area, plot area, and gridlines have been changed.

CHART/PLOT AREAS, GRIDLINES

Value axis   *Chart title*

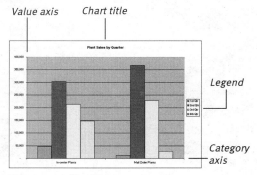

Legend

Category axis

Figure 14.22 The title, legend, and axes on a chart.

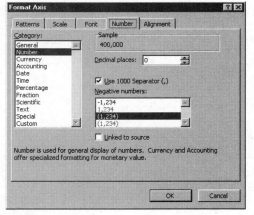

Figure 14.23 Select a category in the Format Axis dialog box.

Modifying the Title, Axes, and Legend

You can format the a chart's title, axes, and legend separately.

To modify the chart title format:

1. Double-click the chart title (**Figure 14.22**).

2. In the Format Chart Title dialog box, click the Patterns tab and enter new settings to change the border surrounding the title, its color, and any fill effects.

3. Click the Font tab and enter new settings to change the font characteristics.

4. Click the Alignment tab, and change the alignment or orientation of the title text. (The title text box cannot be resized with the handles.)

5. Click OK.

To modify an axis format:

1. Double-click an axis.

2. In the Format Axis dialog box, use the Patterns, Scale, Font, Number, and Alignment tabs to format those aspects of the axis (**Figure 14.23**).

3. Click OK.

To modify the legend format:

1. Double-click the legend.

2. In the Format Legend dialog box, use the Patterns, Scale, Font, Number, and Alignment tabs to change any of those aspects of the legend.

3. Click OK.

   The legend is modified (**Figure 14.24**).

✔ Tips

■ The Alignment tab in the Format Legend dialog box contains the controls for the placement of the legend in the chart area. If you want to format only one of the legend entries, click it to select it, and use the Select Legend Entry dialog box to format its font characteristics.

■ To delete elements such as the title or legend, click the border of the element and press Delete, or right-click the element and choose Clear from the shortcut menu.

■ You can also use buttons on the Chart toolbar to add or delete a legend or angle axis text upward or downward.

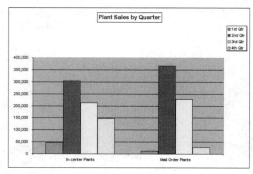

Figure 14.24 The legend has been reformatted.

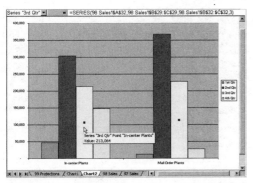

Figure 14.25 The chart with a data series selected.

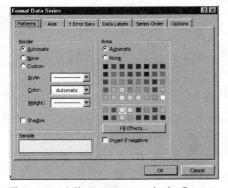

Figure 14.26 Choose a pattern in the Format Data Series dialog box.

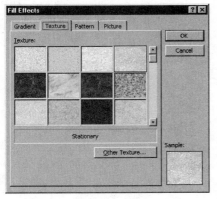

Figure 14.27 Choose a fill effect.

Modifying a Data Series

A data series is a group of related values, such as all the data values in a row or column of the datasheet. You can modify each data series separately.

To modify a data series:

1. Click a data series in the chart (**Figure 14.25**).

   References to the cells that contain data for that series appear in the edit line above the chart, and a tip window appears defining the data point you clicked.

2. Edit the references in the edit line.

To modify a data series format:

1. Double-click the data series.

2. In the Format Data Series dialog box, use the tabs to change virtually any aspect of the data series (**Figure 14.26**).

3. Click Fill Effects on the Patterns tab to choose an effect (**Figure 14.27**).

(continued)

MODIFYING A DATA SERIES

4. Click the Options tab and adjust the overlap and gap width (**Figure 14.28**).

5. Click OK.

The series displays the new formatting (**Figure 14.29**).

✔ Tip

■ Click the By Row or By Column button on the Chart toolbar to specify whether each series is a row or a column of data in the sheet containing the data cells.

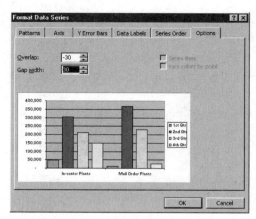

Figure 14.28 Change the overlap and gap width on the Options tab.

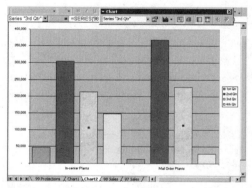

Figure 14.29 The data series has a textured look and the overlap and gap have been modified for all series.

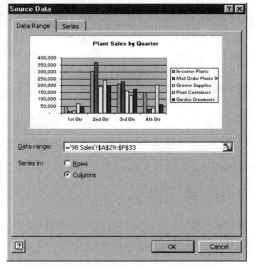

Figure 14.30 Choose Source Data from the Chart menu.

Figure 14.31 The data range extended in the Source Data dialog box.

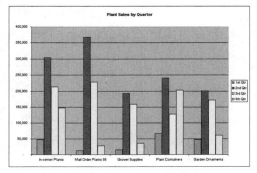

Figure 14.32 The data range includes three more columns.

Adding Data to a Chart

Once a chart has been created, you might want to extend it to include more data.

To add data to a chart:

1. Select a chart.

2. From the Chart menu, choose Source Data (**Figure 14.30**).

3. In the Source Data dialog box, add more rows using the Series tab or extend the data range to include more columns using the Data Range tab (**Figure 14.31**).

4. Click OK.

   The new rows or columns are added to the chart (**Figure 14.32**).

Adding Data Tables and Trendlines

You can add a table of the data that is represented by the chart and add a trendline that shows the general trend, such as growth or decline, that emerges in the data.

To add a data table:

◆ Click the Data Table button on the Chart toolbar (**Figure 14.33**).

The Data Table appears below the chart (**Figure 14.34**).

✔ Tip

■ To modify the format of the data table, double-click the data table and, in the Format Data Table dialog box, edit the line styles and font characteristics.

Data Table button

Figure 14.33 Click the Data Table button on the Chart toolbar.

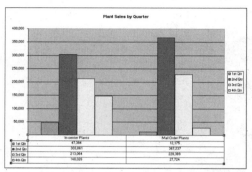

Figure 14.34 The data table appears below the chart.

Figure 14.35 Choose Add Trendline from the Chart menu.

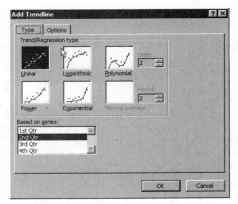

Figure 14.36 Select a type in the Add Trendline dialog box.

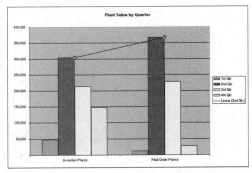

Figure 14.37 The trendline is added to the data series.

To add a trendline:

1. Click a data series for which you want to add a trendline.

2. From the Chart menu, choose Add Trendline (**Figure 14.35**).

3. In the Add Trendline dialog box, define the kind of trendline you want and set the options (**Figure 14.36**).

4. Click OK.

   The trendline is added (**Figure 14.37**).

DATA TABLES AND TRENDLINES

Creating a PivotTable Report

PivotTable and PivotChart reports can help you look at data in different ways. Once the reports are created, you can swap rows with columns for different views.

To create a PivotTable report:

1. Click in the selected data area.

2. From the Data menu, choose PivotTable and PivotChart Report to start the Pivot-Table and PivotChart Wizard (**Figure 14.38**).

3. Select the PivotTable report, specify the data source, and indicate whether you want the report to be placed on a new worksheet or an existing one (**Figure 14.39**).

4. Position the table items to create the view you want (**Figure 14.40**).

   The row and columns items are listed below the button area on the PivotTable toolbar.

Figure 14.38 Choose PivotTable and PivotChart Report from the Data menu.

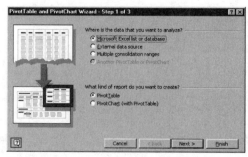

Figure 14.39 The first step of the PivotTable and PivotChart Wizard.

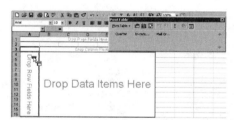

Figure 14.40 Place the PivotTable items.

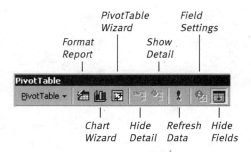

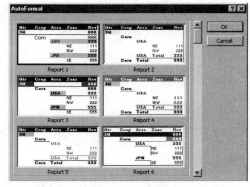

Figure 14.41 The PivotTable toolbar.

Figure 14.42 Select a format in the AutoFormat dialog box.

5. Click the Format Report button on the PivotTable toolbar (**Figure 14.41**).

6. Choose a format from the AutoFormat dialog box (**Figure 14.42**).

7. Click OK.

✔ Tip

■ If your workbook already contains a PivotTable or PivotChart report, you can base this new report on the previous one.

Creating a PivotChart Report

When you create a PivotChart report, Excel creates the PivotTable report as well. The PivotChart report presents the data graphically, and you can swap rows and columns in either the table or the chart.

To create a PivotChart report:

1. Click in the selected data area.

2. Choose PivotTable and PivotChart Report from the Data menu to start the PivotTable and PivotChart Wizard.

3. Select the PivotChart report, specify the data source, and indicate whether you want the report to be placed on a new worksheet or an existing one (**Figure 14.43**).

4. Position the chart items to create the view you want (**Figure 14.44**).

✔ Tip

■ Modify the format of any PivotChart element just as you would any other chart.

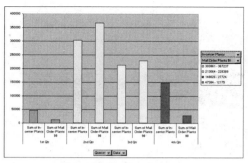

Figure 14.43 The PivotChart Report showing data ordered by quarter.

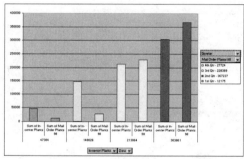

Figure 14.44 The PivotChart Report showing data ordered by in-center plants.

EXCEL DATABASE TECHNIQUES

	A	B	C	D	E	F
				Vacation Days 1998		
1						
2						
3	LastName	Initials	Employee No.	Status	Total Vacation Days	Vacation Days Used
4	Warkworth	B.	3750	Permanent	20	5
5	Elston	M.Y.	3751	Permanent	15	4
6	Timosian	A.R.	3752	Temporary	0	0
7	Wyclyff	C.P.	3753	Permanent	10	1
8	Swanston	G.E.	3754	Temporary	15	0
9	Crawford	L.D.	3755	Permanent	20	2
10	Lange	T.J.	3756	Permanent	15	9

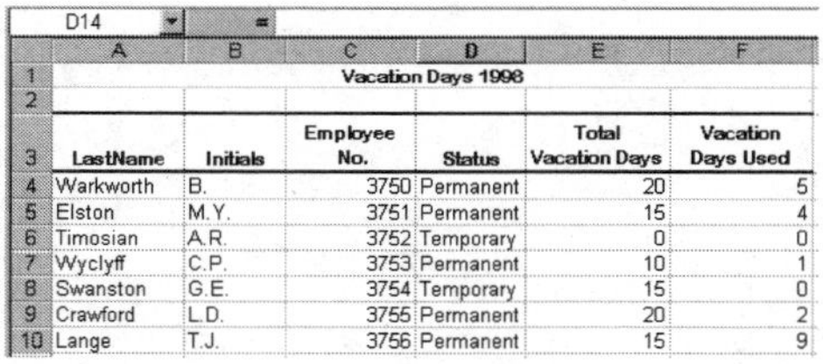

Figure 15.1 Each record of information occupies a row and each column is a field.

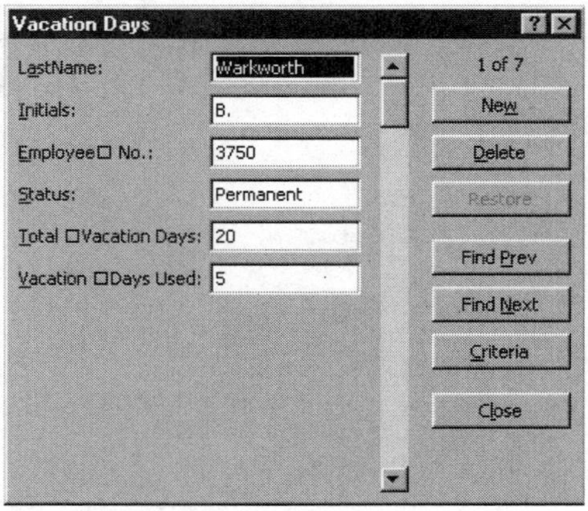

Figure 15.2 A data form.

Unless you work with extremely large databases (thousands and thousands of sets of data) or you need a complex database structure, Excel can provide all the database power you'll need.

In Excel, you enter data in rows. Each row is a record (one complete set of information). Each column in the row, called a field, contains one particular type of information in the record (**Figure 15.1**).

Rather than enter information directly in the cells of a sheet, you can also create a fill-in-the-blanks data form to make it easier to enter, edit, delete, and search through information (**Figure 15.2**).

After you enter the data, you can search through it, sort it, and pull out only the information that matches particular criteria.

Setting Up the Database

Set up the database in the same way you would create other ranges in a spreadsheet.

To set up a database:

1. Enter the field names at the top of a group of adjacent columns (**Figure 15.3**).

2. Enter the data in rows below the field names (**Figure 15.4**).

✔ Tips

- Press Tab when you complete a cell to move to the next cell to the right.

- Press Enter when you complete a cell to move to the next cell below.

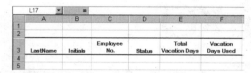

Figure 15.3 The field names for the database.

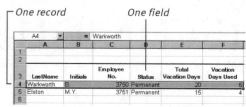

Figure 15.4 Enter the data in rows (records) below the field names.

Figure 15.5 Click any cell in the database.

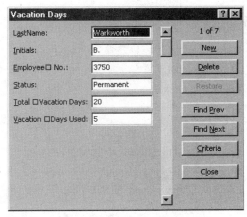

Figure 15.6 Choose Form from the Data menu.

Figure 15.7 The form for this database.

Creating a Form

You can use a form to add new records, edit and delete existing records, and search through information.

To create a form:

1. Click in any cell that contains data (**Figure 15.5**).

2. From the Data menu, choose Form (**Figure 15.6**).

3. In the Worksheet Form dialog box, click New and fill in the fields for a new record.

   or

   Use the Find Prev and Find Next buttons on the form to find records to edit (**Figure 15.7**).

4. Click Close to put away the form.

✔ Tips

- Press Tab to move from field to field on a form.

- Press Shift+Tab to return to the previous field on a form.

Sorting the Database

You can sort the data alphabetically and numerically, using up to three sort keys.

To sort the database:

1. Click in any cell in the database (**Figure 15.8**).

2. From the Data menu, choose Sort (**Figure 15.9**).

3. In the Sort dialog box, choose a field name from the Sort By drop-down list (**Figure 15.10**).

4. To further sort the data using the entries in second and third fields, choose additional fields from the two Then By drop-down lists in the Sort dialog box.

5. For each Sort By, to sort from smallest to largest, earliest to latest, or alphabetically from A to Z, click Ascending. To sort from largest to smallest, latest to earliest, or alphabetically from Z to A, click Descending.

6. Click OK to see the sorted data (**Figure 15.11**).

✔ Tip

- You can quickly sort by any column in the database (or in any other spreadsheet range) by clicking the Sort Ascending or Sort Descending button on the Standard toolbar (**Figure 15.12**).

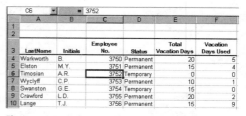

Figure 15.8 Click any cell in the database.

Figure 15.9 Choose Sort from the Data menu.

Figure 15.10 Select fields in the Sort dialog box.

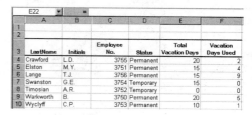

Figure 15.11 The sorted data.

Figure 15.12 The Sort Ascending and Sort Descending buttons on the Standard toolbar.

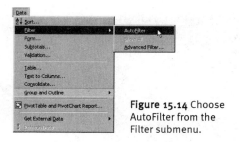

	D6		=	Permanent		
	A	B	C	D	E	F
1						
2						
3	**LastName**	**Initials**	**Employee No.**	**Status**	**Total Vacation Days**	**Vacation Days Used**
4	Crawford	L.D.	3755	Permanent	20	2
5	Elston	M.Y.	3751	Permanent	15	4
6	Lange	T.J.	3756	Permanent	15	9
7	Swanston	G.E.	3754	Temporary	15	0
8	Timosian	A.R.	3752	Temporary	0	0
9	Warkworth	B.	3750	Permanent	20	5
10	Wyclyff	C.P.	3753	Permanent	10	1

Figure 15.13 Click in any cell in the database.

Figure 15.14 Choose AutoFilter from the Filter submenu.

	D6		=	Permanent		
	A	B	C	D	E	F
1						
2						
3	**LastName**	**Initials**	**Employee No.**	**Status**	**Total Vacation Day**	**Vacation Days Used**
4	Crawford	L.D.	37	(All)	20	2
5	Elston	M.Y.	37	(Top 10...)	15	4
6	Lange	T.J.	37	(Custom...)	15	9
7	Swanston	G.E.	37	Permanent	15	0
8	Timosian	A.R.	3752	Temporary	0	0
9	Warkworth	B.	3750	Permanent	20	5
10	Wyclyff	C.P.	3753	Permanent	10	1

Figure 15.15 Select an entry from one of the pull-down lists.

	H25		=			
	A	B	C	D	E	F
1						
2						
3	**LastName**	**Initials**	**Employee No.**	**Status**	**Total Vacation Day**	**Vacation Days Used**
4	Crawford	L.D.	3755	Permanent	20	2
5	Elston	M.Y.	3751	Permanent	15	4
6	Lange	T.J.	3756	Permanent	15	9
9	Warkworth	B.	3750	Permanent	20	5
10	Wyclyff	C.P.	3753	Permanent	10	1
11						
12						

Figure 15.16 Only records that match the selected entry appear.

Extracting Data

You can use criteria to extract all the records that match the criteria and then use the extracted data in other parts of your worksheet or in reports.

To extract data from the database:

1. Click in any cell in the database (**Figure 15.13**).

2. From the Data menu, choose Filter and then choose AutoFilter (**Figure 15.14**).

3. Click any of the arrow buttons next to the field names to display a list of the entries in that field (**Figure 15.15**).

4. Choose an entry on the list to view only those records that match the entry (**Figure 15.16**).

5. Continue to filter by using the arrow buttons, if necessary.

✔ Tips

■ To stop filtering, choose AutoFilter from the Filter submenu again.

■ When the database is filtered, the fields on which the database is filtered show a blue arrow button.

■ To extract the data to another location, choose Advanced Filter from the Filter pop-up menu and then choose Copy to Another Location in the Advanced Filter dialog box.

Totaling Numeric Data in a Database

For any numeric list in the database, you can create subtotals and totals.

To total numeric data in the database:

1. Select any cell in the database.

2. From the Data menu, choose Subtotals (**Figure 15.17**).

3. In the Subtotal dialog box, select a field from the At Each Change In drop-down list (**Figure 15.18**).

4. Click OK.

   A subtotal appears each time this field changes value. A grand total appears at the bottom of the list (**Figure 15.19**).

✔ Tips

■ In the gray area to the left of the table, click the minus button next to a line to show only the subtotal on that line.

■ To remove the totals and subtotals, choose Subtotals again and click Remove All in the Subtotal dialog box.

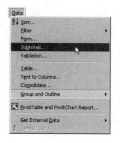

Figure 15.17 Choose Subtotals from the Data menu.

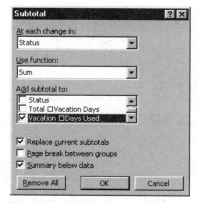

Figure 15.18 Select the fields in the Subtotal dialog box.

Minus buttons

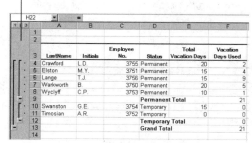

Figure 15.19 Click the minus buttons to hide detail and show only the totals.

SPECIAL
EXCEL TECHNIQUES

Each Excel workbook can contain multiple worksheets. If you want, you can use just the first worksheet for all your data and calculations. But you also might want to organize your information by placing certain data on each worksheet and using one of the sheets to consolidate data from other sheets.

In this chapter, you'll learn how to take advantage of multiple sheets and other, more advanced Excel tasks and capabilities.

Changing to Another Sheet

You can use the worksheet tabs visible at the bottom of the current sheet to switch easily from sheet to sheet (**Figure 16.1**).

To change to another sheet:

◆ Click the tab of the sheet you want to display (**Figure 16.2**).

✔ Tips

■ If the tab is not visible, use the Tab scrolling buttons to scroll through the sheets (**Figure 16.3**).

■ You can rearrange the order of sheets by dragging their tabs to the left or right.

Figure 16.1 A workbook containing five worksheets.

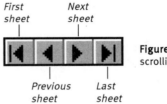

Figure 16.2 To bring a worksheet to the front, click its tab.

Figure 16.3 The Tab scrolling buttons.

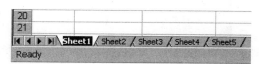

Figure 16.4 Double-click a tab and type over the highlighted name to rename the sheet.

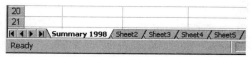

Figure 16.5 The new name appears on the tab.

Naming Sheets

You can replace the default sheet names (Sheet1, Sheet2, and so on) with useful, informative names (for example, Marketing, Manufacturing, Personnel).

To name a sheet:

1. Double-click the tab of the sheet you want to rename (**Figure 16.4**).

2. Type the new name over the current name in the sheet tab (**Figure 16.5**).

✔ Tips

- You can also choose Sheet and then Rename from the Format menu to select the sheet name in the tab of the current sheet, ready to be typed over.

- Sheet names can be up to 31 characters long and can include spaces.

NAMING SHEETS

Referring to Data from Other Sheets in Formulas

While you are building a formula, you can include data from another sheet.

To build a formula using data from another sheet:

1. Click the destination cell for the formula.

2. Start the formula by typing an equal sign, a left parenthesis, a cell, and then an operator (**Figure 16.6**).

3. Refer to cells on another sheet by switching to the sheet and then selecting the cell or cells (**Figure 16.7**).

4. Press Enter when you finish building the formula (**Figure 16.8**).

   You will be returned to the sheet on which you started the formula and the formula appears (**Figure 16.9**).

✔ Tip

■ If you've named ranges in other sheets, you can enter the range names in the formula without worrying about which sheet the data is on. Excel will find the range on any sheet in the workbook.

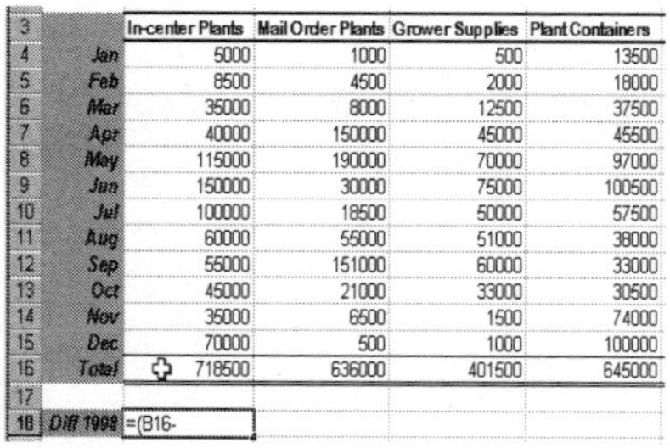

		In-center Plants	Mail Order Plants	Grower Supplies	Plant Containers
4	Jan	5000	1000	500	13500
5	Feb	8500	4500	2000	18000
6	Mar	35000	8000	12500	37500
7	Apr	40000	150000	45000	45500
8	May	115000	190000	70000	97000
9	Jun	150000	30000	75000	100500
10	Jul	100000	18500	50000	57500
11	Aug	60000	55000	51000	38000
12	Sep	55000	151000	60000	33000
13	Oct	45000	21000	33000	30500
14	Nov	35000	6500	1500	74000
15	Dec	70000	500	1000	100000
16	Total	718500	636000	401500	645000
17					
18	Diff 1998	=(B16-			

Figure 16.6 Type the formula.

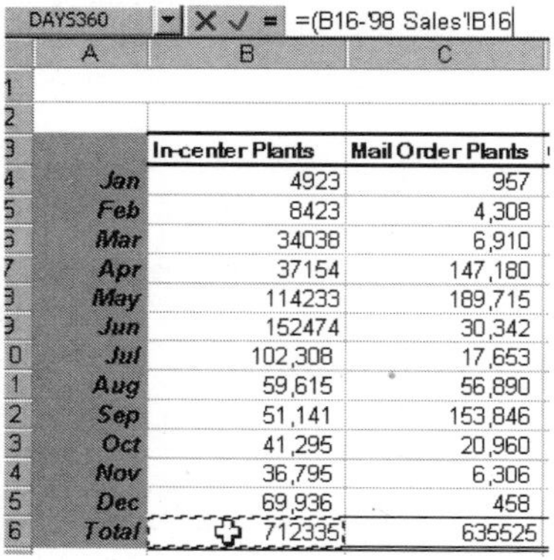

DAYS360 ▼ X ✓ = =(B16-98 Sales'!B16|

	A	B	C
1			
2			
3		In-center Plants	Mail Order Plants
4	Jan	4923	957
5	Feb	8423	4,308
6	Mar	34038	6,910
7	Apr	37154	147,180
8	May	114233	189,715
9	Jun	152474	30,342
10	Jul	102,308	17,653
11	Aug	59,615	56,890
12	Sep	51,141	153,846
13	Oct	41,295	20,960
14	Nov	36,795	6,306
15	Dec	69,936	458
16	Total	712335	635525

Figure 16.7 Switch to another sheet and select the cell or cells to include in the formula.

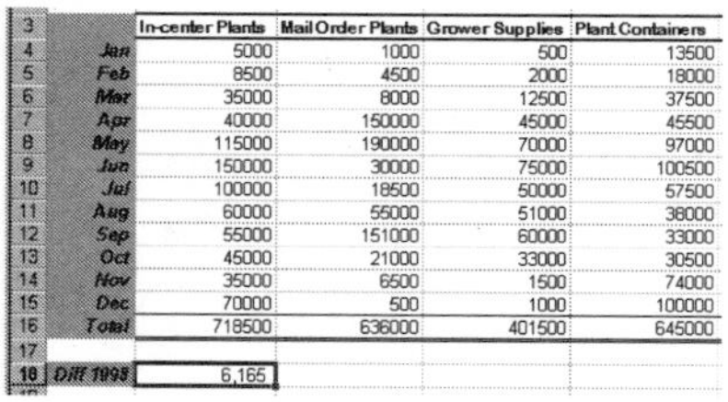

		In-center Plants	Mail Order Plants	Grower Supplies	Plant Containers
4	Jan	5000	1000	500	13500
5	Feb	8500	4500	2000	18000
6	Mar	35000	8000	12500	37500
7	Apr	40000	150000	45000	45500
8	May	115000	190000	70000	97000
9	Jun	150000	30000	75000	100500
10	Jul	100000	18500	50000	57500
11	Aug	60000	55000	51000	38000
12	Sep	55000	151000	60000	33000
13	Oct	45000	21000	33000	30500
14	Nov	35000	6500	1500	74000
15	Dec	70000	500	1000	100000
16	Total	718500	636000	401500	645000
17					
18	Diff 1998	6,165			

Figure 16.8 Press Enter to complete the formula.

Cell reference	Sheet name	Cell reference

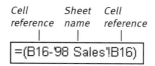

=(B16-98 Sales'!B16)

Figure 16.9 The formula.

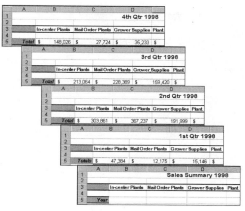

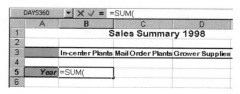

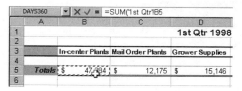

Figure 16.10 3-D referencing.

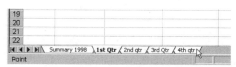

Figure 16.11 Click the destination for the formula and type the formula as usual.

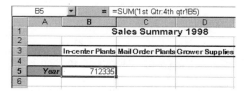

Figure 16.12 Select the cell or range on the first sheet.

Figure 16.13 While pressing the Shift key, click the tab for the last range.

Figure 16.14 The result of the formula.

Consolidating to a Sheet

When successive sheets of a workbook contain the exact same arrangement of data, you can sum ranges that extend "down" from sheet to sheet data rather than across a single sheet. This process is called 3-D referencing (**Figure 16.10**).

To consolidate using data from other sheets:

1. On the consolidation sheet, click in the destination cell for the formula and start the formula as usual (**Figure 16.11**).

2. Select the range or cell on the first sheet in the range of sheets (**Figure 16.12**).

3. Press and hold the Shift key on the keyboard.

4. Click the tab of the last sheet in the range (**Figure 16.13**).

5. Press Enter to see the result of the formula (**Figure 16.14**).

Naming Ranges

When you assign a name to a range, you can use the range name in formulas rather than the range address (**Figure 16.15**). Range names make it easier to refer to data and easier to understand formulas.

To name a range:

1. Select the range that you want to name (**Figure 16.16**).

2. From the Insert menu, choose Name, and then choose Define from the Name submenu (**Figure 16.17**).

3. Enter the name in the Define Name dialog box (**Figure 16.18**).

4. Click OK.

✔ Tips

■ To use the name in a formula, choose Paste from the Name submenu (**Figure 16.19**).

■ You can assign a name to an individual cell or to a range of cells.

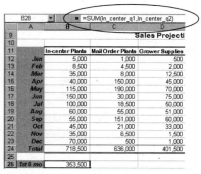

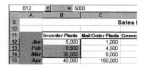

Figure 16.15 Using range names in a formula.

Figure 16.16 Select the range to name.

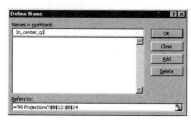

Figure 16.17 Choose Define from the Name submenu.

Figure 16.18 Type the range name in the Define Name dialog box.

Figure 16.19 Choose Paste from the Name submenu to paste a name into a formula.

NAMING RANGES

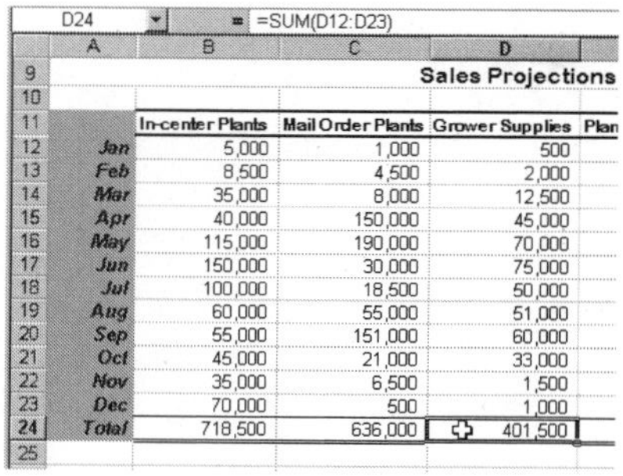

Figure 16.20 Select the formula or formulas to trace.

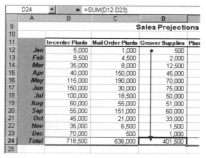

Figure 16.21 Choose Trace Precedents from the Auditing submenu.

Figure 16.22 Arrows show the links between a formula and the cells that supplied the data for it.

Trace Precedents   *Remove All Arrows*

Figure 16.23 The Auditing toolbar.

Auditing a Workbook

To avoid bogus results from incorrect formulas, you can have Excel identify the cells that have supplied data for a formula. That way, you can easily see whether all the cells you wanted have been included in the calculation.

To trace the precedents for a formula:

1. Select the cell or cells that contain the formulas (**Figure 16.20**).

2. From the Tools menu, choose Auditing, and then choose Trace Precedents from the Auditing submenu (**Figure 16.21**).

3. Choose Trace Precedents again to view an additional level of precedents, if one exists.

✔ Tips

- To clear the arrows that have appeared to show the cells that are included in the formula (**Figure 16.22**), choose Remove All Arrows from the Auditing submenu menu.

- The Auditing toolbar contains Trace Precedents and Remove All Arrows buttons (**Figure 16.23**). To view the Auditing toolbar, choose Show Auditing Toolbar from the Auditing submenu.

Seeking Goals

Use goal seeking to force a particular result in a calculation by changing one of the calculation's components. For example, if you know the percentage growth you are looking for, you can use Goal Seeking to determine the changes that would be necessary to produce that result.

To seek a goal:

1. From the Tools menu, choose Goal Seek (**Figure 16.24**).

2. In the Goal Seek dialog box, specify the cell whose value you want to set (this should be a cell whose value is usually calculated through a formula), the value you want that cell to have, and the cell whose value can vary to make the result come out to the value you want (**Figure 16.25**).

3. Click OK.

   If a solution is possible, the Goal Seek Status dialog will tell you, and the variable cell you specified will change.

4. Click OK to accept the change or click Cancel to reject it (**Figure 16.26**).

Figure 16.24 Choose Goal Seek from the Tools menu.

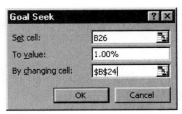

Figure 16.25 Specify the cell to set, the value, and the cell to change in the Goal Seek dialog box.

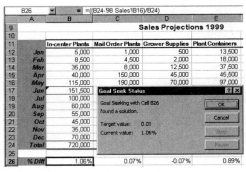

Figure 16.26 The result of the goal seeking.

SEEKING GOALS

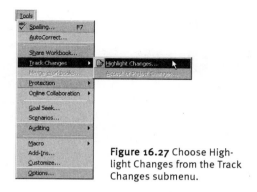

Figure 16.27 Choose Highlight Changes from the Track Changes submenu.

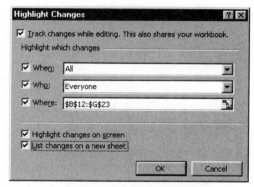

Figure 16.28 Make choices in the Highlight Changes dialog box.

Tracking Changes

You can share Excel workbooks with others and automatically track the changes they make. This capability makes managerial review especially easy.

To track changes:

1. From the Tools menu, choose Track Changes, and then choose Highlight Changes from the submenu (**Figure 16.27**).

2. In the Highlight Changes dialog box, use the selections to specify which changes to highlight (**Figure 16.28**).

3. To fill in the Where box, you can simply drag through the relevant cells.

4. Click OK.

✔ Tips

- Tracked cells with changes display a colored triangle in the upper left corner. To see a change notation, move the cursor onto the cell (**Figure 16.29**).

- Check List Changes on a New Sheet in the Highlight Changes dialog box to have the changes listed in a History sheet added to your workbook.

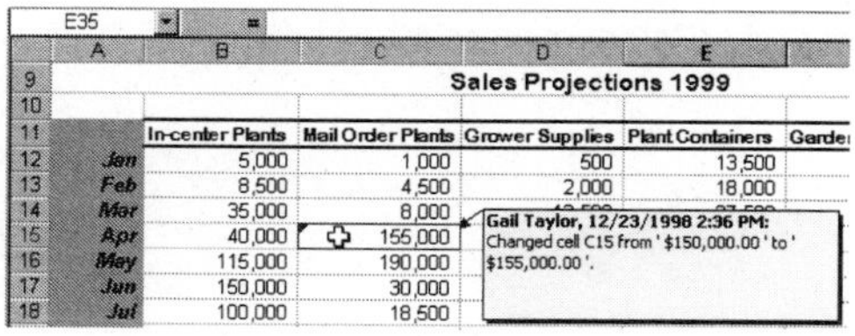

Figure 16.29 A cell change notice.

Reviewing Changes

When someone else has changed cells that have been set up for tracking changes, you can accept or reject those changes.

To review changes:

1. From the Tools menu, choose Track Changes, and then choose Accept or Reject Changes (**Figure 16.30**).

2. In the Select Changes to Accept or Reject dialog box, use the When, Who, and Where controls to specify which changes to review (**Figure 16.31**).

3. To fill in the Where box, you can drag through the relevant cells.

4. Click OK.

5. Click a cell that matches the criteria defined in step 2 to display the Accept or Reject Changes dialog box (**Figure 16.32**).

6. In the Accept or Reject Changes dialog box, use the buttons (Accept, Reject, Accept All, Reject All) to exercise your choices.

7. Click Close to finish.

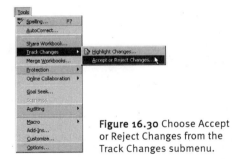

Figure 16.30 Choose Accept or Reject Changes from the Track Changes submenu.

Figure 16.31 Select the changes to review.

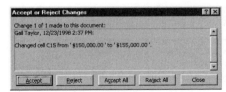

Figure 16.32 Accept or reject a change in the Accept or Reject Changes dialog box.

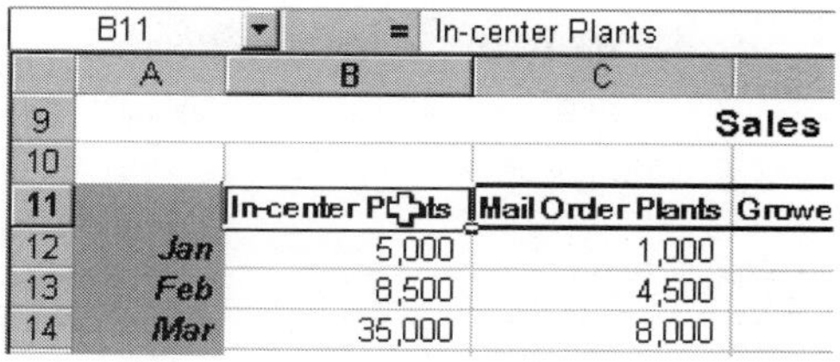

Figure 16.33 Select a cell.

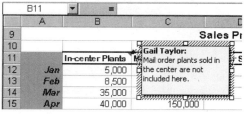

Figure 16.34 Choose Comment from the Insert menu.

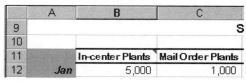

Figure 16.35 Type a comment in the Comment text box.

Figure 16.36 The comment marker.

Inserting Comments

A comment is an annotation that you attach to a cell to provide information about the cell's contents. This capability enables several people to review the same worksheet and attach their comments.

To insert a comment:

1. Select the cell to which you want to attach a comment (**Figure 16.33**).

2. From the Insert menu, choose Comment (**Figure 16.34**).

3. In the yellow text box that opens and displays your name, type the text for the comment (**Figure 16.35**).

4. Click in another cell to close the text box.

✔ Tips

■ A comment is indicated by a comment marker (a small red triangle) at the upper right corner of the cell (**Figure 16.36**). To view the comment, pass the cursor over the cell.

■ To remove a comment, right-click in the cell, and choose Delete Comment from the shortcut menu.

INSERTING COMMENTS

Protecting and Sharing a Workbook

You can allow others to work on portions of your workbook or all of your workbook, but it's a good idea to set up cell formatting options in advance so that they don't make changes inadvertently.

To unlock cells so that other people can edit the cell contents:

1. Select the cells that will be editable and choose Cells from the Format menu or right-click and choose Format Cells from the shortcut menu.

2. On the Protection tab in the Format Cells dialog box, clear the Locked check box (**Figure 16.37**).

3. Click OK.

✔ Tip

■ To hide formulas, check Hidden on the Protection tab in the Format Cells dialog box (**Figure 16.37**).

To protect a workbook:

1. From the Tools menu, choose Protection, and choose Protect Sheet from the submenu (**Figure 16.38**).

2. In the Protect Sheet dialog box, you can assign a password so that you are the only one who can remove the protection (**Figure 16.39**).

3. Click OK.

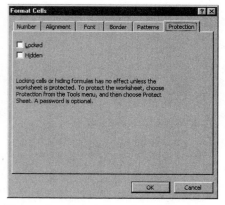

Figure 16.37 Unlock the cells in the Format Cells dialog box.

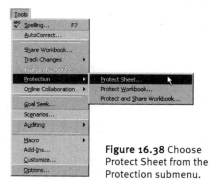

Figure 16.38 Choose Protect Sheet from the Protection submenu.

Figure 16.39 Specify the protection and an optional password in the Protect Sheet dialog box.

Figure 16.40 Choose Share Workbook from the Tools menu.

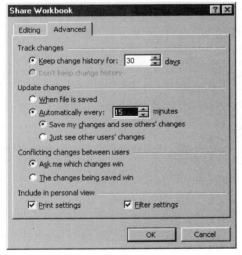

Figure 16.41 Specify update settings on the Advanced tab of the Share Workbook dialog box.

To share a workbook:

1. From the Tools menu, choose Share Workbook (**Figure 16.40**).

2. On the Editing tab in the Chart Workbook dialog box, enable changes by more than one user.

3. On the Advanced tab, specify when you want the changes updated and how you want conflicts handled (**Figure 16.41**).

4. Click OK.

✔ Tips

- To return the workbook to its unshared state, choose Share Workbook from the Tools menus and clear the Allow Changes check box.

- You can protect and share in one step by choosing Protect and Share Workbook from the Protection submenu.

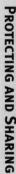

PROTECTING AND SHARING

Merging Workbooks

Another approach to sharing work is to maintain multiple copies of a shared workbook and track the changes in each for the same period of time. At the end of that time, you can merge the copies.

To merge workbooks:

1. From the Tools menu, choose Merge Workbooks (**Figure 16.42**).

2. Select the workbooks to merge into the current one (**Figure 16.43**).

3. Click OK.

Figure 16.42 Choose Merge Workbooks from the Tools menu.

Figure 16.43 Select the files in the Select Files to Merge into Current Workbook dialog box.

EXCEL
AND THE WEB

Excel can read worksheets that have been saved to the Web as Web pages and save worksheets as Web pages, too. This lets the people on a corporate intranet, or those who can connect to a Web site on the Internet, share Excel data easily using only their Web browsers

When you save a workbook as a Web page, others can see the workbook in a Web browser just as it looked to you in Excel.

When you use a Web browser to open a workbook that has been saved as a Web page, you can choose to edit the worksheet in Excel and then save it on your machine as a standard Microsoft Excel Workbook.

Opening a Document on the Web

You can open a document on the Web so that you can edit it in Excel.

To open a Web page as an Excel worksheet:

1. From the File menu, choose Open (**Figure 17.1**).

2. Choose Web Folders from the Places bar and Web Pages as the type of file.

3. Double-click a Web folder or enter the URL in the File Name text box of the Open dialog box (**Figure 17.2**).

4. Click Open.

   Your computer logs onto the Web server and displays the file in Excel.

✔ Tips

- If your system administrator or Internet service provider has set up a Web server that supports Web folders, you can use the Add Web Folder Wizard to create a folder that serves as a shortcut.

- To save the Web page on your computer, choose Edit with Microsoft Excel from the File menu of the Web browser and then, in Excel, choose Save As. By choosing from the Save as Type drop-down list, you can save the file as a Microsoft Excel Workbook or as a Web page (**Figure 17.3**).

- If the Web toolbar is visible, you can also type in the URL and press Enter to have your default browser download and display a Web document (**Figure 17.4**).

Figure 17.1 Choose Open from the File menu.

Figure 17.2 Type the URL in the File Name text box.

Figure 17.3 Type-the name in the Save As dialog box.

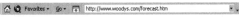

Figure 17.4 Type a URL in the Address box on the Web toolbar.

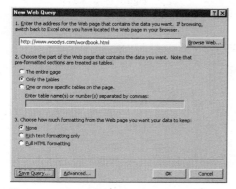

Figure 17.5
Choose New
Web Query from
the Get External
Data submenu.

Figure 17.6 Enter the address in the New Web Query dialog box.

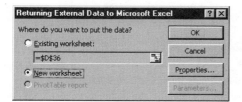

Figure 17.7 Select a destination for the external data.

Figure 17.8 The list of queries in the Run Query dialog box.

Running a Web Query

You can use a Web query to retrieve data from a Web page instead of the entire contents of the page. You can then analyze the data in Excel.

To run a Web query:

1. From the Data menu, choose Get External Data, and then choose New Web Query from the submenu (**Figure 17.5**).

2. In the New Web Query dialog box, type the Web address (URL) or click Browse and browse the Web for the file. When you reach the page on the Web, click in the Address box in the New Web Query dialog box (**Figure 17.6**).

3. In the Returning External Data to Microsoft Excel dialog box, specify a destination for the query results (**Figure 17.7**).

4. Click OK.

✔ Tip

■ You can save the query and later choose Run Saved Query from the Get External Data submenu to open the Run Query dialog box (**Figure 17.8**).

Saving a Workbook as a Web Page

If you plan to make your workbook available for viewing in a browser, you can save it as a Web page.

To save a workbook as a Web page:

1. From the File menu, choose Save As Web Page (**Figure 17.9**).

2. In the Save As dialog box, choose the file name and location (**Figure 17.10**).

3. Click the Change Title button and, in the Set Page Title dialog box, enter the title to be displayed in the Web browser's title bar (**Figure 17.11**).

4. Click OK.

5. In the Save As dialog box, click Save.

✔ Tips

- All extra files that make up the Web page created are stored in a folder. If you move the Web page you create, be sure to move the folder with it (**Figure 17.12**).

- If your system administrator or Internet service provider (ISP) has set up a Web server that supports Web publishing, you can save the Web page to a Web folder by selecting the Web folder in the Save As dialog box.

Figure 17.9 Choose Save As Web Page from the File menu.

Figure 17.10 Type the name in the Save As dialog box.

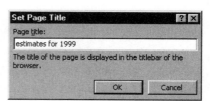

Figure 17.11 Type the title in the Set Page Title dialog box.

Folder   File

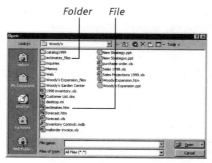

Figure 17.12 The file and its folder in the Open dialog box.

Part 4
Microsoft
PowerPoint

Part 4
Microsoft
PowerPoint

INTRODUCING POWERPOINT 2000

18

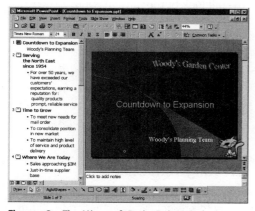

Figure 18.1 The Microsoft PowerPoint window.

PowerPoint 2000 is the presentation graphics part of the Microsoft Office suite. Using PowerPoint, you can create charts and graphs, slides, handouts, overheads, and any other presentation materials you can imagine using. PowerPoint even creates slide shows, which are electronic presentations that you can run on your computer screen or on a projection device in front of an audience. You can also publish slide shows on the Web.

PowerPoint comes with dozens of professionally designed templates that take care of the look of a presentation so that you can focus on the message. It even comes with a selection of sample presentation outlines from which you can choose to get a start on the presentation content.

Bulleted text slides, graphs, tables, organization charts, clip art, and drawing tools are all elements in PowerPoint's powerful arsenal.

The Steps to a PowerPoint Presentation

Getting started building a presentation

PowerPoint offers not one, but several different ways to start a presentation, including various design and content templates and an AutoContent Wizard that let you choose a presentation outline first.

Creating the slides

You can develop the slides in Outline view, where you can see the text for the entire presentation, or you can work in Normal view, where you can see each slide along with the full outline in side-by-side window panes. You can also generate slides one at a time, typing text into special text placeholders on the slides as you go. Creating slides using PowerPoint is no more difficult than filling in the blanks. If you've outlined your presentation in Word, you can even transfer the outline to a new PowerPoint presentation automatically.

Creating charts and tables

If the information you need to convey is numeric, you might want to consider using a chart slide. PowerPoint lets you create organization charts and tables to depict other types of information visually.

Customizing the presentation

In Slide Sorter view, you get a bird's-eye view of the entire presentation. You can rearrange slides, change the overall design, and delete extraneous slides. In Slide view or Normal view, you can add a logo or change the color or design of the background, change the font and color schemes, or change the template, which governs the overall look of the presentation.

Adding special graphics

PowerPoint's sophisticated drawing tools and commands make it easy to embellish slides with special graphics. You can even import a scanned photograph or a graphic from another application.

Creating a slide show

PowerPoint's big payoff comes when you're ready to present. You can generate 35mm slides and handouts just as you'd expect, but you can also create an on-screen, electronic presentation known as a slide show, complete with TV-like special effects and transitions, and with sound. You can then send the slide show, along with the special PowerPoint Viewer that can display it, to a computer user not fortunate enough to have PowerPoint. You can also publish your slide show on the Web or on a corporate intranet.

Figure 18.2 You can start PowerPoint from the Start menu.

Figure 18.3 Click an option in the PowerPoint dialog box.

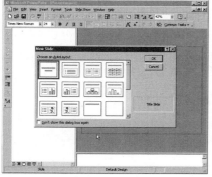

Figure 18.4 Choose a layout for the first slide in the default presentation design.

Starting PowerPoint

You start PowerPoint in the same way that you start every application in the Microsoft Office suite.

To start PowerPoint:

1. From the Start menu, choose Programs, and then choose Microsoft PowerPoint (**Figure 18.2**).

2. Select an action from the PowerPoint Startup dialog box (**Figure 18.3**).

✔ Tips

■ If PowerPoint is already started, click its icon on the taskbar to restore the window.

■ You can also start PowerPoint by double-clicking any PowerPoint document listed in the Open Office Document dialog box.

■ If you choose not to display the Power-Point Startup dialog box, PowerPoint begins with the first slide choice of a default presentation (**Figure 18.4**). To turn the Startup dialog box on again, choose Options from the Tools menu, and check Startup Dialog on the View tab of the Options dialog box.

STARTING POWERPOINT

The PowerPoint Window

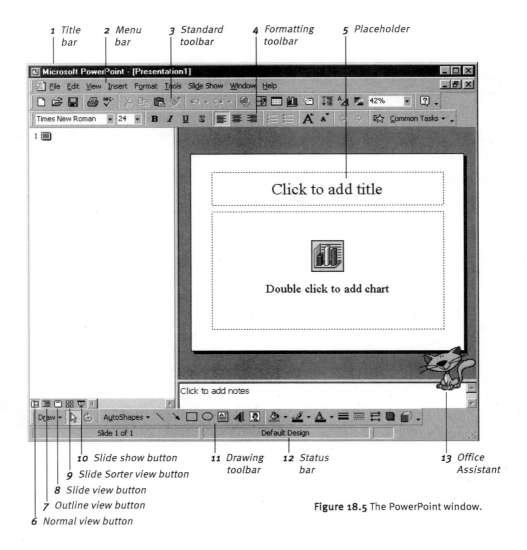

1 *Title bar* 2 *Menu bar* 3 *Standard toolbar* 4 *Formatting toolbar* 5 *Placeholder*

10 *Slide show button*
9 *Slide Sorter view button*
8 *Slide view button*
7 *Outline view button*
6 *Normal view button*

11 *Drawing toolbar* 12 *Status bar* 13 *Office Assistant*

Figure 18.5 The PowerPoint window.

Key to the PowerPoint Window

1 Title bar

Displays the presentation name. Drag the title bar to move the window.

2 Menu bar

Click any name on the menu bar to pull down a menu.

3 Standard toolbar

Toolbar with buttons for file management, editing, and proofing commands.

4 Formatting toolbar

Toolbar with buttons for formatting text.

5 Placeholder

Click or double-click a placeholder to add an element to a slide.

6 Normal view button

Click this button to switch to Normal view, which combines the Outline, Slide, and Notes views.

7 Outline view button

Click this button to switch to Outline view, which shows the text of the presentation in outline form.

8 Slide view button

Click this button to switch to Slide view, which shows a single slide.

9 Slide Sorter view button

Click this button to switch to Slide Sorter view, which shows thumbnail views of your slides arranged in a grid.

10 Slide Show button

Click this button to view the slides of the presentation in sequence, as a slide show.

11 Drawing toolbar

Toolbar with buttons for adding graphic objects to slides.

12 Status bar

Shows the current slide number.

13 Office Assistant

Click the Office Assistant for online help.

THE POWERPOINT WINDOW

BUILDING A
PRESENTATION

When you first start PowerPoint, the PowerPoint dialog box gives you several options for starting a new presentation. The first option, AutoContent Wizard, offers a menu of presentations that already contain sample content. These presentations are also preformatted using appropriate designs. If you choose Design Template in the PowerPoint dialog box, you can choose a design for the presentation and then enter your own content. The last option, Blank Presentation, gives you the least help. You start with a single blank slide and build the presentation from scratch.

Starting a New Presentation

When you start a new presentation, PowerPoint offers several options in the New Presentation dialog box. To concentrate on content first, choose one of the suggested presentation outlines offered by the AutoContent Wizard. If you don't need the interactive assistance of the AutoContent Wizard, try one of the predefined templates on either of the other two tabs.

To start a new presentation:

1. Click the New button on the Standard toolbar to view a choice of slide layouts (**Figure 19.1**).

or

From the File menu, choose New (**Figure 19.2**).

2. On the General tab of the New Presentation dialog box, double-click Blank Presentation or AutoContent Wizard (**Figure 19.3**).

or

On the Design Templates tab of the New Presentation dialog box, select a presentation design on the Design Templates tab (**Figure 19.4**).

or

On the Presentations tab of the New Presentation dialog box, select a type of presentation (**Figure 19.5**).

3. Click OK.

✔ Tip

■ To start with a blank presentation and add formatting later, select Blank Presentation.

Figure 19.1 Click the New button.

Figure 19.2 Choose New from the File menu.

Figure 19.3 Choose an option in the New Presentation dialog box.

Figure 19.4 The Design Templates tab.

Figure 19.5 The Presentations tab.

Figure 19.6 Choose a presentation type.

Figure 19.7 Choose an output type.

Figure 19.8 Fill in title and footer information.

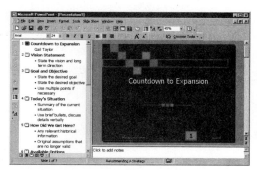

Figure 19.9 A sample presentation with content supplied by the AutoContent Wizard.

Using the AutoContent Wizard

The AutoContent Wizard offers a choice of sample presentation outlines and then drops you off in Normal view, where you can replace the sample text provided by the wizard with your own content.

To start a presentation using the AutoContent Wizard:

1. From the File menu, choose New.

2. Select AutoContent Wizard from the General tab.

3. In the AutoContent Wizard dialog box, click Next.

4. On the presentation type page, click a type button, scroll down to select a type of presentation, and click Next (**Figure 19.6**).

5. On the output page, click the type of output you will create, and click Next (**Figure 19.7**).

6. On the title and footer page, enter information for your title slide and click Next (**Figure 19.8**).

7. Click the Finish button.

    The presentation you've chosen appears (**Figure 19.9**).

✔ Tips

- To return to a previous step, click Back.

- To skip steps and accept default settings, click Finish.

- Each sample presentation outline generates a presentation with a preset look. You can change the look by choosing a different design template later.

AUTOCONTENT WIZARD

Using a Design Template

Templates can provide either the graphic design and color scheme of a presentation (design template) or suggest content and structure, using a set of slides whose text you edit (sample presentation).

To start with a design template:

1. From the File menu, choose New.

2. Select a template from the Design Templates tab of the New Presentation dialog box (**Figure 19.10**).

3. Click OK.

4. In the New Slide dialog box, click the appropriate layout icon for your first slide (**Figure 19.11**).

5. Click OK.

   A new presentation opens in Normal view in the selected design: it contains one slide (**Figure 19.12**).

✔ Tips

- The design templates make no suggestions regarding content or organization; you can add as many slides as you want, containing any combination of elements (text, tables, charts, pictures, and so on).

- You can change the look of a presentation at any time by choosing a different design template.

Figure 19.10 Choose a design from the Design Templates tab.

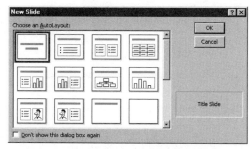

Figure 19.11 Choose a layout for the first slide in the New Slide dialog box.

Figure 19.12 The presentation begins with the selected design.

Figure 19.13 Choose a sample presentation.

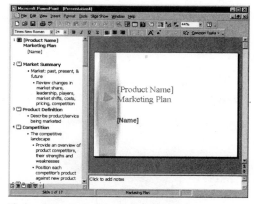

Figure 19.14 First slide and outline of the new presentation in Normal view.

Using a Sample Presentation

If you want suggestions about the content of your presentation and how it might be organized, PowerPoint offers a set of content templates, which provide sample slides with sample text and charts.

To start with a sample presentation:

1. From the File menu, choose New.

2. Select a presentation from the Presentations tab of the New Presentation dialog box (**Figure 19.13**).

3. Click OK.

   A new presentation opens in Normal view (**Figure 19.14**). Each slide contains suggestions for text.

✔ Tips

■ Use the suggested content for inspiration. It's easiest to change the content and rearrange the slides in Outline view.

■ You can change the look of the presentation without changing the content at any time by choosing a different template.

SAMPLE PRESENTATION

Changing Views

Each new presentation opens in Normal view, which combines the outline of the presentation with a view of the current slide, as well as quick access to notes.

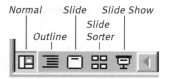

Figure 19.15 The View buttons.

To change to another view:

◆ Click the appropriate button at the lower left corner of the presentation window (**Figure 19.15**).

Outline view displays only the text of the presentation in outline form, allowing you to work easily with the content (**Figure 19.16**).

Normal view displays three panes that show the outline, the slide, and an area into which you can enter speaker's notes (**Figure 19.17**).

Slide Sorter view displays thumbnail views of your slides so that you can reorganize the slides and change the overall look of the presentation. In this view, you can also add and edit the transition effects for the slide show (**Figure 19.18**).

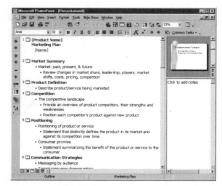

Figure 19.16 Outline view.

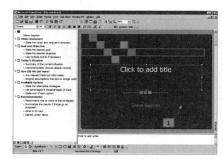

Figure 19.17 Normal view.

Figure 19.18 Slide Sorter view.

Figure 19.19 Slide Show view.

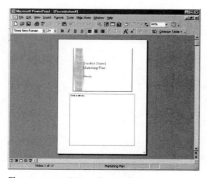

Figure 19.20 Choose Notes Page from the View menu.

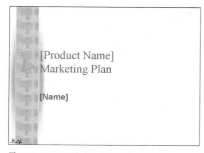

Figure 19.21 Notes Page view.

Figure 19.22 The Slide Show shortcut menu.

Slide Show view displays the presentation one slide at a time in sequence as an automatic slide show (electronic presentation) (**Figure 19.19**).

Notes Page view, which is available only from the View menu, lets you enter and edit speaker's notes for the presenter.

To change to Notes Page view:

◆ From the View menu, choose Notes Page (**Figures 19.20** and **19.21**).

✔ Tips

■ Each view shows a different aspect of the same presentation.

■ You can switch from one view to another at any time.

■ Right-click in Slide Show view or click the button at the lower-left corner of the current slide to display the Slide Show shortcut menu (**Figure 19.22**).

CHANGING VIEWS

Adding Slides

You can add a slide at any point during the design phase of a creating a presentation.

To add a slide:

1. Click Common Tasks on the toolbar.

2. Choose New Slide from the Common Tasks pull-down menu (**Figure 19.23**).

   or

   Press Ctrl+M.

3. In the New Slide dialog box, double-click a slide layout (**Figure 19.24**).

✔ Tips

- You can also choose New Slide from the Insert menu (**Figure 19.25**).

- If the New Slide Dialog option is turned off (at the bottom of the New Slide dialog box), a blank slide will appear each time you click the New Slide button. To turn the New Slide Dialog option on again, choose Options from the Tools menu, and check New Slide Dialog on the View tab.

- If you choose the wrong slide layout, choose Slide Layout from the Common Tasks pull-down menu and then choose the correct layout in the Slide Layout dialog box.

Figure 19.23 Choose New Slide from the Common Tasks pull-down menu.

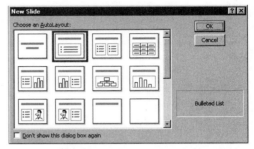

Figure 19.24 Choose a layout for the new slide in the New Slide dialog box.

Figure 19.25 Choose New Slide from the Insert menu.

ADDING SLIDES

OUTLINING THE PRESENTATION

Figure 20.1 Outline view.

Outline view shows only the text in outline form so that you can focus on the content of the presentation rather than the appearance (**Figure 20.1**). In Outline view, you can rearrange the flow, add or delete topics, and refine the wording of slides. You can also start working in Outline view and enter the text of a presentation before switching to Slide view to add charts and graphs, tables, drawings, and other elements to individual slides.

Switching to Outline View

Even if you've already created a full presentation in Slide view, you can still switch to Outline view temporarily to focus on the text.

To switch to outline view:

◆ Click the Outline View button at the lower-left corner of the PowerPoint window (**Figure 20.2**).

✔ Tip

■ The AutoContent Wizard starts you in Normal view automatically, where you can adjust the panes to enlarge the outline portion of your presentation (**Figure 20.3**).

Outline View button

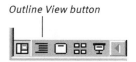

Figure 20.2 Click the Outline View button.

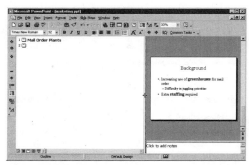

Figure 20.3 The outline portion enlarged in the Normal view.

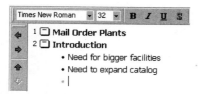

Slide icon

Figure 20.4 Type the slide title and press Enter.

Figure 20.5 Press Tab and type bulleted items.

Figure 20.6 Press Shift+Tab to type the next slide's title.

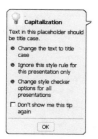

Figure 20.7 Click a light bulb to see a tip.

Figure 20.8 Click OK to close the tip.

Entering the Text

You can enter text most conveniently in Outline view.

To enter text:

1. Type the title for a slide next to the slide icon and press Enter (**Figure 20.4**).

2. Type the title of the next slide and press Enter.

or

Press Tab, type the first bulleted text line for the current slide, and press Enter.

3. Type other bulleted text items, pressing Enter after each (**Figure 20.5**).

or

Press Shift+Tab to start a new slide (**Figure 20.6**).

4. Continue as above to create new slides or add bulleted text points to the current slide.

✔ Tips

■ If you are using the Office Assistant and you see a light bulb on the view of the slide, click it to display a tip about your latest action (**Figures 20.7** and **20.8**).

■ To create a slide for a graph, an organization chart, a table, or a drawing, simply type a slide title without entering bulleted text items underneath.

Replacing Existing Text

If you start with a presentation with the AutoContent Wizard or with a sample presentation, you will need to replace the sample text with your own.

To replace text:

1. Click a bullet to select a bulleted text line (**Figure 20.9**).

   or

   Triple-click anywhere on a bulleted text line.

2. Type replacement text (**Figure 20.10**).

✔ Tip

■ Click a slide icon to select all the text on a slide. Then type replacement text, slide title and all (**Figure 20.11**).

Click here

Figure 20.9 Click a bullet.

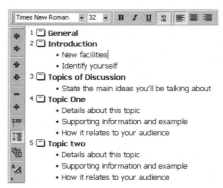

Figure 20.10 Type a replacement.

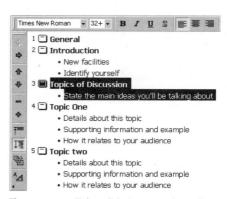

Figure 20.11 Click a slide icon to select all the text on a slide.

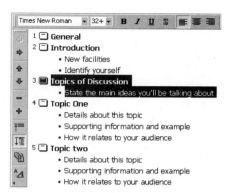

Figure 20.12 Click a slide icon.

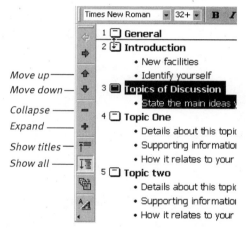

Figure 20.13 A horizontal line indicates the new position for the slide.

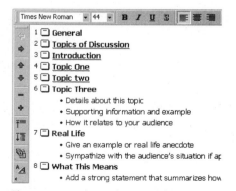

Figure 20.14 Release the mouse button to drop the slide text.

Reorganizing the Slides

You can reorganize the slides in Outline view by dragging and by using buttons on the Outlining toolbar.

To move a slide:

1. Click a slide icon (**Figure 20.12**).

2. Drag the icon up or down in the outline (**Figure 20.13**).

    or

    Click the Move Up or Move Down button on the Outlining toolbar.

3. Release the mouse button to drop the slide at its new position (**Figure 20.14**).

✔ Tip

■ You can click the bullet at the beginning of a text item and then click the Move Up or Move Down button to move a single line on an individual slide.

Showing the Slide Titles Only

You can temporarily show only the slide titles to work with the presentation's overall structure and disregard the detail in an outline.

To show the slide titles only:

1. Select the slides whose details you want to hide.

2. Click the Show Titles button on the Outlining toolbar (**Figure 20.15**).

✔ Tips

■ To redisplay the text on one or more of the slides, select the slides to be expanded and click the Show All button on the Outlining toolbar.

■ To hide or display text on a single slide, click the slide icon and then click the Collapse Selection button on the Outlining toolbar (**Figure 20.16**). To redisplay hidden text, click the Expand Selection button.

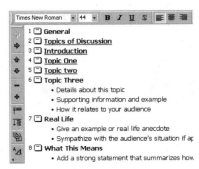

Figure 20.15 Lines under the slide titles indicate that text is collapsed underneath.

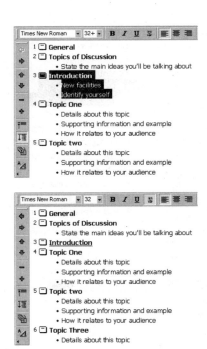

Figure 20.16 Before and after: collapsing the text of the slide.

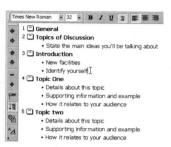

Figure 20.17 Click at the end of a slide.

Figure 20.18
Choose New Slide.

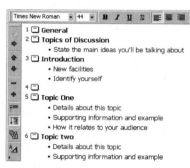

Figure 20.19 The blank slide appears.

Figure 20.20 Click a slide icon and press Delete.

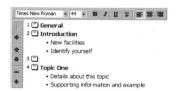

Figure 20.21 The slide is deleted.

Inserting and Deleting Slides

As you create the outline of a presentation, you can insert and delete slides as needed.

To insert a slide:

1. Click at the end of the last line of a slide (**Figure 20.17**).

2. Choose New Slide from the Common Tasks pull-down menu (**Figure 20.18**).

3. In the Slide Layout dialog box, double-click the layout of the new slide.

   The new slide appears (**Figure 20.19**).

To delete a slide:

1. Click a slide icon to select an entire slide.

2. Press the Del key to delete the slide (**Figures 20.20** and **20.21**).

CREATING
TEXT SLIDES

Unlike Outline view, which shows a list of slides in text-only form, Slide view shows a single slide as it will appear when printed or presented. In Slide view, you can work directly on the slide and add text, charts, graphics, clip art, and other objects.

You may also choose to work in Normal view, which displays both the outline and the slide in side-by-side panes. All the information in this chapter also applies to working in the slide pane in Normal view.

Creating a Text Slide

Instead of using Outline view to enter the text of slides, you can create text slides in Slide view or enlarge the slide pane of Normal view to work in the Slide pane.

To create a text slide:

1. From the Common Tasks pull-down menu, choose New Slide (**Figure 21.1**).

   or

   From the Insert menu, choose New Slide. (**Figure 21.2**)

   or

   Press Ctrl+M.

2. In the New Slide dialog box, double-click the second layout option, Bulleted List (**Figures 21.3** and **21.4**).

Figure 21.1 Choose New Slide from the Common Tasks pull-down menu.

Figure 21.2 Choose New Slide from the Insert menu.

Bulleted List layout

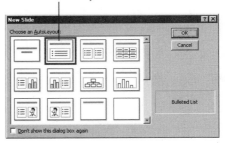

Figure 21.3 Choose an AutoLayout in the New Slide dialog box.

Figure 21.4 The Bulleted List layout.

CREATING A TEXT SLIDE

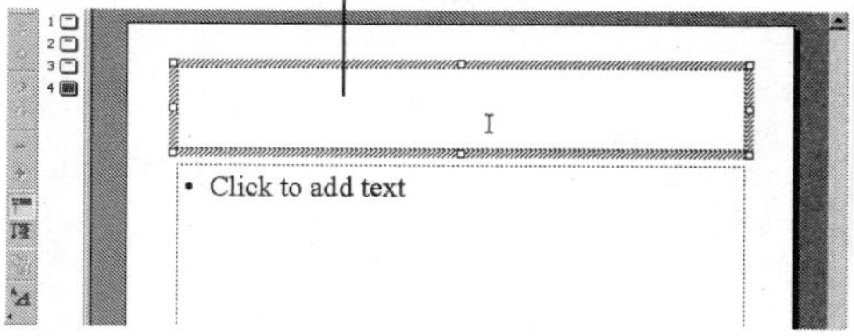

Click a placeholder

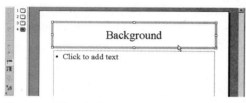

Figure 21.5 Click in the top text box.

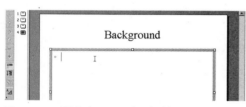

Figure 21.6 Type text.

Background

Figure 21.7 Click the next placeholder.

Filling in Text Placeholders

PowerPoint reminds you to fill in place-holders by prompting for replacement text.

To fill in text placeholders:

1. Click a "Click to add title" or "Click to add text" placeholder (**Figure 21.5**).

2. Type your replacement text (**Figure 21.6**).

3. Click the next placeholder and type your replacement text (**Figure 21.7**).

✔ Tips

■ When you finish typing text into a placeholder, press Ctrl+Enter to jump to the next placeholder.

■ When you finish entering the text in the last placeholder on the page, you can press Ctrl+Enter to add a new bulleted list slide.

FILLING TEXT PLACEHOLDERS

Selecting Text Blocks

Selecting characters, words, or paragraphs within a text block is just like selecting them in a Word document.

If you want to move or format an entire text block, however, PowerPoint makes it easy to select the entire text block.

To select a text block:

◆ Click anywhere on a text block. Handles appear (**Figure 21.8**).

✔ Tips

■ Click within a selected text block to select text within the block.

■ To select a bulleted item in a text block, click the bullet.

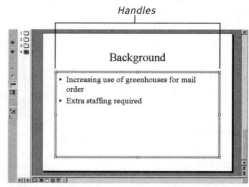

Figure 21.8 When you click the text block, handles appear.

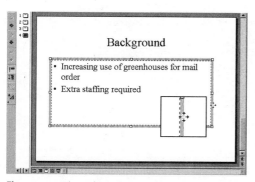

Figure 21.9 Place the pointer on the border.

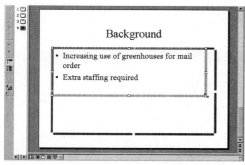

Figure 21.10 Place the pointer on a handle.

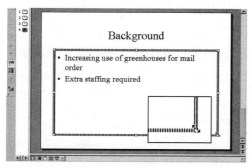

Figure 21.11 Drag the handle to resize a text block.

Moving and Resizing Text Blocks

You can use the borders of a text block to move or resize it.

To move a text block:

1. Position the pointer on the border surrounding a selected text block (**Figure 21.9**).

2. Hold down the mouse button and drag the mouse.

3. Release the mouse button when the block is in the new position.

To resize a text block:

1. Position the pointer on a handle (**Figure 21.10**).

2. Hold down the mouse button and drag the mouse (**Figure 21.11**).

3. Release the mouse button when the block is resized.

✔ Tips

- The text inside a text block rewraps to fit within the new size of the block.

- Hold down the Ctrl key as you resize a text block to resize the block around its center point .

MOVING/RESIZING BLOCKS

Formatting Text

You can format selected words or all the text in a text block.

To format text:

1. Select the text within a text block that you want to format (**Figure 21.12**).

   or

   Select the text block you want to format.

2. Click a text formatting button on the Formatting toolbar (**Figure 21.13**).

   or

   From the Format menu, choose the type of formatting.

   or

   Right-click selected text and make a selection from the shortcut menu.

3. If you chose a selection on the Format menu, make selections in the formatting dialog box that has appeared (**Figures 21.14** and **21.15**).

4. Click OK.

✔ Tips

- Any text formatting changes you make are preserved when you choose a different template to change the overall design of the presentation.

- To change the font uniformly across all slides, drag to select the text in Outline view (or in the Outline pane in Normal view), and then switch to Slide view to see the result.

- In Normal view, you can use the Format Painter to copy formatting to text on other slides.

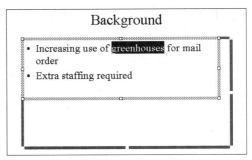

Figure 21.12 Select text to format.

Figure 21.13 Click a button on the Formatting toolbar.

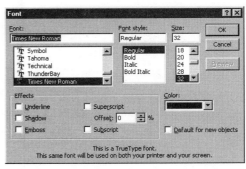

Figure 21.14 Select formatting in the Font dialog box.

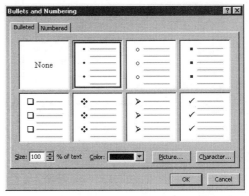

Figure 21.15 Select formatting in the Bullets and Numbering dialog box.

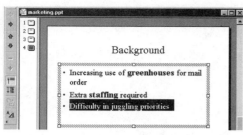

Figure 21.16 Click a bulleted item.

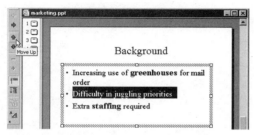

Figure 21.17 The text moved to its new location.

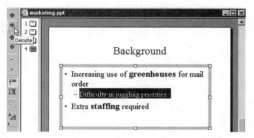

Figure 21.18 Text moved to the right one level appears indented.

Rearranging Text in a Block

You can move the items within a text block and demote or promote them in the hierarchy.

To rearrange text in a block:

1. Click a bulleted text item (**Figure 21.16**).

2. Use the Outlining toolbar to move the text item up, down, left, or right (**Figure 21.17**).

✔ Tips

- When you move a text item to the right one level, it appears indented under the previous text item (**Figure 21.18**).

- When you move a text item to the left or right, you move the text item to a different level. Each level can have a different default text format and bullet style.

- You can also simply drag an item up or down to change its position.

REARRANGING TEXT

CREATING CHART SLIDES

A carefully crafted chart can make even complex numeric information visually accessible and therefore easy to interpret and communicate.

When you create or edit a chart, PowerPoint uses Microsoft Graph, the same charting module used by Excel. Graph creates a chart, and while doing so it commandeers the PowerPoint window, replacing PowerPoint's menus and toolbars with its own. When you click outside the border of the completed chart, the PowerPoint menus and toolbars reappear.

Starting a Chart

You can begin a new slide, or you can insert a chart in an existing slide.

To start a chart:

1. Choose New Slide from the Common Tasks pull-down menu.

2. In the New Slide dialog box, select one of the three layouts that includes a chart placeholder: Chart, Text & Chart, Chart & Text (**Figure 22.1**).

3. Click OK.

4. Double-click the "Double click to add chart" placeholder (**Figure 22.2**).

   or

1. Display the slide to which you'd like to add a chart.

2. Click the Insert Chart button on the Standard toolbar (**Figure 22.3**).

   or

   From the Insert menu, choose Chart.

   The default sample chart and its datasheet appear on the slide (**Figure 22.4**).

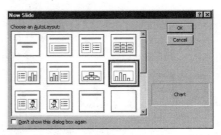

Figure 22.1 Choose a chart AutoLayout from the New Slide dialog box.

Figure 22.2 Double-click the chart placeholder.

Insert Chart button

Figure 22.3 To add a chart to an existing slide, click the Insert Chart button.

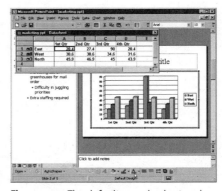

Figure 22.4 The default sample chart and datasheet appear.

STARTING A CHART

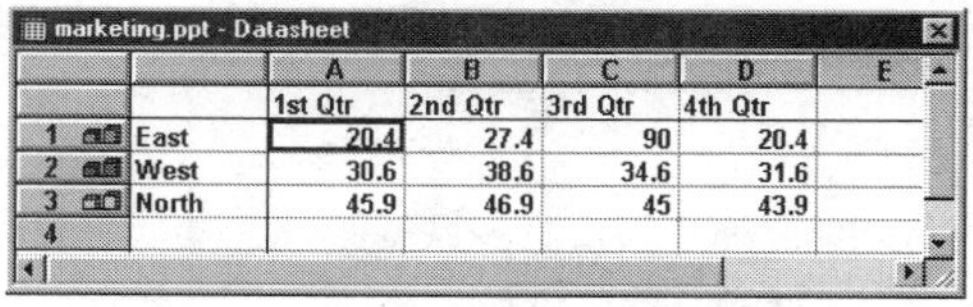

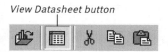

Figure 22.5 Click any cell in the datasheet.

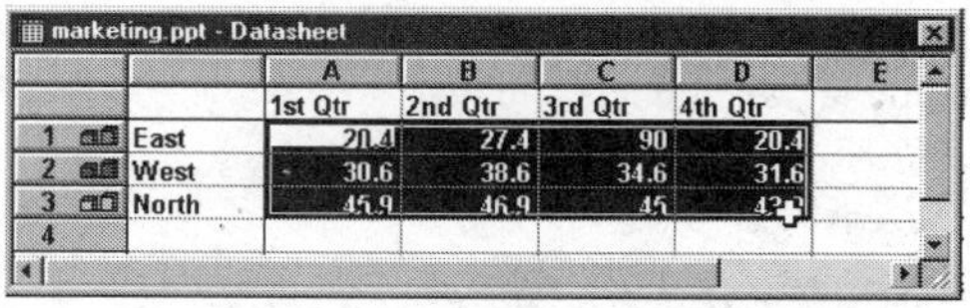

Figure 22.6 Select the cells that contain data you want to replace.

View Datasheet button

Figure 22.7 Click the View Datasheet button to show or hide the datasheet.

Row heading button   *Column heading button*

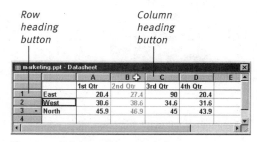

Figure 22.8 Column B is excluded.

Replacing the Sample Data on a Datasheet

Each chart begins with the same sample data placeholders. You can extend the rows and columns to suit your needs.

To replace the sample data:

1. Click any cell in the Excel-like grid and type over its contents (**Figure 22.5**).

   or

   Select all the cells that contain data (a range) and begin typing new data in columns (**Figure 22.6**).

2. Press Enter after typing each new heading or number. If you select a range, when the cell pointer reaches the bottom of a column, it jumps to the top of the next column automatically.

✔ Tips

- Click the View Datasheet button in the Graph Standard toolbar to hide the datasheet (**Figure 22.7**).

- To exclude a row or column of data from the graph, double-click the row or column heading button (**Figure 22.8**).

REPLACING SAMPLE DATA

Changing the Chart Type

The most basic commands to format a new chart are available as buttons on the Graph Standard toolbar.

To change the chart type:

1. Double-click the chart to make it active, if necessary (**Figure 22.9**).

   Handles appear.

2. Click the Chart Type arrow button on the Graph toolbar (**Figure 22.10**).

3. Click a chart type on the drop-down menu.

   The chart type is changed (**Figure 22.11**).

✔ Tips

■ Choosing Chart Type from the Chart menu gives you many more chart type options (**Figure 22.12**).

■ You can create a Chart Type toolbar by positioning the pointer on the Chart Type arrow button, holding down the mouse button, and then dragging to another point on the screen.

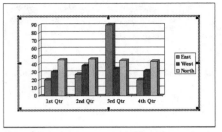

Figure 22.9 Double-click the chart you want to format, and handles appear.

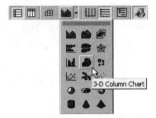

Figure 22.10 Select a chart type from the Chart Type drop-down list.

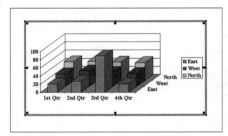

Figure 22.11 The modified chart.

Figure 22.12 Choose Chart Type from the Chart menu to view more options.

Figure 22.13 Choose Chart Type to save a custom type.

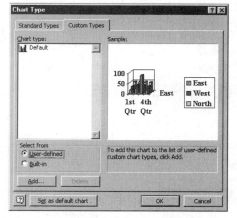

Figure 22.14 Open the Custom Types tab in the Chart Type dialog box.

Figure 22.15 Add a name in the Add Custom Chart Type dialog box.

Saving a Custom Chart Format

If you customize a chart format and want to use it for other charts in the future, you can save it for selection later.

To save a custom chart format:

1. Format the chart the way you want it.

2. From the Chart menu, choose Chart Type (**Figure 22.13**).

3. In the Chart Type dialog box, click the Custom Types tab (**Figure 22.14**).

4. Click the User-defined radio button, and click Add.

5. In the Add Custom Chart Type dialog box, type a name for your custom chart, and add a description, if you want (**Figure 22.15**).

6. Click OK in both dialog boxes.

✔ Tips

- Your custom-defined chart type will be available in the Custom Types list for future charts.

- To delete custom chart types from the list, select one of the charts on the Custom Types tab of the Chart Type dialog box, and then click Delete.

- To make one of your custom chart types the default type, select one of the charts on the Custom Types tab of the Chart Type dialog box, and then click Set as Default Chart.

CUSTOM CHART FORMAT

Displaying a Legend and Gridlines

You can display or hide the legend and gridlines by clicking buttons on the Graph toolbar.

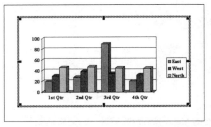

Figure 22.16 Click the chart to make it active.

To turn the legend on or off:

1. Click the chart to make it active, if necessary (**Figure 22.16**).

2. Click the Legend button on the Graph toolbar (**Figure 22.17**).

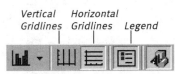

Figure 22.17 Click a button to turn the gridlines and legend on or off.

To turn gridlines on or off:

1. Click the chart to make it active, if necessary.

2. Click the Vertical Gridlines or Horizontal Gridlines button on the Graph toolbar (**Figure 22.17**).

Figure 22.18 Choose Chart Options for additional changes.

✔ Tips

- You can also alter or add a legend or gridlines by pulling down the Chart menu and choosing Chart Options (**Figure 22.18**).

- When you add gridlines from the Chart Options dialog box, you can choose Major Gridlines that mark major intervals along the axis or Minor Gridlines for each axis (**Figures 22.19** and **22.20**).

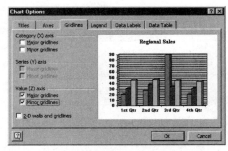

Figure 22.19 Change the gridline display through the Chart Options dialog box.

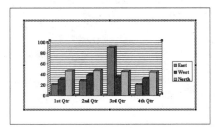

Figure 22.20 A chart that displays the minor value axis gridlines.

Figure 22.21 Choose Chart Options to begin adding a title.

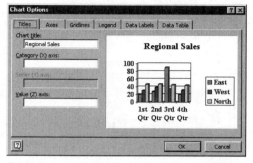

Figure 22.22 Add the title on the Titles tab of the Chart Options dialog box.

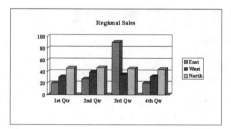

Figure 22.23 The title added to the chart.

Adding Chart Titles

Although in many instances the slide title is sufficient, you can add a chart title.

To add a chart title:

1. Click the chart to make it active, if necessary.

2. From the Chart menu, choose Chart Options (**Figure 22.21**).

3. In the Chart Options dialog box, click the Titles tab (**Figure 22.22**).

4. Enter the titles you want.

5. Click OK to add the title to the chart (**Figure 22.23**).

✔ Tips

■ To remove a title, choose the Titles tab in the Chart Options dialog box, and clear the title or click on the title to select it and press Del.

■ As you edit elements in the Chart Options dialog box, you can keep an eye on the changes in the Preview chart on the right to be sure you're editing the intended field.

ADDING CHART TITLES

Adding Data Labels

Depending on how the data is arranged, each column (if ordered by row) or row (if ordered by column) represents a data series. You can add data labels to every series or to a single series.

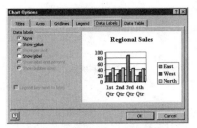

Figure 22.24 Use the Data Labels tab to add data labels for every series.

To turn on data labels for every series in the chart:

1. Click the chart to make it active, if necessary.

2. From the Chart menu, choose Chart Options.

3. In the Chart Options dialog box, click the Data Labels tab.

4. Click the check boxes to select the desired labels (**Figure 22.24**).

5. Click OK to see the data labels appear on your chart (**Figure 22.25**).

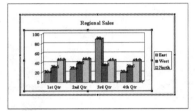

Figure 22.25 Every series has data labels.

To turn on data labels for a single series:

1. Double-click a data series.

2. In the Format Data Series dialog box, click the options you want to invoke (**Figure 22.26**).

3. Click OK.

   The reformatted chart reflects your selections (**Figure 22.27**).

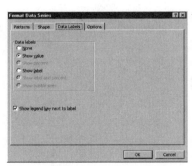

Figure 22.26 Pick a label for a single series.

✔ Tips

- To remove data labels, choose None on the Data Labels tab of the Chart Options dialog box.

- To format data labels, double-click one of the labels and then make changes in the Format Data Labels dialog box.

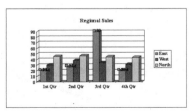

Figure 22.27 Only one series has data labels.

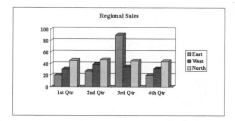

Figure 22.28 The data for the charts in Figures 22.29 and 22.30.

Arranging Data by Row vs. by Column

The sets of data that you need to chart are arranged either in rows or in columns on the data sheet (**Figures 22.28–22.30**). To inform Graph how your data is arranged, use the By Row button or the By Column button on the Standard toolbar.

To change the data arrangement:

1. Click the chart to make it active, if necessary.

2. Click the By Column button or the By Row button (**Figure 22.31**).

   or

   From the Data menu, choose Series in Rows or Series in Columns (**Figure 22.32**).

✔ Tip

- Choosing an alternative view of the data (By Row rather than By Column, or vice versa) is legitimate only when both the columns and the rows of the datasheet hold related series of data (such as sales numbers over time).

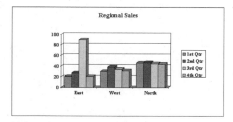

Figure 22.29 Data arranged by row.

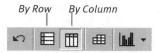

Figure 22.30 Data arranged by column.

By Row   By Column

Figure 22.31 The By Row and By Column buttons.

Figure 22.32 Choose Series in Rows or Series in Columns from the Data menu.

ARRANGING DATA

FORMATTING CHARTS

The charts you add to slides are given a default appearance by PowerPoint. Each chart type has its own default settings. The color and fonts used in the chart are determined by the design template applied to the presentation. For any particular chart, you can override any of the default settings by selecting elements in the chart and then changing their formatting.

Formatting Chart Elements

You can format the appearance of any individual element of the chart (one set of bars, one line, an axis, and so on). You can also change the style of any series in the chart by formatting a data series.

To format a chart element:

1. Click the chart to make it active, if necessary.

2. Double-click the chart element you want to format (**Figure 23.1**).

3. The appropriate dialog box for the element you've chosen appears. Choose formatting settings on the appropriate tab or tabs (**Figure 23.2**).

4. Click OK.

✔ Tips

■ You can also select a chart element and choose the first command on the Format menu, Selected Chart Element.

■ After you format one chart element, you can double-click a different chart element to format.

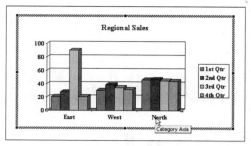

Figure 23.1 Double-click the chart element you want to format.

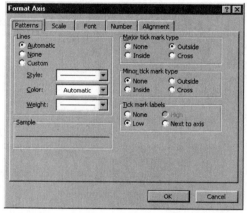

Figure 23.2 Use the tabs in the Format Axis dialog box to format the element that you selected.

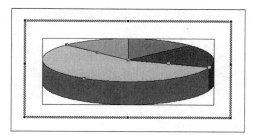

Figure 23.3 Click the pie to select it.

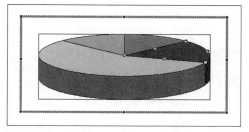

Figure 23.4 Click the slice to cut.

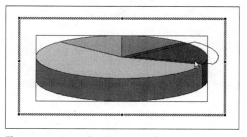

Figure 23.5 Drag the slice away from the pie.

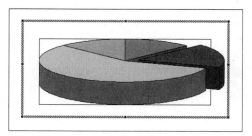

Figure 23.6 The cut slice.

Cutting a Pie Chart Slice

The pie chart type gives you an extra way to highlight data by cutting away a slice.

To cut a pie chart slice:

1. Click the chart to make it active, if necessary.

2. Click the pie once to select the entire pie (**Figure 23.3**).

3. Click the slice to cut (**Figure 23.4**).

4. Drag the slice away from the pie (**Figures 23.5** and **23.6**).

✔ Tip

■ To rejoin the slice with the pie, drag the slice back toward the center of the pie.

CUTTING A PIE CHART SLICE

Creating High-Low-Close Charts

High-low-close charts that display the high, low, and closing prices of stocks are called stock charts in PowerPoint.

To create a high-low-close chart:

1. Click the chart to make it active, if necessary.
2. On the datasheet, make sure the columns are ordered high-low-close (**Figure 23.7**).
3. From the Data menu, choose Series in Columns (**Figure 23.8**).
4. From the Chart menu, choose Chart Type.
5. On the left on the Standard Types tab of the Chart Type dialog box, choose Stock.
6. On the right, choose the type of stock chart you want (**Figure 23.9**).
7. Click OK.

   The stock chart appears (**Figure 23.10**).

✔ Tips

- The first column can be either dates or a list of securities.
- You can add a column for Opening Price before the High column (**Figure 23.11**). You can also add a column for Volume, but it must be the first data series to be properly charted.

marketing.ppt - Datasheet

		A	B	C	D	E	F
		High	Low	Close			
1	12-Apr	41.6	39.2	40.7			
2	19-Apr	40.3	37.9	39.6			
3	26-Apr	45.5	38.7	44.1			
4							

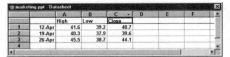

Figure 23.7 Edit the datasheet for a High-Low-Close chart.

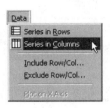

Figure 23.8 Choose Series in Columns from the Data menu.

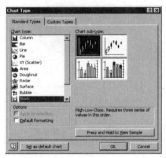

Figure 23.9 Select Stock as the type and choose a subtype.

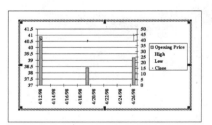

Figure 23.10 The high-low-close chart.

marketing.ppt - Datasheet

		A	B	C	D	E	F	G
		Opening P	High	Low	Close			
1	12-Apr	40.9	41.6	39.2	40.7			
2	19-Apr	38.4	40.3	37.9	39.6			
3	26-Apr	39.2	45.5	38.7	44.1			
4								
5								

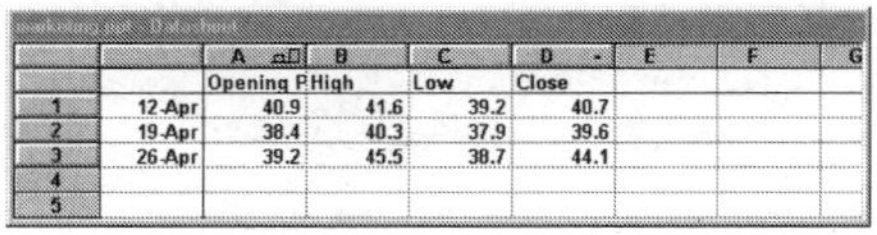

Figure 23.11 Opening Price column added.

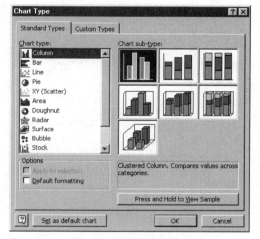

Figure 23.12 Choose Chart Type from the Chart menu.

Figure 23.13 Choose a different sub-type.

Switching Between 2-D and 3-D Chart Types

For most chart types, you can select either a 2-D or a 3-D style.

To change a chart style:

1. Click the chart to make it active, if necessary.

2. From the Chart menu, choose Chart Type (**Figure 23.12**).

3. On the left in the Chart Type dialog box, select a chart type.

4. On the right, select the sub-type you want (**Figure 23.13**).

    For chart types in which 2-D and 3-D styles exist, you will see both versions among the Chart sub-type thumbnails on the right.

5. Click OK to see your changes (**Figure 23.14**).

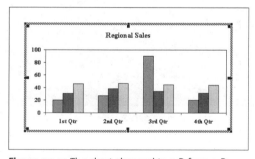

Figure 23.14 The chart changed to 2-D from 3-D.

2-D AND 3-D CHART TYPES

Changing the View of 3-D Charts

You can adjust many view settings for any 3-D chart.

Figure 23.15 Choose 3-D View from the Chart menu.

To change the view of a 3-D chart:

1. Click the 3-D chart to make it active, if necessary.

2. From the Chart menu, choose 3-D View (**Figure 23.15**).

3. In the 3-D View dialog box, click the large arrows to change elevation. Click the rotation axes to change the angle on the horizontal plane (**Figure 23.16**).

4. If you want to change the depth of the perspective, clear the Right Angle Axes check box and click the perspective arrows (**Figure 23.17**).

5. Click OK.

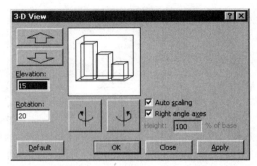

Figure 23.16 Click the arrows to change elevation or rotation.

✔ Tips

- To change the proportions of the chart, clear the Auto Scaling check box and change the Height of Base percentage.

- For more precision, you can change the values in any of the text boxes.

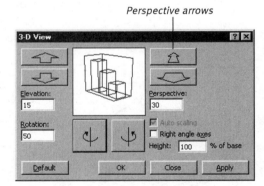

Figure 23.17 Adding perspective.

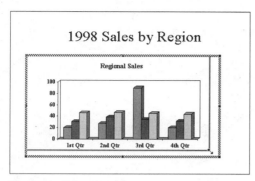

Figure 23.18 Drag to resize.

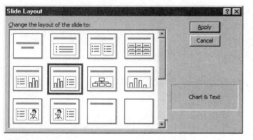

Figure 23.19 Choose Slide Layout from the Common Tasks pull-down menu.

Figure 23.20 Select a different chart layout.

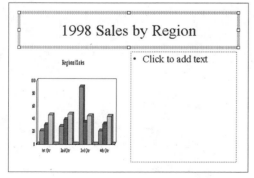

Figure 23.21 The chart repositioned.

Moving and Resizing Charts

Whenever the handles of a chart are visible, you can reposition the chart or resize it in the same way as for any other object (**Figure 23.18**).

You can also change the slide layout to another chart type.

To change the slide layout:

1. From the Common Tasks pull-down menu, choose Slide Layout (**Figure 23.19**).

2. Choose a different chart layout (**Figure 23.20**).

3. Click Apply (**Figure 23.21**).

MOVING/RESIZING CHARTS

CREATING ORG CHARTS AND TABLES

24

An org chart (also called an organization chart) depicts the hierarchical structure of an organization. A table displays text and numbers formatted neatly in side-by-side columns. Both org charts and tables are easy to add to existing slides, but if you create a new slide especially for an org chart or a table, you can choose an org chart or a table autolayout, which contains a placeholder you can click to start an org chart or table easily.

Starting an Organization Chart

PowerPoint includes a special program called Microsoft Organization Chart that helps you create organization charts.

To start an organization chart:

1. Choose New Slide from the Common Tasks pull-down menu to start a new slide (**Figure 24.1**).

2. In the New Slide dialog box, double-click the Org Chart layout (**Figure 24.2**).

3. On the new slide, double-click the "Double click to add org chart" placeholder (**Figure 24.3**).

✔ Tip

■ Org charts are created by a module called Microsoft Organization Chart, which appears in a separate window (**Figure 24.4**).

Figure 24.1 Choose New Slide from the Common Tasks pull-down menu.

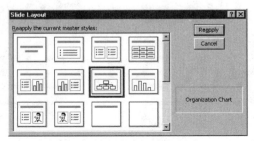

Figure 24.2 Select the Org Chart layout in the New Slide dialog box.

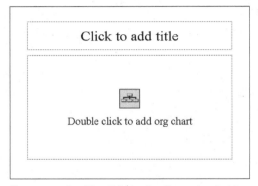

Figure 24.3 Double-click the Org Chart placeholder.

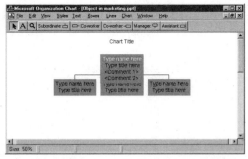

Figure 24.4 The default org chart in the Microsoft Organization Chart window.

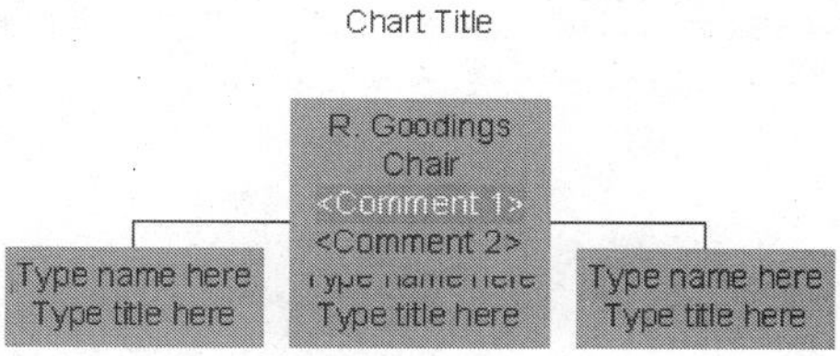

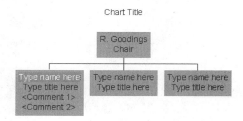

Figure 24.5 Type to replace placeholders and press Tab to move to next line.

Figure 24.6 Press Ctrl+Down arrow to move to the next box.

Entering Names and Titles

The default set of four boxes contains text placeholders.

To enter names and titles:

1. In the box at the top of the hierarchy, type the name of the head of the hierarchy.

2. Press Tab to highlight the next line within the same box, and type the organization member's title (**Figure 24.5**).

   or

   Click in a different box and type a name.

   or

   Press Ctrl+Down arrow to move to the box below and type a name (**Figure 24.6**).

3. If you want to enter additional information in the same box, press Tab to highlight each successive line and then type over the prompt text.

✔ Tips

■ The default size for all boxes at the same level changes to accommodate the number of lines of text and the longest line of text in any box at that level.

■ To edit the information in a box, click the box, pause briefly, and then click again to position an insertion point in the box. If you double-click without pausing between the clicks, the program thinks that you intend to select the box and others at the same level.

ENTERING NAMES/TITLES

Adding Members

The initial org chart structure contains only four organization members: a manager and three subordinates. To build a more complete structure, you will need to add other members.

To add a subordinate:

1. Click the Subordinate button (**Figure 24.7**).

2. Position the mouse pointer on a box that requires a subordinate (**Figure 24.8**).

3. Click to add a subordinate (**Figure 24.9**).

To add a coworker, a manager, or an assistant:

1. Click one of the Coworker buttons (left or right) or the Manager or Assistant button (**Figure 24.10**).

2. Position the mouse pointer on a box that requires a new member connected to it (**Figure 24.11**).

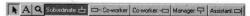
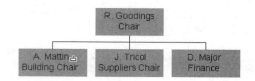

Figure 24.7 Click the Subordinate button.

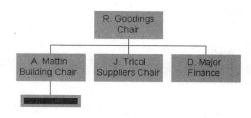

Figure 24.8 Position the mouse pointer on a box.

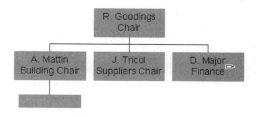

Figure 24.9 Click to add a subordinate.

Figure 24.10 Click a button to add a member.

Figure 24.11 Position the mouse pointer on a box and click to add the member.

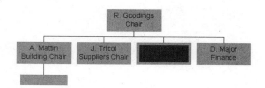

Figure 24.12 Coworker added to the left.

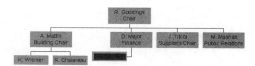

Figure 24.13 Assistant added.

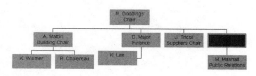

Figure 24.14 Manager added.

3. Click to add a new member
(**Figures 24.12–24.14**).

✔ Tips

■ To add several members in a category, click the button several times (once for each member to add) and then click an organization member.

■ To move a subordinate to another organization member, drag the subordinate on top of the other member's box and then release the mouse button.

■ To delete a box, click the box to highlight it and press Del or choose Cut from the Edit menu.

Formatting the Boxes, Text, and Lines

You can apply formatting to the boxes, the text within them, and the lines connecting them.

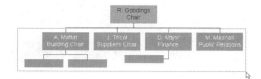

Figure 24.15 Drag to select boxes.

To format a box or boxes:

1. Click a box or drag a selection box that encloses multiple boxes to format (**Figure 24.15**).

2. Choose one of the Box options on the Boxes pull-down menu and choose a setting from the submenu that appears (**Figure 24.16**).

Figure 24.16 Choose an option from a submenu.

To format text:

1. Click a box or drag a selection box that encloses multiple boxes to format.

2. Choose an option on the Text pull-down menu and then choose a setting for the option (**Figure 24.17**).

3. Click OK to finish selecting font or color.

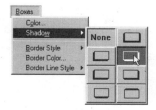

Figure 24.17 Choose from the Text menu to format the text in selected boxes.

To format the connecting lines:

1. Click a line or drag a selection box that encloses multiple lines to format.

2. Choose one of the line options on the Lines menu (**Figure 24.18**).

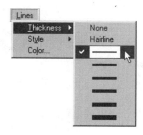

Figure 24.18 Choose from the Lines menu to format the connecting lines.

✔ Tips

- To select multiple objects (boxes or connecting lines), you can also hold down the Shift key while clicking each one.

- Double-click a box to select all boxes at the same level.

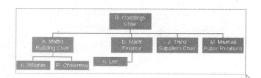

Figure 24.19 Drag to select boxes.

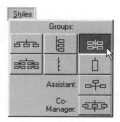

Figure 24.20 Choose from the Styles menu.

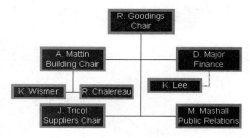

Figure 24.21 The new style applied.

Rearranging the Org Chart

You can rearrange all or part of your chart by selecting boxes and choosing a style for the selection.

To apply a new style:

1. Drag a selection box that encloses multiple boxes (**Figure 24.19**).

2. Pull down the Styles menu and click a style (**Figures 24.20** and **24.21**).

REARRANGING THE CHART

Finishing the Chart and Leaving Microsoft Organization Chart

To return to PowerPoint, you need to update the presentation and quit Microsoft Organization Chart.

To update the presentation and return to PowerPoint:

1. Complete the chart (**Figure 24.22**).

2. From the File menu, choose Update Presentation Name (**Figure 24.23**).

3. From the File menu, choose Quit and Return to *Presentation Name* (**Figure 24.24**).

4. Drag the chart or drag the chart's handles to move or resize the chart on the PowerPoint slide as necessary (**Figure 24.25**).

✔ Tip

■ Any time you want to edit an existing chart, double-click the chart.

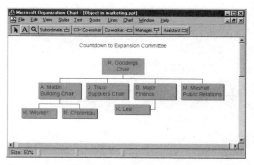
Figure 24.22 The finished org chart.

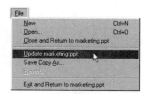
Figure 24.23 Choose Update the presentation.

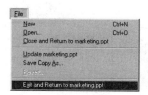
Figure 24.24 Choose Exit and return to the presentation.

Figure 24.25 Use the handles to resize or move the chart.

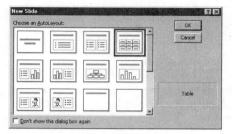

Figure 24.26 Click New Slide.

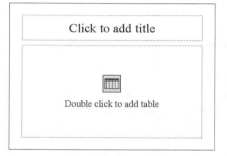

Figure 24.27 Choose the table layout from the New Slide dialog box.

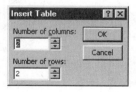

Click to add title

Double click to add table

Figure 24.28 The Table placeholder.

Figure 24.29 Select the number of columns and rows.

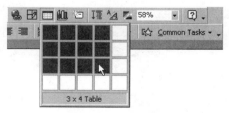

Figure 24.30 Click the table button and drag to select columns and rows.

Starting a Table

To add a table to your presentation, you can insert the table in an existing slide or begin a new slide using a table layout.

To begin a new slide using a table layout:

1. Click the New Slide button to start a new slide (**Figure 24.26**).

2. In the New Slide dialog box, double-click the Table autolayout (**Figure 24.27**).

3. Double-click the "Double click to add table" placeholder on the new slide (**Figure 24.28**).

4. In the Insert Table dialog box, set the number of columns and number of rows (**Figure 24.29**).

5. Click OK.

To insert a table in an existing slide:

1. View the slide to which you want to add a table.

2. Click the Insert Table button on the Standard toolbar and drag across the number of rows and columns you want in the new table (**Figure 24.30**).

   or

   Choose Table from the Insert menu.

Entering the Data and Formatting the Table

While you are creating or editing the table, Microsoft Word's Tables and Borders toolbar is available (**Figure 24.31**). Enter data and edit the table just as you would in Microsoft Word.

To format the table:

1. Choose Table from the Format menu (**Figure 24.32**).

2. Use the tabs available to format the Borders, Fill, and Text Box (**Figure 24.33**).

3. Click OK.

4. Click outside the frame to finish editing the table.

✔ Tip

■ You can also use any of the Tables and Borders toolbar buttons to format the table.

Figure 24.31 The Tables and Borders toolbar appears.

Figure 24.32 Choose Table from the Format menu.

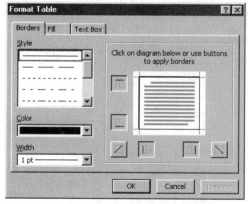

Figure 24.33 Click a tab to format Borders, Fill, or Text Box.

ENTERING DATA/FORMATTING

CUSTOMIZING A PRESENTATION

25

When you apply a design template to a presentation, the template makes a comprehensive set of formatting changes to the slides. You might want to modify the design of the presentation to achieve a custom look—for example, to develop a design that matches your corporate standard or the colors of a new product logo.

In this chapter, you'll learn to go beyond the basic designs provided by templates and create a unique look of your own.

Selecting a New Design

Changing a presentation's template can give a presentation an entirely new look, perhaps for a different audience.

A template contains a color scheme (a combination of colors used for text and other foreground presentation elements) and a slide master design (a background color, a selection of text fonts and formatting, and a background graphic design).

To select a new design:

1. Choose Apply Design Template from the Common Tasks pull-down menu (**Figure 25.1**).

   or

   From the Format menu, choose Apply Design Template.

   or

   Right-click outside the placeholder areas in Slide or Normal view and choose Apply Design Template from the shortcut menu.

2. In the Apply Design Template dialog box, click each design you want to consider, and note its appearance in the Preview frame on the left (**Figure 25.2**).

3. When you find the design you want to use, click Apply (**Figure 25.3**).

✔ Tips

■ The name of the current design template appears in the status bar at the bottom of the presentation window.

■ A change in design template overrides any color scheme or background changes you have made.

Figure 25.1 Choose Apply Design Template from the Common Tasks pull-down menu.

Figure 25.2 Preview the designs in the Apply Design Template dialog box.

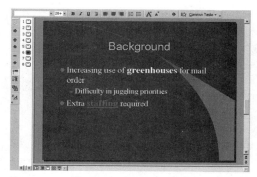

Figure 25.3 The new design is applied.

Figure 25.4 Choose Slide Color Scheme from the Format menu.

Figure 25.5 Select a color scheme on the Standard tab...

Figure 25.6 ...or create a custom color scheme on the Custom tab.

Figure 25.7 The new color scheme.

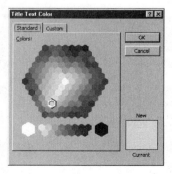

Figure 25.8 Changing the title color.

Changing the Color Scheme

The eight colors of the color scheme are the colors used by all the elements on slides unless you change the color of a specific element. The color scheme is stored in a template, so when you switch templates, you end up switching color schemes as well.

You can select predefined color schemes or create your own.

To change the color scheme:

1. From the Format menu, choose Slide Color Scheme (**Figure 25.4**).

   or

   Right-click outside the placeholder areas in Slide or Normal view and choose Slide Color Scheme from the shortcut menu.

2. In the Color Scheme dialog box, click the Standard or Custom tab (**Figures 25.5** and **25.6**).

3. Choose a standard color scheme on the Standard tab or create one of your own on the Custom tab.

4. Click Apply to All to change the color scheme for all slides, or click Apply to change it for a single slide (**Figure 25.7**).

✔ Tips

- To change a color in the color scheme, on the Custom tab in the Color Scheme dialog box, click one of the Scheme colors and click Change Color. Then choose a color in the color dialog box that appears (**Figure 25.8**).

- If you change the color scheme after you have applied a design template, the remaining design elements are retained.

CHANGING THE COLOR SCHEME

Switching to Slide and Title Master Views

The Slide Master view displays the elements common to all slides except the title slide, which has its own master. You can set the background and the text elements in this view as well as add graphical elements, and all slides types added through the Slide Layout dialog box will have the settings, except for the title slide type.

The Title Master view displays the elements common to all title slide types.

To switch to Slide Master view:

◆ From the View menu, choose Master and then choose Slide Master from the submenu (**Figure 25.9**).

or

Hold down the Shift key as you click the Slide view button.

To switch to Title Master view:

◆ From the View menu, choose Master, and then choose Title Master from the submenu

Slide Master view shows the text placeholders and a Slide Miniature box displaying the current slide. You can change the default text formatting for the slide titles and main text items as well as the background design (**Figure 25.10**).

✔ Tips

■ To return to the presentation, click Close on the Master toolbar (**Figure 25.11**) or click any view button.

■ To switch to Title Master view,

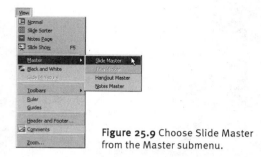

Figure 25.9 Choose Slide Master from the Master submenu.

Figure 25.10 The Slide Master view with the Slide Miniature box.

Figure 25.11 Click Close on the Master toolbar.

Figure 25.12 Choose Background from the Format menu.

Figure 25.13 Choose Fill Effects for the background.

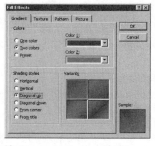

Figure 25.14 Try various fill effects for the background.

Figure 25.15 The background change applied.

Changing the Background Color and Shading

You can change the background color and shading for the current slide or for all slides. You can make the change in Slide Master or Title Master view or in any other view.

To change the background color and shading:

1. From the Format menu, choose Background (**Figure 25.12**).

   or

   Right-click outside the placeholder areas in Slide, Normal, or a Master view and choose Background from the shortcut menu.

2. In the Background dialog box, pull down the Background Fill menu and choose a solid color or Fill Effects (**Figure 25.13**).

3. In the Fill Effects dialog box, click through the tabs and select the features you want (**Figure 25.14**).

4. Click OK.

5. In the Background dialog box, click Apply to All to change the background for all slides or click Apply to change it for a single slide (**Figure 25.15**).

✔ Tips

- To see the new background shading while the Slide Background dialog box is still open, click the Preview button and then move the dialog box to the side.

- If you apply the change in Slide Master view, all slide types except the title type are changed. If you apply the change in Title Master view, only the title type is changed.

CHANGING THE BACKGROUND

Changing the Text Fonts

By changing the fonts on the slide master, you can change the fonts all the way through the presentation.

To change the text fonts:

1. From the View menu, choose Master and then choose Slide Master from the submenu.

   or

   Hold down the Shift key as you click the Slide View button.

2. Select the text in the Title Area or any of the text levels in the Object Area of the slide master (**Figure 25.16**).

3. From the Format menu, choose Font (**Figure 25.17**).

   or

   Right-click the text and choose Font from the shortcut menu.

4. In the Font dialog box, make formatting changes (**Figure 25.18**).

5. Click OK.

6. To switch to another view, click Close on the Master toolbar or click any view button.

✔ Tip

■ The color of the text is determined by the color scheme, but changing the color of text in Slide Master view overrides the color scheme.

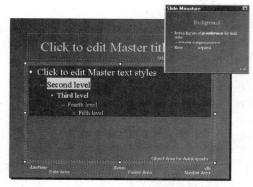

Figure 25.16 Click a text item in Slide Master view.

Figure 25.17 Choose Font from the Format menu.

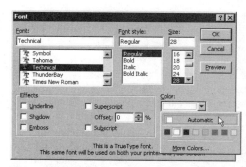

Figure 25.18 Make changes to the font for the text level selected.

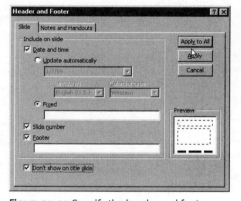

Figure 25.19 Choose Header and Footer from the View menu.

Figure 25.20 Specify the header and footer information.

Changing Header and Footer Information

You can change the header and footer details at any time in your presentation design.

To change header and footer information:

1. From the View menu, choose Header and Footer (**Figure 25.19**).

2. In the Header and Footer dialog box, click to turn the data and time and slide number on or off, and specify any text to appear on the slides (**Figure 25.20**).

3. Click Apply to All to apply your changes to all slides, or click Apply to apply them to a single slide.

✔ Tip

■ Click Don't Show On Title Slide to omit the information from the title slide.

CHANGING HEADER/FOOTER

Adding a Logo to the Background

A logo can give a stock presentation that important made-to-order look. You can draw a logo, or you can insert a graphic file.

To add a logo to the background:

1. From the View menu, choose Master, and then choose Slide Master from the submenu.

   or

   Hold down the Shift key as you click the Slide View button.

2. With PowerPoint's drawing tools on the Drawing toolbar, modify the existing background graphic objects or add new objects.

   or

   From the Insert menu, choose Picture, and then choose From File from the submenu (**Figure 25.21**).

3. In the Insert Picture dialog box, locate the file to insert (**Figure 25.22**).

4. Click Insert.

5. Position the logo on the slide master (**Figure 25.23**).

6. To switch to another view, click Close on the Master toolbar or click any view button.

✔ Tip

■ You can copy and paste a graphic image from another program onto the slide master, or copy and paste graphics from the slide master of another presentation onto the slide master of the current presentation.

Figure 25.21 Choose From File from the Picture submenu.

Figure 25.22 Find the file to insert and click Insert.

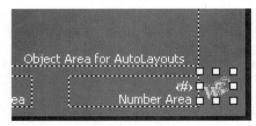

Figure 25.23 Position the picture on the slide master.

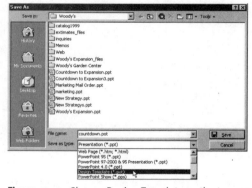

Figure 25.24 Choose Save As from the File menu.

Figure 25.25 Choose Design Template as the type.

Saving a Custom Design

You can open a template, make any or all of the changes detailed in this chapter, and then save the custom template for use with future presentations.

To save a custom design:

1. Make formatting changes to the color scheme and slide master of a presentation or template.

2. From the File menu, choose Save As (**Figure 25.24**).

3. In the Save As dialog box, pull down the Save as Type menu and choose Design Template (**Figure 25.25**).

4. Enter the name of the template and choose the location where you want to save it.

5. Click Save.

✔ Tip

■ You can use any presentation as a template.

Working in Slide Sorter View

Slide Sorter view displays rows of thumbnail views of slides, much the way you arrange 35mm slides in rows on a light table to get an overview of the presentation. In Slide Sorter view, you can rearrange slides, delete or duplicate slides, and change the template to change the overall look of the presentation.

To switch to Slide Sorter view:

◆ Click the Slide Sorter View button (**Figure 25.26**).

or

From the View menu, choose Slide Sorter (**Figure 25.27**).

PowerPoint shows the presentation in Slide Sorter view (**Figure 25.28**).

✔ Tip

■ To switch to a view of a single slide, double-click the slide or click the slide and then click the Slide View button.

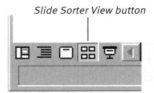

Slide Sorter View button

Figure 25.26 Click the Slide Sorter View button.

Figure 25.27 Choose Slide Sorter from the View menu.

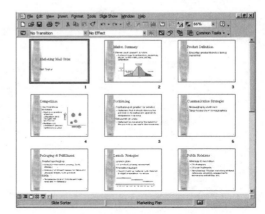

Figure 25.28 Slide Sorter view.

SLIDE SORTER VIEW

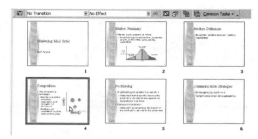

Figure 25.29 Select a slide.

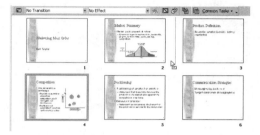

Figure 25.30 The line shows the new location.

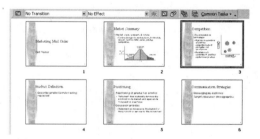

Figure 25.31 The slide moved to the new location.

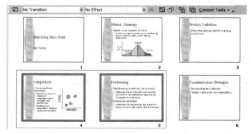

Figure 25.32 Drag a selection box to select several slides.

Reordering Slides

At any point in the design of your presentation, you can change the order of the slides.

To reorder the slides:

1. Position the mouse pointer on the slide to reposition in the presentation (**Figure 25.29**).

2. Hold down the mouse button and drag the slide to a new position.

    A vertical line appears to indicate where the slide will drop when you release the mouse button (**Figure 25.30**).

3. Release the mouse button to drop the slide (**Figure 25.31**).

✔ Tips

■ You can select several slides to move by drawing a selection box around the group of slides and then dragging the group to the new position (**Figure 25.32**).

■ You can also select several slides by holding down the Shift key and selecting the first and last slides in the series.

■ To gather slides from different parts of a presentation, hold down the Ctrl key as you click each slide. Drag any one slide in the group to a new point in the presentation. All the selected slides will appear in sequence and in the same relative order at the new position.

Changing the Design in Slide Sorter View

When you apply a new design template in Slide Sorter view, you can see at a glance how various layouts are affected. You can also change the background or color scheme for all the slides or for selected slides.

To apply a new design template:

1. Choose Apply Design Template from the Common Tasks pull-down menu (**Figure 25.33**).

   or

   From the Format menu, choose Apply Design Template.

2. In the Apply Design Template dialog box, select a new design (**Figure 25.34**).

3. Click Apply (**Figure 25.35**).

Figure 25.33 Choose Apply Design Template from the Common Tasks pull-down menu.

Figure 25.34 Select a template by viewing options in the Preview window.

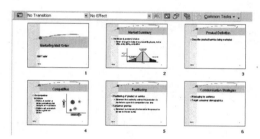

Figure 25.35 The new template applied.

Figure 25.36 Choose Background from the Format menu.

To change the background or color scheme:

1. Select the slide or slides you want to change.

2. Choose Background or Slide Color Scheme from the Format menu (**Figure 25.36**).

3. Make the change in the Color Scheme dialog box or the Background dialog box (**Figures 25.37** and **25.38**).

4. Click Apply to change only the selected slide or slides, or click Apply to All to change all slides (**Figure 25.39**).

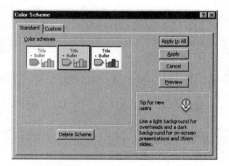

Figure 25.37 Select a different background and click Apply or Apply to All.

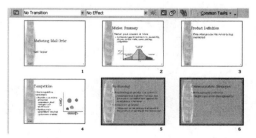

Figure 25.38 Select a different color scheme and click Apply or Apply to All.

CHANGING THE DESIGN

Figure 25.39 The background for two slides has been changed.

Duplicating and Deleting Slides

You can duplicate and delete selected slides in Slide Sorter view and see the effect on the flow of slides immediately.

To duplicate a slide or slides:

1. Select the slide or slides you want to duplicate (**Figure 25.40**).

2. Press Ctrl+D to duplicate the slide (**Figure 25.41**).

To delete a slide or slides:

1. Select the slide or slides you want to delete.

2. Press Del or Ctrl+X to delete the slide (**Figure 25.42**).

✔ Tip

- You can also choose Duplicate or Delete Slide from the Edit menu.

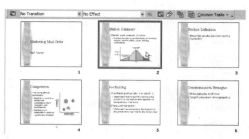

Figure 25.40 Select the slide to duplicate or delete.

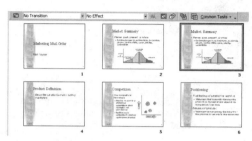

Figure 25.41 The slide duplicated.

Figure 25.42 The slide deleted.

DRAWING ON SLIDES

26

In Microsoft PowerPoint, you can add graphics to your presentation in several ways. You can choose an image from the substantial collection of clip art included in the Microsoft Office installation. You can also use PowerPoint's drawing tools to create your own graphics.

Be careful when you are scanning graphics to include in your presentations. Most graphics that have been published are copyrighted and cannot legally be used without the permission of the copyright holder. Exceptions are books of royalty-free clip art that you can buy at art supply stores or collections of clip art that are distributed electronically or on disk.

Drawing Shapes and Lines

You can draw lines and shapes directly on a slide in Normal or Slide view, or you can draw in one of the Master views.

To draw a shape or line:

1. In Slide view, click one of the drawing tools or menus on the Drawing toolbar (**Figure 26.1**).

2. Drag with the mouse pointer to create the shape or line (**Figures 26.2** and **26.3**).

3. Click the shape and choose Colors and Lines from the Format menu (**Figure 26.4**).

4. In the Colors and Lines dialog box, choose a fill color, line color, and line style (**Figure 26.5**).

5. Click OK.

Figure 26.1 Click a drawing tool.

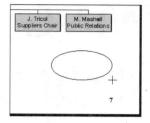

Figure 26.2 Drag to create the shape.

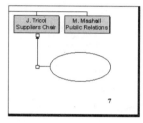

Figure 26.3 Click and drag other tools to add other elements.

Figure 26.4 Choose Colors and Lines from the Format menu.

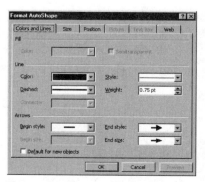

Figure 26.5 Choose a fill color, line color, and line style.

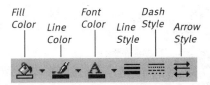

Fill Color *Line Color* *Font Color* *Line Style* *Dash Style* *Arrow Style*

Figure 26.6 The Style buttons on the Drawing toolbar.

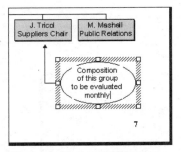

J. Tricol
Suppliers Chair

M. Mashall
Public Relations

Composition
of this group
to be evaluated
monthly|

7

Figure 26.7 You can type text within a shape.

✔ Tips

■ To keep a shape regular (a square instead of a rectangle, or a circle instead of an oval, for example), hold down the Shift key while dragging through the area to create the shape.

■ You can also click Style buttons on the Drawing toolbar (**Figure 26.6**).

■ To add text inside a shape, click the shape and then begin typing (**Figure 26.7**).

■ To delete a line or shape, click it so that the handles appear, and press Del.

DRAWING SHAPES/LINES

Adding Predefined Shapes and Text Boxes

You can use AutoShapes to quickly add graphic objects to your worksheet, and you can create text as a graphic object and then edit the size, shape, color, and other aspects of the text box, just as you can edit other kinds of graphics.

Figure 26.8 Choose an AutoShape from a pop-out palette.

To draw a predefined shape:

1. Click and hold down the mouse button on the AutoShapes button on the Drawing toolbar and select an item on the list.

2. Choose one of the shapes in the pop-out palette that appears (**Figure 26.8**).

3. Position the mouse pointer at one corner of an imaginary rectangle that would contain the shape, hold down the mouse button, drag to the opposite corner of the rectangle, and release the mouse button (**Figure 26.9**).

   The shape appears.

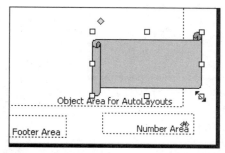

Figure 26.9 Click and drag to place the Autoshape on your slide.

To add a text box:

1. Click the Text Box button on the Drawing toolbar (**Figure 26.10**).

2. Click in the slide where you want the text box to appear (**Figure 26.11**).

3. Type the text.

   The box expands to surround the text. Press Enter to create a new line of text within the box.

Text Box button

Figure 26.10 Click the Text Box button.

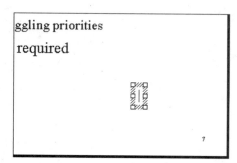

Figure 26.11 Click where you want the text box to appear.

SHAPES AND TEXT BOXES

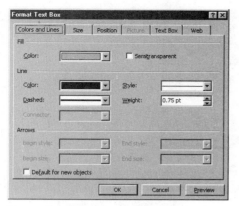

Figure 26.12 Select formatting for the text box.

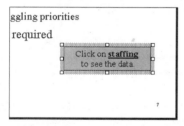

Figure 26.13 The formatted text box.

4. For precise control over the parameters of the text box (fill and line color, word wrapping, internal margins, position, and so on), double-click one of the sides of the object to format the object.

5. In the Format Text Box dialog box, select the formatting you want (**Figure 26.12**).

6. Click OK (**Figure 26.13**).

✔ Tips

- To keep a shape you are drawing regular, hold down the Shift key as you drag to draw the shape.

- After you've entered the text, you can change the shape of the text box by dragging the side handles.

- Change the location of the text box by clicking one of the sides (not at a handle) and dragging the box to the new location.

- To delete a text box, click one of the sides so that the insertion point inside disappears, and press Del.

- You can also add text to any other shape by clicking in the shape and typing.

SHAPES AND TEXT BOXES

Adding Shadows and 3-D Effects

You can add shadow or 3-D effects to any of the lines or shapes you create.

To add a shadow or a 3-D effect:

1. Click a line or shape to select it. Handles appear.

2. Click the Shadow button and choose the location and direction of the shadow to add to the shape (**Figures 26.14** and **26.15**).

   or

   Click the 3-D button and select an effect (**Figures 26.16** and **26.17**).

✔ Tip

- You can't use both shadow and 3-D effects on the same object.

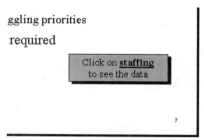

Figure 26.14 Select a shadow for the shape.

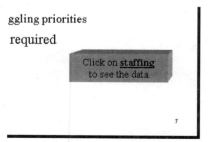

Figure 26.15 A shadow applied to the text box.

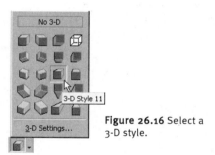

Figure 26.16 Select a 3-D style.

ggling priorities

required

Click on **staffing** to see the data.

Figure 26.17 A 3-D style applied to the text box.

Insert WordArt button

Figure 26.18 Click the Insert WordArt button.

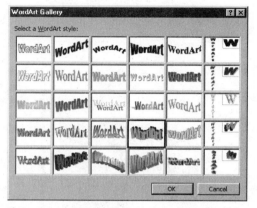

Figure 26.19 Click a style in the WordArt gallery.

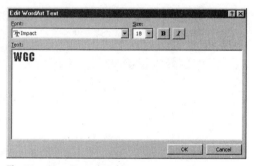

Figure 26.20 Type the text.

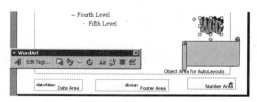

Figure 26.21 The WordArt and the WordArt toolbar.

Making Text Conform to Shapes

WordArt is specially formatted text that Excel can display in a number of preset styles. Several tools are available to help you create and edit WordArt.

You can move, resize, and reshape the WordArt using the handles that appear, just as you adjust other graphics.

To insert WordArt:

1. Click the Insert WordArt button on the Drawing toolbar (**Figure 26.18**).

2. Click a style in the WordArt Gallery dialog box (**Figure 26.19**).

3. In the Edit WordArt Text dialog box, replace "Your Text Here" with your own text (**Figure 26.20**).

4. Set the font, size, and style you want.

5. Click OK.

   The WordArt and the WordArt toolbar appear (**Figure 26.21**).

To modify the WordArt:

◆ Change the shape of the curve or curves to which the WordArt is bound by clicking the WordArt Shape button on the WordArt toolbar and choosing from the palette that appears (**Figures 26.22** and **26.23**).

✔ Tip

■ For precise control over the appearance of the WordArt, click the Format WordArt button on the toolbar (**Figure 26.24**) and make changes in the Format WordArt dialog box.

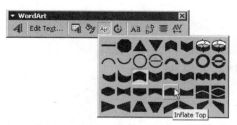

Figure 26.22 Select from the Shape palette.

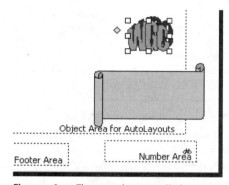

Figure 26.23 The new shape applied.

Format WordArt button

Figure 26.24 Click the Format WordArt button to format the WordArt.

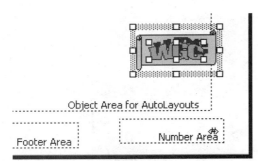

Figure 26.25 Draw a selection box around the objects.

Figure 26.26 Choose Group from the Draw submenu.

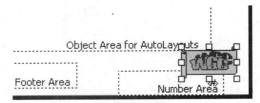

Figure 26.27 The objects are now grouped.

Grouping and Ungrouping Shapes

By grouping several objects, you can treat them as a single object. Simply select and then move, copy, or format the group.

To group several objects:

1. Hold down the Shift key as you click each object for the group.

or

Using the Selection tool on the Drawing toolbar, draw a selection box that entirely encloses just the objects you want to group (**Figure 26.25**).

2. From the Drawing toolbar, choose Group (**Figure 26.26**).

A single set of handles now surrounds the objects in the group (**Figure 26.27**).

✔ Tip

■ To ungroup objects, select the group and then choose Ungroup from the Drawing toolbar.

GROUPING/UNGROUPING

Rearranging and Rotating Shapes

Once they are created, you can align, rotate, and overlap shapes.

To align shapes on the slide:

1. Select the objects you want to align.

2. From the Draw menu, choose Align and then choose a command on the submenu (**Figure 26.28**).

To rotate a shape:

1. Select the object you want to rotate.

2. From the Draw menu, choose Rotate or Flip and choose a command on the submenu (**Figures 26.29** and **26.30**).

To overlap a shape:

1. Select an object to move above or below other overlapping objects.

2. From the Draw menu choose Order, and then, from the Order submenu, choose Send to Back, Send to Front, Bring Forward (one level) or Send Backward (one level) (**Figure 26.31**).

✔ Tips

- Objects align with the object that extends farthest from the center of the slide.

- If you click Free Rotate on the Drawing toolbar, position the mouse pointer on a corner handle and draw an arc to rotate the object through.

Figure 26.28 The Align and Distribute commands.

Figure 26.29 The Rotate and Flip commands.

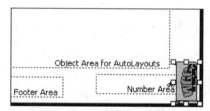

Figure 26.30 The group rotated.

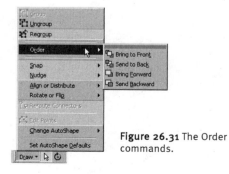

Figure 26.31 The Order commands.

Figure 26.32 Choose Clip Art from the Picture submenu.

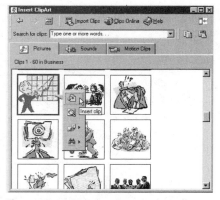

Figure 26.33 With the picture selected, click Insert Clip.

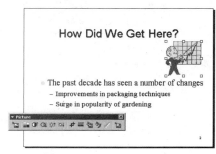

Figure 26.34 The picture and the Picture toolbar.

Using Clip Art

You can choose from a library of clip art included with Office 2000, and you can use any additions you've made to that library from other sources. After you insert a picture, you can use the Format Picture dialog box to change parameters.

To insert a picture:

1. From the Insert menu, choose Picture and then choose Clip Art from the pop-out menu (**Figure 26.32**).

2. In the Insert ClipArt window, click a category.

3. Click a picture (you can scroll to view all the options) or use the Back arrow in the upper left corner to return to select another category.

4. When you find a suitable picture, click Insert Clip to insert the picture in your worksheet (**Figure 26.33**).

   The picture and the Picture toolbar appear in the document (**Figure 26.34**).

✔ Tip

■ To format the picture, click the Format Picture button on the Picture toolbar or right-click the picture and choose Format Picture from the shortcut menu.

USING CLIP ART

CREATING SLIDE SHOWS

Slide shows are the payoff for all your hard work creating slides in PowerPoint. Slide shows are animated presentations that you display on a computer monitor or projection system. They can include eye-catching transition effects between slides and sophisticated animations displayed on individual slides. Individual lines of text can slide into view, and even the charts on slides can be animated, with bars growing or pie slices being added right on the screen. Slide shows can also contain audio clips, music, narration, and video. All these features play as the show progresses.

Adding Transition Effects

Transition effects are the dissolves, splits, wipes, and other film-like effects that a slide show can use to bring each new slide into view. Switch to Slide Sorter view to add effects (**Figure 27.1**).

To add a transition effect:

1. Click the slide for which you want to change the transition effect.

2. Click the arrow button next to the Transition Effects drop-down list on the Slide Sorter toolbar and select a transition effect from the list (**Figure 27.2**).

   or

   Click the Transition button on the Slide Sorter toolbar (**Figure 27.3**).

   or

   Right-click the slide and choose Transition Effects from the shortcut menu.

3. In the Slide Transition dialog box, choose a transition effect from the drop-down list, a speed (slow, medium, or fast) and the advance option (on mouse click or after a period of time) (**Figure 27.4**).

4. Click Apply to All to add this transition effect to all slides, or click Apply to add it only to the selected slide.

✔ Tips

- To apply the same transition effect to multiple slides, hold down the Shift key while you click the slides and then choose a transition effect.

- To preview the transition effect in Slide Sorter view, click the transition icon that appears below each slide that has a transition effect (**Figure 27.5**).

Slide Sorter View button

Figure 27.1 Click the Slide Sorter View button.

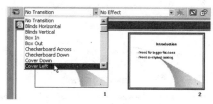

Figure 27.2 Choose a transition effect for the selected slide.

Transition button

Figure 27.3 Click the Transition button on the Slide Sorter toolbar.

Figure 27.4 Choose options in the Slide Transition dialog box.

Figure 27.5 Click the transition icon.

Transition icon

Figure 27.6 Choose a preset animation for the selected slide.

Figure 27.7 Choose a preset animation from the Preset Animation submenu.

Animation icon

Figure 27.8 Click the animation icon to see the effect.

Figure 27.9 The Animation Effects toolbar.

Adding Preset Animation

Preset animation can bring slide title and bulleted text into view using a special effect. Experiment with the various available effects.

To choose a preset animation:

1. In Slide Sorter view, click the slide that requires preset animation.

2. From the Preset Animation list on the Slide Sorter toolbar, select an effect (**Figure 27.6**).

   or

   From the Slide Show menu, choose Preset Animation and then choose an effect from the pop-out menu (**Figure 27.7**).

   or

   Right-click the slide, choose Preset Animation from the shortcut menu, and then choose an effect from the pop-out menu.

✔ Tips

- To preview the animation effect in Slide Sorter view, click the animation icon that appears below each slide that has an animation effect (**Figure 27.8**).

- You can also apply effects using the buttons on the Animation Effects toolbar (**Figure 27.9**). Choose Toolbars from the View menu and then choose Animation Effects from the pop-out menu.

- To apply the same preset animation effect to multiple slides, hold down the Shift key and click the slides and then choose an effect.

ADDING PRESET ANIMATION

Creating Custom Animations

For more control over the animation of text and objects on a slide, you can create a custom animation. Custom animations can be created only in Slide view.

To create a custom animation:

1. In Slide view, display the slide that requires custom animation.

2. From the Slide Show menu, choose Custom Animation (**Figure 27.10**).

   or

   Right-click the slide and choose Custom Animation from the shortcut menu.

3. In the Custom Animation dialog box, check the items you want to animate and set the order and timing (**Figure 27.11**).

4. On the Effects tab, select an effect from the drop-down list and, if text is in your checked list, set the way the text is introduced (**Figure 27.12**).

5. Click Preview to display the animation in the small Preview window.

6. Click OK.

✔ Tip

■ You can also preview an animation by clicking the Animation Preview button on the Animation Effects toolbar.

Figure 27.10 Choose Custom Animation from the Slide Show menu.

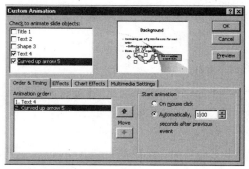

Figure 27.11 Click the slide items to animate in the Custom Animation dialog box.

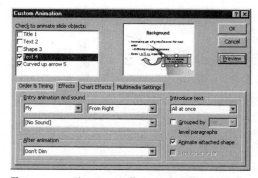

Figure 27.12 Choose an effect on the Effects tab.

Figure 27.13 Choose Sound from File from the Movies and Sounds submenu.

Figure 27.14 Find the sound file and click OK.

Figure 27.15 Position the sound icon on the slide.

Figure 27.16 Choose an action from the shortcut menu.

Adding Audio and Video

You can add sounds to the transition effects and to the preset animation. You can also add audio and video to your presentation by inserting files from the Clip Gallery or from other folders available to you.

To add an audio file:

1. In Slide view, display the slide to which you want to add the audio file.

2. From the Insert menu, choose Movies and Sounds, and then choose Sound from File (**Figure 27.13**).

3. In the Insert Sound dialog box, type in a filename or browse through your folders to find the sound file you want (**Figure 27.14**).

4. Click OK.

5. Answer Yes to have the sound play automatically or No to have it play when you click it.

   The sound icon appears in the middle of the slide (**Figure 27.15**). You can move it as you would any object.

✔ Tip

■ If you right-click the sound icon, you can choose Play Sound or Edit Sound Object from the shortcut menu (**Figure 27.16**).

ADDING AUDIO AND VIDEO

To add a video file:

1. In Slide view, display the slide to which you want to add the video file.

2. From the Insert menu, choose Movies and Sounds and then choose Movie from File (**Figure 27.17**).

3. In the Insert Movie dialog box, type in a filename or browse through your folders to find the video file you want (**Figure 27.18**).

4. Click OK.

5. Answer Yes to have the video play automatically or No to have it play when you click it.

   The first frame of the video appears in the middle of the slide (**Figure 27.19**). You can move it as you would any object.

✔ Tip

■ If you right-click the first frame, you can choose Play Movie or Edit Movie Object from the shortcut menu (**Figure 27.20**).

Figure 27.17 Choose Movie from File from the Movies and Sounds submenu.

Figure 27.18 Find the video file and click OK.

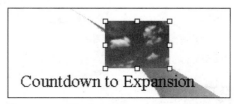

Figure 27.19 The first frame of the video file.

Figure 27.20 Choose an action from the shortcut menu.

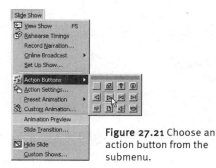

Figure 27.21 Choose an action button from the submenu.

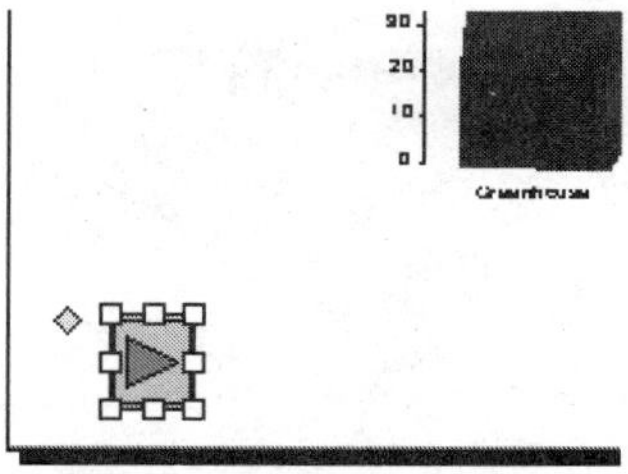

Figure 27.22 The action button on the slide.

Figure 27.23 Choose an action in the Action Settings dialog box.

Figure 27.24 Choose a sound to play on the Mouse Over or the Mouse Click tab.

Adding Action Buttons

If you plan to allow your show to be viewed in an interactive way, you can add action buttons so that your viewers can control the flow and play sounds and video by clicking the buttons.

To add an action button:

1. In Normal, Outline, or Slide view, select the slide to which you want to add the button.

2. From the Slide Show menu, choose Action Buttons, and then choose a button from the submenu (**Figure 27.21**).

3. Position the button in on your slide (**Figure 27.22**).

   The Action Settings dialog box is displayed.

4. On the Mouse Click tab of the Action Settings dialog box, select an action (**Figure 27.23**).

5. On the Mouse Over tab, you can select a different action that will occur when the user passes the mouse over the button (**Figure 27.24**).

6. Click OK.

✔ Tip

- You can add actions to other objects simply by selecting them and then choosing Action settings from the Slide Show menu.

Setting Up the Show

You can set up the slide show in Normal, Outline, Slide, or Slide Sorter view. You can also hide slides from the show.

To set up the slide show:

1. From the Slide Show menu, choose Set Up Show (**Figure 27.25**).

2. In the Set Up Show dialog box, choose the type of show, which slides are to be shown, and the method used to advance slides (**Figure 27.26**).

3. Click OK.

To hide a slide:

1. In Slide Sorter view, select the slide you want to hide.

2. Choose Hide Slide from the Slide Show menu or click the Hide Slide button on the Slide Sorter toolbar (**Figure 27.27**).

   When a slide is hidden, a hidden slide icon appears below it in Slide Sorter view (**Figure 27.28**).

✔ Tips

- Click the Projector Wizard button in the Set Up Show dialog box for help connecting your computer to a projector.

- Choose Custom Shows from the Slide Show menu to add slides from this presentation to a custom show.

- Even though a slide is hidden, you can display it by clicking a hyperlink or an action button pointing to it.

Figure 27.25 Choose Set Up Show from the Slide Show menu.

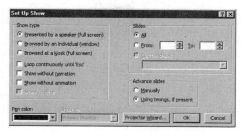

Figure 27.26 Choose show type and the range of slides in the Set Up Show dialog box.

Hide Slide button

Figure 27.27 Click the Hide Slide button on the Slide Sorter toolbar.

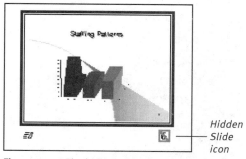

Hidden Slide icon

Figure 27.28 The hidden slide icon.

Slide Show

Figure 27.29 Choose Rehearse Timings from the Slide Show menu.

Rehearse Timings button

Figure 27.30 Click the Rehearse Timings button on the Slide Sorter toolbar.

Figure 27.31 The Rehearsal dialog box.

Slide Show View button

Figure 27.32 Click the Slide Show View button.

Displaying the Show

You can rehearse the delivery of your presentation; PowerPoint times it for you. You can rehearse or view the slide show in Normal, Outline, Slide, or Slide Sorter view.

To rehearse the slide show:

◆ From the Slide Show menu, choose Rehearse Timings (**Figure 27.29**).

or

In Slide Sorter view, click the Rehearse Timings button on the Slide Sorter toolbar (**Figure 27.30**).

The Slide Show begins with the Rehearsal dialog box in the upper left corner (**Figure 27.31**).

To view the slide show:

◆ Click the first slide to view in the show and then click the Slide Show View button (**Figure 27.32**).

or

From the Slide Show menu, choose View Show.

DISPLAYING THE SHOW

✔ Tips

- To use these timings, choose Use Slide Timings in the Set Up Show dialog box.

- To advance through the slide show, click anywhere on the slide. You can also right-click anywhere and choose as action from the shortcut menu (**Figure 27.33**). You can also use keystrokes, as shown in **Table 27.1**.

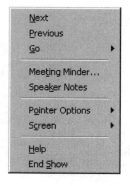

Next
Previous
Go ▶

Meeting Minder...
Speaker Notes

Pointer Options ▶
Screen ▶

Help
End Show

Figure 27.33 The Slide Show shortcut menu.

Table 27.1

Slide Show Keyboard Shortcuts

SLIDE SHOW	KEYSTROKES
Next Action	Spacebar, Enter, N, Page Down, Right arrow
Previous Action	P, Backspace, Page Up, Left arrow
Go to slide number	number+Enter
Black/White screen	B or W (press again to return to show)

PowerPoint and the Web

28

Using PowerPoint's sophisticated new features, you can save an entire presentation as a Web page. The Web page displays a list of the slides and a set of navigation controls you can use to switch from one slide to the next.

Saving a presentation as a Web page allows you to share it with others not fortunate enough to have PowerPoint—they can view the presentation in any Web browser.

Adding a Hyperlink

A hyperlink is specially marked text or a graphic that you click to go to a file or an HTML page on the Web or on an intranet. Add a hyperlink if your presentation will be viewed on screen or in a browser.

Figure 28.1 Select the text to which you want to add a hyperlink.

To add a hyperlink:

1. Select text to which you want to add a hyperlink (**Figure 28.1**).

2. From the Insert menu, choose Hyperlink (**Figure 28.2**).

   or

   Press Ctrl+K

   or

   Click the Insert Hyperlink button on the Standard toolbar (**Figure 28.3**).

Insert Hyperlink button

Figure 28.3 Click the Insert Hyperlink button on the Standard toolbar.

Figure 28.2 Choose Hyperlink from the Insert menu.

To link to another file:

1. In the Insert Hyperlink dialog box, type the destination link (**Figure 28.4**).

   or

   Select from recent files, pages, and links.

   or

   Click the File button and navigate to the file you want in the Link to File dialog box.

   or

   Click the Web Page button and navigate to the Web page you want in the browser window. (You must be connected to the Web to use this method.)

2. Click OK. The text is now colored and underlined (**Figure 28.5**).

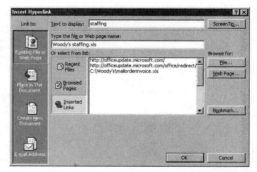

Figure 28.4 Type a filename or browse for the file to link to in the Insert Hyperlink dialog box.

> ## Background
>
> - Increasing use of **greenhouses** for mail order
>   - Difficulty in juggling priorities
> - Extra staffing required

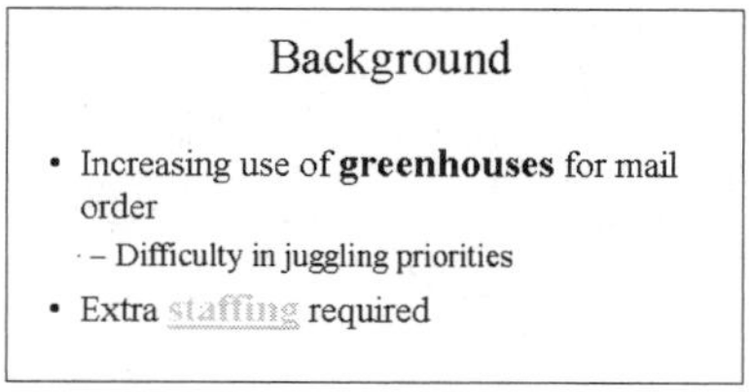

Figure 28.5 The hyperlinked text is colored and underlined.

ADDING A HYPERLINK

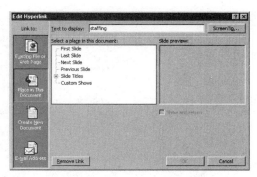

Figure 28.6 Position the hyperlink in the current document.

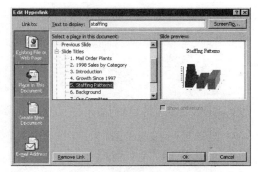

Figure 28.7 Select a slide to serve as the hyperlink destination.

Figure 28.8 Right-click the hyper-linked text to display the shortcut menu.

To link to another slide in the presentation:

1. In the Insert Hyperlink dialog box, click Place in This Document in the Link To bar (**Figure 28.6**).

2. Click the Slide Titles expansion box to select a slide as the destination (**Figure 28.7**).

3. Click OK. The text is now colored and underlined.

✔ Tips

- Use the Recent Files, Browsed Pages, and Inserted Links buttons as shortcuts to help you find recently used pages.

- To edit or remove a hyperlink, right-click the link and choose the appropriate action from the shortcut menu (**Figure 28.8**).

ADDING A HYPERLINK

Opening a Presentation on the Web

You can open a presentation on the Web so that you can edit it in PowerPoint. If you select a Web page that is not a presentation, PowerPoint displays it as a single slide. If the file you open was published from one another Microsoft. Office 2000 application, that application will start, and you can copy or drag information from one application to another.

Figure 28.9 Type a URL in the File Name box or browse for the file.

To open a Web page as a PowerPoint presentation:

1. From the File menu, choose Open.

2. Choose Web Folders from the Places bar and Web pages as the type of file.

3. Open a Web Folder or enter the URL in the File Name text box (**Figure 28.9**).

4. Click Open.

   Your computer logs onto the Web server and displays the file in PowerPoint (**Figure 28.10**).

✔ Tips

■ If your system administrator or Internet service provider has set up a Web server that supports Web folders, you can use the Add Web Folder Wizard to create a folder that serves as a shortcut.

■ If the Web toolbar is visible, you can type in the URL and press Enter to have your default browser download and display a Web document.

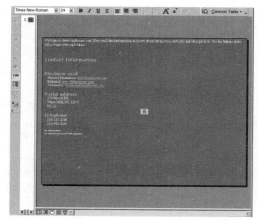

Figure 28.10 The file displayed as a PowerPoint presentation.

Figure 28.11 Choose Web Page Preview from the File menu.

Previewing a Presentation as a Web Page

You can test any presentation to see how it will be displayed in a browser.

To preview a presentation as a Web page:

◆ From the File menu, choose Web Page Preview (**Figure 28.11**).

Your default browser displays your presentation (**Figure 28.12**).

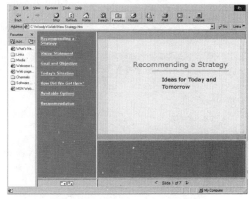

Figure 28.12 The presentation displayed in the default browser.

Saving a Presentation as a Web Page

If you save your presentation as a Web page, you and others can make changes to the presentation and then resave it as a Web page.

To save a presentation as a Web page:

1. From the File menu, choose Save As Web Page.

2. In the Save As dialog box, choose the name and location (**Figure 28.13**).

3. Click Change Title and type the text you want displayed as the title when the page is viewed in a browser (**Figure 28.14**).

4. Click OK to return to the Save As dialog box.

5. Click Save.

✔ Tips

- The extra files created are stored in a subdirectory. If you move the Web page you create, be sure to move the subdirectory with it (**Figure 28.15**).

- If your system administrator or Internet service provider has set up a Web server that supports Web publishing, you can save the Web page to a Web folder.

- To set further Web options or to save only a subset of a presentation, click the Publish button in the Save As dialog box and make changes in the Publish As Web page dialog box (**Figure 28.16**).

Figure 28.13 Save the file as a Web page.

Figure 28.14 Change the title in the Set Page Title dialog box.

Figure 28.15 The Web page and its subdirectory of files.

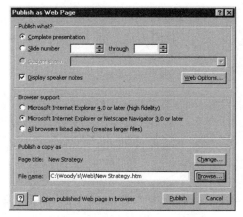

Figure 28.16 Customize the presentation in the Publish as Web Page dialog box.

Part 5
Microsoft Access

Part 5
Microsoft Access

INTRODUCING

ACCESS 2000

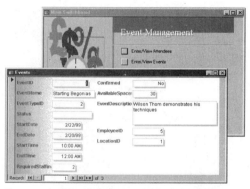

Figure 29.1 Microsoft Access table data displayed in a form.

Microsoft Access 2000 is the database management system (DBMS) within the Microsoft Office suite. It enables you to store and manage large quantities of data, organized in units called records. An Access database consists of the following objects:

◆ Tables—hold the records

◆ Forms—display the records in the tables one by one (**Figure 29.1**)

◆ Queries—locate specific information

◆ Reports—print batches of records

◆ Data access pages—make data available through Web pages

◆ Macros and Visual Basic modules—automate tasks

Access Wizards make it especially easy to set up tables, forms, data access pages, reports, and queries.

An Access database can feed information to a Word mail merge so that you can send a form letter to addresses in a database.

Although Excel also provides database capabilities, its storage capacities are limited. Access can hold a virtually unlimited amount of data.

The Steps to Creating an Access Database

Starting a new database

You can begin with a blank database, or you can also use a database wizard to begin building your database with commonly used database elements corresponding to a variety of business activities.

Setting up a table

All the data in a database is stored in tables, so you need to design the tables first. Access helps you create tables using the Table Wizard, which offers you dozens of common fields for storing the individual bits of information in each record. Mix and match the fields to create the table.

Creating a form

You can type your data directly into a table, but it's much easier to type it into a form, which displays a single record and blank fields. Once again, an Access Wizard helps you create a form with all the controls (fill-in blanks, check boxes, and other items) you'll need.

Finding, sorting, and filtering information

Retrieving the information you need from a database is as easy as entering it. You can simply search for matching text in a field, create a filter to display only selected records, sort the data, or create a complex query, which can pull out information according to special criteria.

Creating a report

The Report Wizard helps you organize database information into presentable pages. It also helps you categorize related information into groups and total numeric information.

Creating a data access page

If you need to present data as a Web page, the Page Wizard helps you design a data access page, with hyperlinks to other places in your database.

Other features

You can also use Access as the source of names and addresses for a Word mail merge.

Figure 29.2 You can start Access from the Start menu.

Starting Access

You start Access in the same way that you start every application in the Microsoft Office suite.

To start Access:

1. From the Start menu, choose Programs, and then choose Microsoft Access (**Figure 29.2**).

2. Select an action in the Microsoft Access dialog box (**Figure 29.3**).

✔ Tips

- If Microsoft Access is already started, click its icon on the taskbar to reopen its window.

- You can also start Access by double-clicking any Access database listed in the Open Office Document dialog box.

- If you see an empty window when Access starts, the Access Startup dialog box is turned off. To turn it back on, choose Options from the Tools menu, and then check Startup Dialog Box on the View tab of the Options dialog box.

Figure 29.3 Click an option in the Microsoft Access startup dialog box.

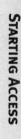

STARTING ACCESS

The Access Window

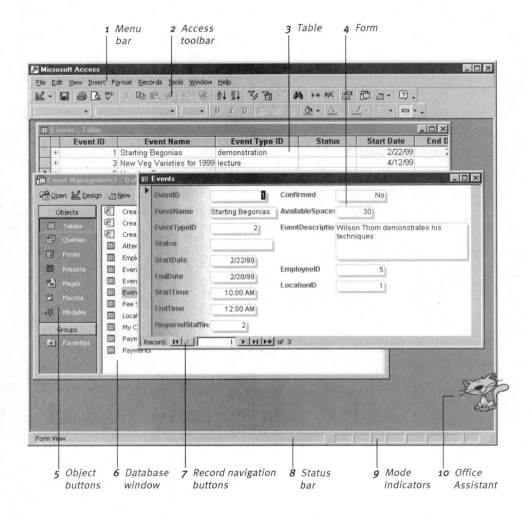

Figure 29.4 The Access window.

THE ACCESS WINDOW

Key to the Access Window

1 Menu bar

Click any name on the menu bar to pull down a menu.

2 Access toolbar

Toolbar with buttons for the most frequently needed commands. Access provides a set of buttons that changes according to the current task as you work in Access.

3 Table

Tables hold the information in a database. A single database can contain many tables, each holding a different set of related records.

4 Form

A fill-in-the-blanks form used to enter, edit, and view the information in a table one record at a time. A single database can contain many different forms, perhaps even more than one form for each table.

5 Object buttons

Click these buttons to change to the tab that shows the object type you want to work with. The objects in a database are tables, forms, reports, queries, macros, and modules.

6 Database window

Displays lists of the objects in a database. The Database window contains tabs that show objects of a certain type. Click a tab, click an object, and then click one of the buttons in the Database window to work with the database.

7 Record navigation buttons

These controls move from record to record in the database. On a form and a table, they display the first, next, previous, or last record. They also display the current record number and the total number of records in the database.

8 Status bar

Shows status information about the current task.

9 Mode indicators

Show special conditions that are in effect, such as a pressed Caps Lock key.

10 Office Assistant

Provides online help and suggestions.

CREATING A DATABASE

30

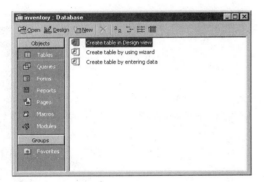

Figure 30.1 A blank database.

When Access starts, you can choose to open an existing database or create a new database. You can start with a blank database (**Figure 30.1**) and then create tables to hold data and forms with which to enter data, or you can use a database wizard that helps you set up a database designed to meet your needs (**Figure 30.2**). You can make this choice in the Access Startup dialog box.

Figure 30.2 A database started using a database wizard.

CREATING A DATABASE

Creating a New Database

When you start a new database, Access closes any other open databases.

To start a new database:

1. On the Database toolbar, click the New button (**Figure 30.3**).

or

Press Ctrl+N.

or

From the File menu, choose New (**Figure 30.4**).

2. In the New dialog box, click Database on the General tab (**Figure 30.5**).

or

Click a wizard on the Databases tab (**Figure 30.6**).

3. Click OK.

✔ Tips

■ When you start with a blank database, you can still use wizards to help you create tables and forms.

■ The two Access projects on the General tab of the New dialog box are databases that rely on a database server on the network, called SQL Server (pronounced "sequel server"). If you are in a corporate setting, you may have SQL Server and the authorization to use it to create an Access project.

New button

Figure 30.3 Click the New button.

Figure 30.4 Choose New from the File menu.

Figure 30.5 Click Database on the General tab.

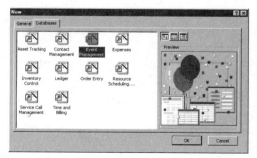

Figure 30.6 Choose a wizard on the Databases tab.

Figure 30.7 Choose a destination and type a name in the File New Database dialog box.

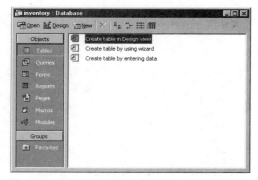

Figure 30.8 The new, blank database.

Saving a New Database

When you create a new database, Access prompts you to save it as your first step.

To save a new database:

1. In the File New Database dialog box, which is displayed automatically, select the folder for the new database (**Figure 30.7**).

2. Type a name for the new database in the File Name box.

3. Click Create.

   After the database has been saved, the Database window displays lists of the objects (tables, forms, reports, and other items) that constitute the database. It also provides buttons you can use to create a new object, open an object, or modify the design of an object. Because this is a new database, each list contains only the tools for creating an object (**Figure 30.8**).

✔ Tip

■ You don't need to save the data you add to a database file. Every change to the data in the database is saved on disk automatically. But you do need to save each of the objects (tables, queries, forms, and reports) that you create within the database.

SAVING A NEW DATABASE

Starting a Database Using a Wizard

When you start a database using an Access wizard, the type of database that you choose determines the selection of tables and forms that the database will contain.

To start a database using a wizard:

1. Create a new database.

2. On the Databases tab of the New dialog box, click one of the wizards.

3. Click OK.

4. Save the new database.

5. In the opening page of the Database Wizard, click Next (**Figure 30.9**).

6. In the next page, select fields for the various tables from the lists and click Next (**Figure 30.10**).

7. In the next page, select a style for screen displays and click Next (**Figure 30.11**).

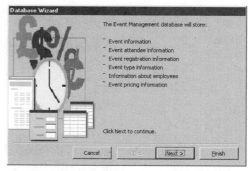

Figure 30.9 The first page of the AutoContent Wizard.

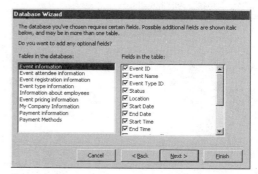

Figure 30.10 Select tables and fields for the new database.

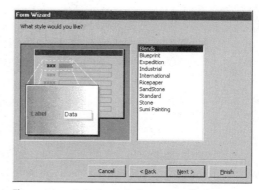

Figure 30.11 Select a style for screen displays.

STARTING USING A WIZARD

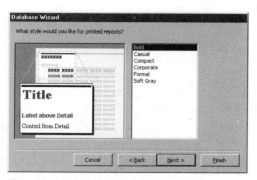

Figure 30.12 Select a style for printed reports.

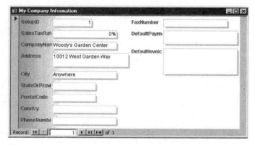

Figure 30.13 Give the database a title.

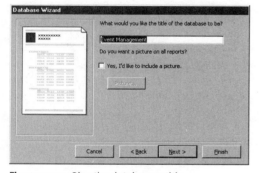

Figure 30.14 Type in your company information.

8. In the next page, select a style for printed reports and click Next (**Figure 30.12**).

9. In the next page, enter a title for the new database and click Next (**Figure 30.13**).

You can add a picture here as well.

10. In the next page, fill in your company information and then click Next (**Figure 30.14**).

11. In the last page of the database wizard, click Finish.

Viewing the Database

If you created a new database using a database wizard, Access displays the Main Switchboard, which provides links to the forms you will use to enter data in the tables (**Figure 30.15**). The relationships between tables are established according to the type of database selected. The Database window is minimized.

To view the Database window:

1. Click the Restore button in the minimized window to restore it to full size (**Figure 30.16**).

2. Click the Tables tab to view the tables in the database (**Figure 30.17**).

To view table relationships:

◆ Click the Relationships button on the Access toolbar (**Figure 30.18**).

or

From the Tools menu, choose Relationships.

The Relationships window opens (**Figure 30.19**)

✔ Tips

■ To see a list of objects of a different type in the Database window, click one of the tabs to the left of the list, such as the Forms tab.

■ To delete an object in the database, select the object in the Database window and press the Del key or choose Delete from the Edit menu.

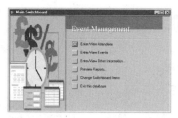

Figure 30.15 The Main Switchboard created by the wizard.

Restore button

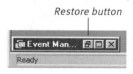

Figure 30.16 Click the Restore button to view the Database window.

Figure 30.17 The Tables tab of the new database.

Relationships button

Figure 30.18 Click the Relationships button on the Database toolbar.

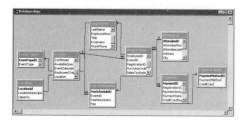

Figure 30.19 The Relationships window.

CREATING
A TABLE

One record   One field

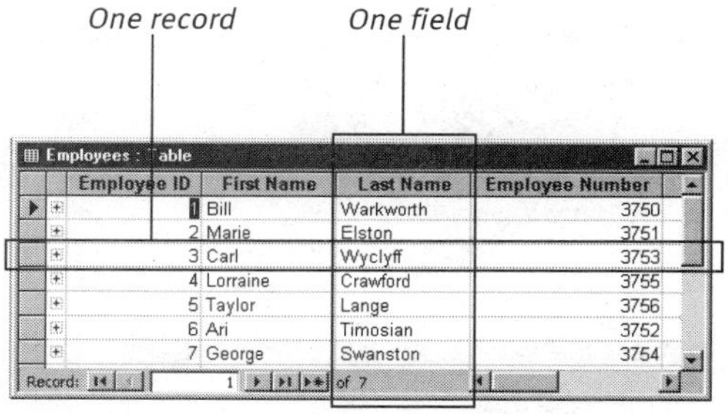

Figure 31.1 The rows of a table are records in the database and the columns are fields.

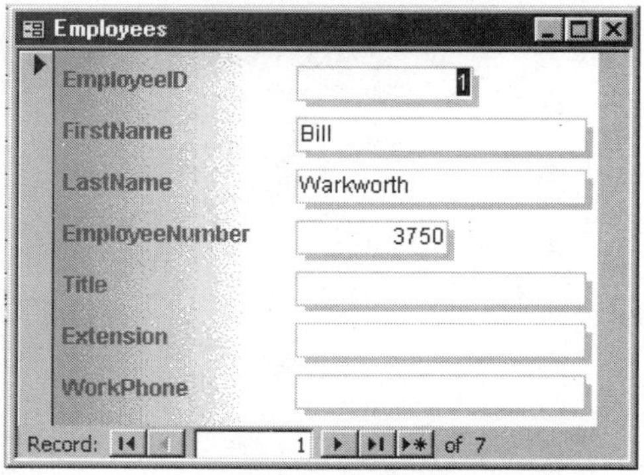

Figure 31.2 A columnar form for entering data.

A table is a complete collection of data displayed in rows and columns. Each row is one set of information, called a record. Each column in the row, called a field, is one part of the information in the record. (**Figure 31.1**).

You can display, edit, or print the data in a table, and you can also create a form to make it easier to add data to the table or update the existing data (**Figure 31.2**).

One field in each table must be a primary key, which holds a unique item that identifies each record—for example, a unique record number.

You can relate tables to other tables as long as they share a common field. For example, you can relate a table of apartments to a table of potential apartment renters if both tables contain a number of rooms field. In one table, the field for the number of rooms contains the number of rooms that are physically present. In the other table, the number of rooms field represents the number of rooms desired.

Entering Data in a Table

To fill a table with data, you enter the data record by record. To complete each record, you enter information into the fields of the record. You probably will want to use a form to enter data into a table, but you can also enter the data directly into the rows and columns of the table.

To enter data in a table:

1. Click the Tables tab in the Database window.

2. Double-click a table name (**Figure 31.3**).

   or

   Select the table to add to and click Open.

3. Click the New Record button on the Access toolbar to add a new record (**Figure 31.4**).

4. Enter data in the first field and then press Tab to move to the next field.

5. If the field shows an arrow button, you can click the button to display the list and then select an entry in the list (**Figure 31.5**).

6. Press Tab after the last field in the record to move to the start of a new record. The record you have completed is saved automatically (**Figure 31.6**).

✔ Tip

■ You do not need to do anything special to save each new record. When you move to the next record, the previous record is saved automatically.

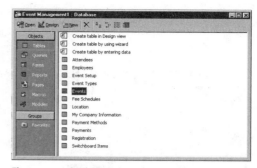

Figure 31.3 Double-click a table on the Tables tab.

New Record button

Figure 31.4 Click the New Record button to add a record.

Figure 31.5 Select from a drop-down list.

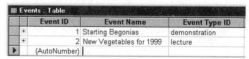

Figure 31.6 The new record is saved when you advance to the next record.

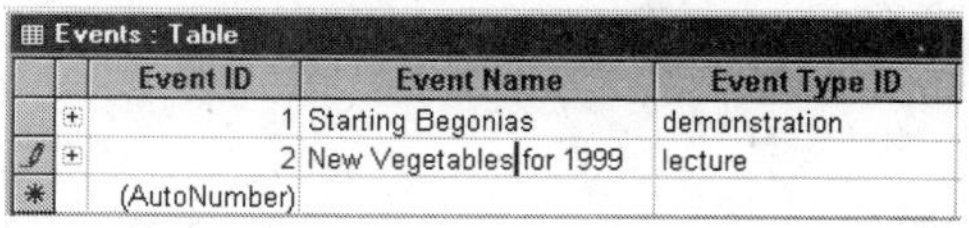

Events : Table		
Event ID	**Event Name**	**Event Type ID**
1	Starting Begonias	demonstration
2	New Vegetables for 1999	lecture
(AutoNumber)		

Figure 31.7 Click in the field you want to edit.

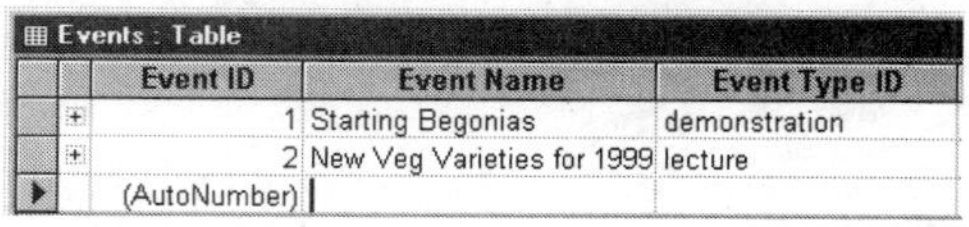

Events : Table		
Event ID	**Event Name**	**Event Type ID**
1	Starting Begonias	demonstration
2	New Veg Varieties for 1999	lecture
(AutoNumber)		

Figure 31.8 The change is saved when you click in another record.

Editing Data in a Table

You can easily change the information in any field of any record.

To edit data in a table:

1. Click any field in the table to position an insertion point in the field (**Figure 31.7**).

   or

   Double-click any word or number in a field to select it.

2. Edit the entry as you would edit text in Word.

3. Click a different record to save the changes (**Figure 31.8**).

✔ Tips

- To select an entire field, click anywhere in the field and press F2.

- To move to the previous field for corrections, press Shift+Tab.

- To replace the entry in a field with the entry in the same field of the previous record, click in the field and press Ctrl+' (Ctrl+apostrophe).

- While you edit a field, the pencil symbol appears to the left of the record to indicate that your changes have not yet been saved.

EDITING DATA IN A TABLE

Printing a Table

To print out the information in a database, you will usually want to create a report, which can be formatted neatly and then printed. But you can also print a table to obtain a quick record of its contents.

To print a table:

1. From the File menu, choose Print (**Figure 31.9**).

   or

   Press Ctrl+P.

   or

   Click the Print button on the Access toolbar.

2. In the Print dialog box, click All to print the entire table.

   or

   Click Pages and specify the page range.

   or

   If you have highlighted records in the table, choose Selected Records (**Figure 31.10**).

3. Click OK.

✔ Tip

- Choose Print Preview from the File menu to preview the print settings; choose Page Setup from the File menu to change settings.

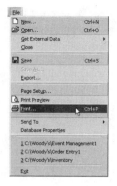

Figure 31.9 Choose Print from the File menu.

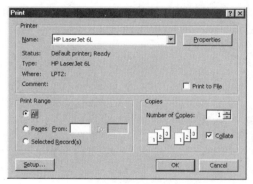

Figure 31.10 Select print options in the Print dialog box.

PRINTING A TABLE

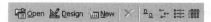

Figure 31.11 Click the New button to create a new table.

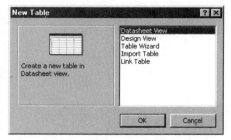

Figure 31.12 Select an option and click OK.

Figure 31.13 Double-click a field name to rename the field.

Figure 31.14 Select a data type for the field.

Figure 31.15 The Create Table options on the Tables tab.

Creating a Table

You can start a new table in Datasheet view or in Design view. You can also start a table using the Table Wizard.

To create a table in Datasheet view:

1. In the Database window, click the Tables tab.

2. Click the New button on the Database window toolbar (**Figure 31.11**).

3. In the New Table dialog box, select Datasheet View (**Figure 31.12**).

4. Click OK.

5. In the new table window, double-click a field name and rename it (**Figure 31.13**).

To create a table in Design view:

1. In the Database window, click the Tables tab.

2. Click the New button on the Database window toolbar.

3. In the New Table dialog box, select Design View.

4. Click OK.

5. Enter the field names and select a data type for each (**Figure 31.14**).

6. Add a description if you want.

✔ Tip

■ You can also create a table by double-clicking one of the three Create Table options at the top of the list of tables (**Figure 31.15**).

Saving a Table

After you create a table, you must save it.

Figure 31.16 Name the table in the Save As dialog box.

To save a table:

1. From the File menu, choose Save.

   or

   Press Ctrl+S.

   or

   Click the Save button on the Access toolbar.

2. In the Save As dialog box, enter a name for the new table (**Figure 31.16**).

3. Click OK.

   The new table is added to the list of tables in the Database window.

✔ Tip

■ To save a table as a form that you can use for data entry or a report that you can print, or to save it with a new name, select the table on the Tables tab in the Database window and then choose Save As from the File menu.

SAVING A TABLE

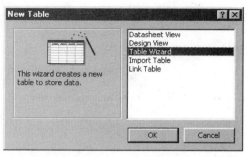

Figure 31.17 Select Table Wizard in the New Table dialog box.

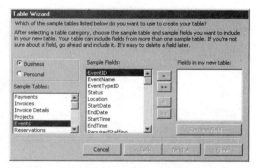

Figure 31.18 Add fields to the new table.

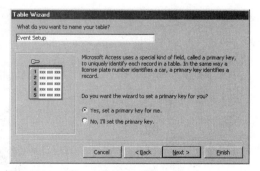

Figure 31.19 Name the new table and select a primary key.

Creating a Table Using the Table Wizard

The Table Wizard helps you start a new table and set up its fields. The wizard provides dozens of sample fields that you might find in both business and personal databases.

To create a table using the Table Wizard:

1. In the Database window, click the Tables tab.

2. Click the New button on the Database window toolbar.

3. In the New Table dialog box, choose Table Wizard from the list (**Figure 31.17**).

4. Click OK.

5. In the first page of the Table Wizard, click Business or Personal to choose a database type.

6. Click a table in the list of Sample Tables, and then double-click a field in the list of sample fields to add the field to your table (**Figure 31.18**).

7. Continue adding other fields from the same sample table or other sample tables until you have all the fields you need, and then click Next.

8. In the next page of the Table Wizard, enter a name for the table and let Microsoft Access set the primary key field or choose to do it yourself, and then click Next (**Figure 31.19**).

   If you choose to set the primary key, you make the decision in a separate Table Wizard step, selecting a field from a drop-down list and then specifying how the numbers are added.

(continued)

USING THE TABLE WIZARD

9. In the next page of the Table Wizard, choose one of the existing tables to relate to the new table, and then click Next (**Figure 31.20**).

If you are establishing a new relationship or changing an existing one, in the Relationships dialog box, choose one of the three options to define a relationship between the two tables, and then click OK (**Figure 31.21**).

10. In the final page of the Table Wizard, choose to modify the design, start entering data, or enter data using a form that the wizard creates, and then click Finish (**Figure 31.22**).

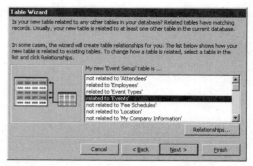

Figure 31.20 Select relationships between the new table and other tables.

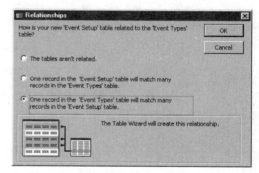

Figure 31.21 Define or change a relationship.

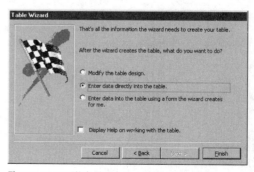

Figure 31.22 Click Finish to set up the table.

Figure 31.23 Double-click a table on the Tables tab.

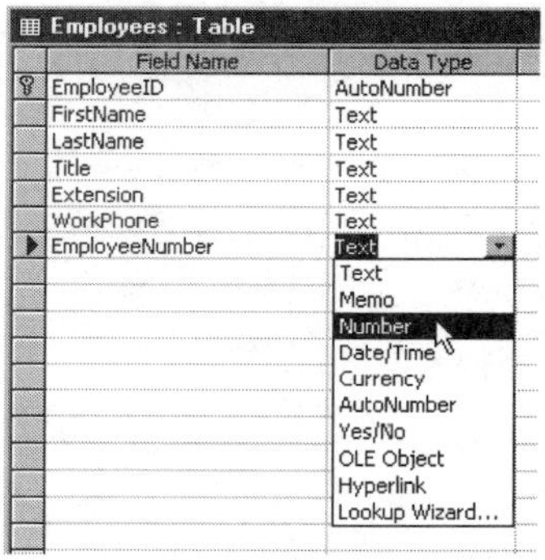

Figure 31.24 Select a data type from the drop-down list.

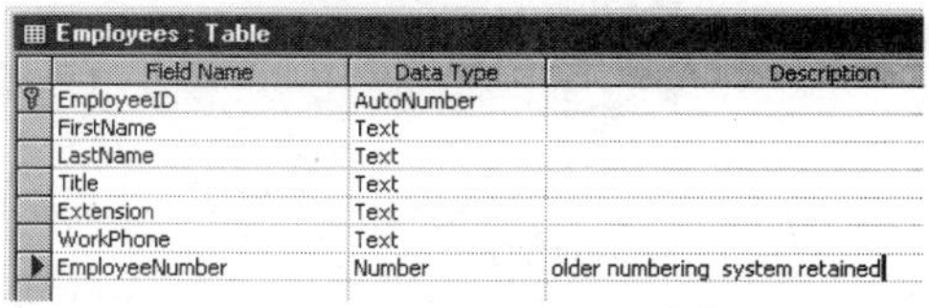

Figure 31.25 Add a description for the field.

Design View button

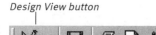

Figure 31.26 Click the Design View button on the Access toolbar.

Adding a Field to the Table in Design View

However the table was created, you can add a field in Design view.

To add a field to a table:

1. On the Tables tab of the Database window, choose a table and click the Design button (**Figure 31.23**).

2. In the Table window, click a blank row in the Field Name column.

3. Enter a field name and press the Tab key to move to the next column.

4. Choose a data type from the drop-down list in the Data Type column (**Figure 31.24**).

5. Press the Tab key to move to the next column and enter a description for the field in the Description column (**Figure 31.25**).

6. Save the changes to the table design.

✔ Tips

■ If a table is already open for data entry and editing, you can click the Design View button on the Access toolbar to switch to Design view (**Figure 31.26**).

■ To move a field up or down, click once in the field's far left column and then click again and drag the field.

■ To insert a field between two other fields in the list, click the name of the field that should be just below the new field and then click the Insert Row button. Click a row and then click the Delete Row button to delete a field.

Setting the Field Size and Format

If the field data type is text, you can set the number of characters allowed and specify formatting rules. If the field data type is a numeric value, you can choose the range of numbers to be accepted and the number of decimal places to be stored.

To set the field size and format:

1. On the Tables tab of the Database window, choose a table and click the Design button.

2. In the Table window, click the name of the field to format.

3. Click the Field Size text box and then enter a number if the field is text, or choose from the drop-down list of options if the field is numeric or some other data type. See **Table 31.1** for the Number Field Size options.

4. Click the Format box and then, if the field is a text field, enter one of the symbols shown in **Table 31.2**. (**Figure 31.27**).

5. Save the changes to the table design.

✔ Tips

- For a text field, you can enter any field size between 0 and 255. The default is 50.

- When you are setting the field size for a Number field, choose the option that requires the fewest number of bytes but that is still suitable for your data.

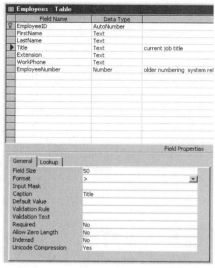

Figure 31.27 Set the field size and format for a field.

Table 31.1

Number Field Size Options

NUMBER TYPE	FIELD SIZE OPTION
Integer	Accepts numbers from −32,768 to 32,767. Occupies 2 bytes.
Long	Accepts numbers from −2,147,483,648 to 2,147,483,647. Occupies 4 bytes.
Single	Stores numbers with 6 digits of precision, from −3.402823E38 to 3.402823E38. Occupies 4 bytes.
Double	Stores numbers with 10 digits of precision, from −1.79769313486232E308 to 1.79769313486232E308. Occupies 8 bytes.

Table 31.2

Text Field Codes

SYMBOL	RESULT
@	A text character is required in the field (either a character or a space).
&	A text character is not required.
‹	All characters entered will become lowercase.
›	All characters entered will become uppercase.

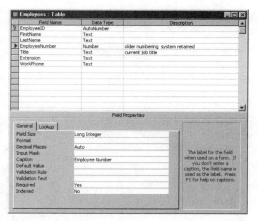

Figure 31.28 Add a caption and a default value for a field.

Entering a Caption and Default Value for a Field

A caption appears at the top of a field in the table and next to the field on a form. For example, next to the field named "fname" in which you enter someone's first name, you can create a caption that reads "First Name." Entering a default entry allows you to set a value for a field that the user can still override. For example, you can set the default value for a Yes/No field to Yes.

To enter a caption and default value:

1. On the Tables tab of the Database window, choose a table and click the Design button.

   or

   If the table is already open, click the Design View button.

2. In the Table window, click the name of the field to format (**Figure 31.28**).

3. Click the Caption box and enter the text that will be used to label the field on the form.

4. Click the Default Value box and then enter the default value.

5. Save the changes to the table design.

✔ Tip

■ If you don't set a caption name, the field name is used.

Requiring and Indexing a Field

A required field must have an entry before the record can be saved. An indexed field is specially prepared so that its information can be searched through more quickly when you later search the database.

To set a field as required and indexed:

1. On the Tables tab of the Database window, choose a table and click Design.

   or

   If the table is already open, click the Design View button.

2. In the Table window, click the name of the field to format.

3. Click the Required box and choose Yes or No from the drop-down list.

4. Click the Indexed box and choose an option from the drop-down list. See **Table 31.3** for the Index options (**Figure 31.29**).

5. To save changes to the table design, click the Save button on the Access toolbar, or press Ctrl+S, or choose Save from the File menu.

✔ Tips

- Primary key fields are automatically indexed.

- To view a list of fields that are indexed, click the Indexes button on the Access toolbar while the table is shown in Design view (**Figures 31.30** and **31.31**).

Figure 31.29 Make the field a required and indexed field.

Figure 31.30 Click the Indexes button on the Access toolbar.

Figure 31.31 The indexed fields in the table.

Table 31.3

Index Options	
OPTION	**RESULT**
No	This field is not indexed.
Yes (Duplicates OK)	This field is indexed and duplicates are allowed.
Yes (No Duplicates)	This field is indexed and each entry is unique.

CREATING
A FORM

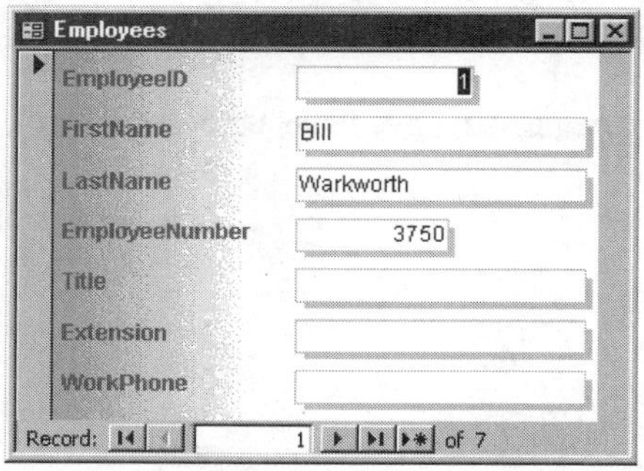

Figure 32.1 A columnar form.

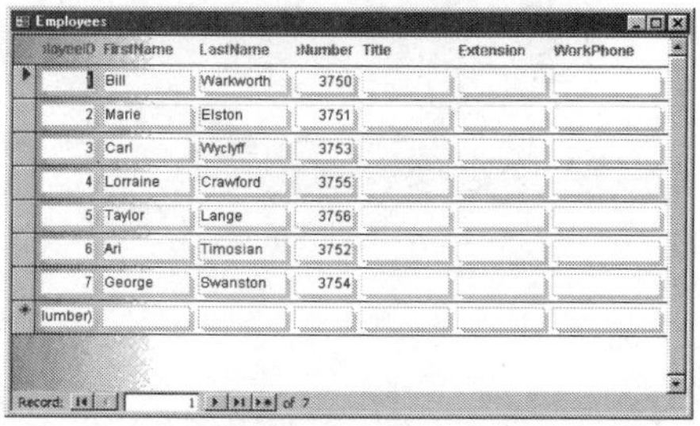

Figure 32.2 A tabular form.

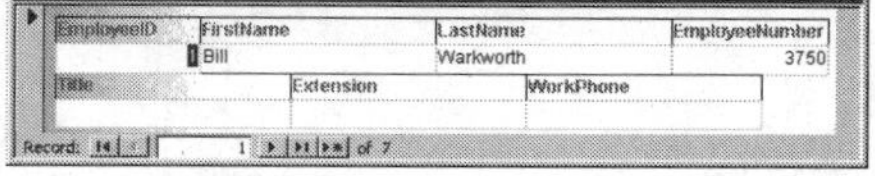

Figure 32.3 A justified form.

Forms enable you and others to enter and edit data in a table in a convenient way, and they can also provide helpful instructions.

When you create a form (**Figures 32.1–32.3**), you add objects called controls, which can be labels, text boxes, blanks, empty fields, check boxes, buttons, radio buttons, and several other types of graphical objects. The controls on a form are displayed when you are entering or editing a table using the form, and they are also printed when you print the form.

When you use the Form Wizard to create a form, it places controls on the form automatically. You can modify the controls or add new controls in Design view.

Entering Data in a Form

A form provides blank fields and other controls that allow you to add data to a table easily.

To enter data in a form:

1. Click the Forms tab in the Database window.

2. Double-click the form that you want to add data to (**Figure 32.4**).

   or

   Select a form and click Open on the Database window toolbar.

   The form, if it is columnar or justified, displays the first record (**Figure 32.5**). If the form is tabular in format, it shows all records.

3. Click the New Record button on the Access toolbar (**Figure 32.6**).

4. Enter data in the first blank field on the form and press Tab.

5. Continue entering data and pressing Tab to move to the next field (**Figure 32.7**).

6. Press Tab after the last field to move to the start of a new record.

✔ Tips

■ To move to the previous field on a form, press Shift+Tab.

■ To jump to a field, click the field.

■ You do not need to save each record. The completed record is saved automatically when you move to the next record.

Figure 32.4 Double-click the name of the form to which you want to add data.

Figure 32.5 The first record of a form is shown in columnar format.

New Record button

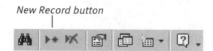

Figure 32.6 Click the New Record button to add a record.

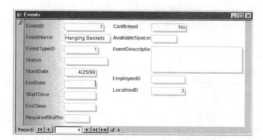

Figure 32.7 Press Tab to move to the next field.

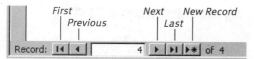

Figure 32.8 The navigation buttons.

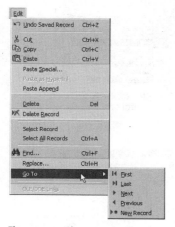

Figure 32.9 Choose an action from the Go To submenu.

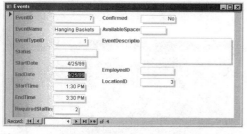

Figure 32.10 Select the text in a field to edit it.

Viewing and Editing Records Using a Form

You can use a form to view each record in a table and edit its fields.

To view and edit records with a form:

1. Open the form by double-clicking the form name on the Forms tab of the Database window.

2. Use the Next or Previous button to move forward or backward record by record through the database (**Figure 32.8**).

   or

   Press the Page Down or Page Up key.

   or

   From the Edit menu, choose Go To, and then choose Next or Previous from the submenu (**Figure 32.9**).

3. Edit the entry as you would edit text in Word (**Figure 32.10**).

4. Click a different record to save your changes.

✔ Tips

- To jump to the first or last record, click the First or Last button, press Ctrl+Up arrow or Ctrl+Down arrow, or choose First or Last from the Go To menu.

- To jump to a specific record number, select the current record number, type a replacement number, and press Enter.

VIEWING /EDITING RECORDS

Creating and Saving a Form

You can create a form for every table in your database, and you can create forms that allow you to add data to more than one table or query at a time. Each time you make changes to the design of a table, you can create a new form to reflect the changes or modify the form design.

To create a form:

1. Click the Forms tab in the Database window.

2. Click the New button on the Database window toolbar.

3. In the New Form dialog box, choose a method from the list.

4. If you choose one of the AutoForms, select a table or query from the pull-down list (**Figure 32.11**).

5. Click OK.

   The AutoForms Wizard creates a form in the default style, using all the fields defined in the table (**Figure 32.12**).

✔ Tips

■ The Design View option in the New Form dialog box displays a blank form in Design view, with the Forms toolbox available for adding controls (**Figure 32.13**).

■ The last two items in the New Form dialog box, Chart Wizard and Pivot Table Wizard, give you graphical representations of the data rather than a means for entering data.

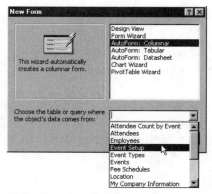

Figure 32.11 Select a table or query to create a form using the AutoForm Wizard.

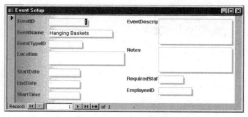

Figure 32.12 A columnar form with default style and fields.

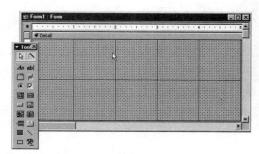

Figure 32.13 A blank form in Design view.

Figure 32.14 Name the form in the Save As dialog box.

To save the form:

1. To save the form, click the Save button on the Access toolbar.

or

Press Ctrl+S.

or

Choose Save from the File menu.

2. In the Save As dialog box, name the new form (**Figure 32.14**).

3. Click OK.

✔ Tip

■ To save a form as a report or a form with another name, select the form on the Forms tab and then choose Save As from the File menu.

CREATING/SAVING A FORM

Creating a Form Using the Form Wizard

The Form Wizard makes it easy for you to select controls for your form from more than one table or query.

To create a form with the Form Wizard:

1. Click the Forms tab in the Database window.

2. Click the New button on the Database window toolbar.

3. In the New Form dialog box, choose Form Wizard from the drop-down list.

4. Click OK.

5. In the first page of the Form Wizard, select a table or query and then double-click each field you want to include (**Figure 32.15**).

   or

   Click the >> button to include all the fields in the table.

6. Select another table or query and add further fields, if needed.

7. When you have finished adding fields, click Next.

8. In the next page of the Form Wizard, choose a layout for the form and then click Next (**Figure 32.16**).

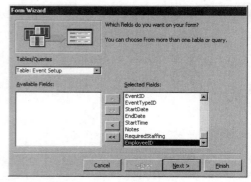

Figure 32.15 Select a table and then select fields in the table.

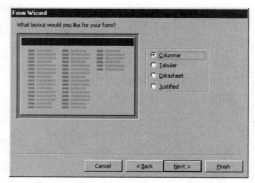

Figure 32.16 Choose a layout for the new form.

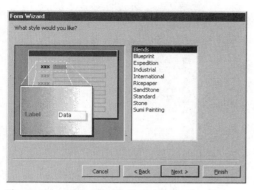

Figure 32.17 Choose a display style for the new form.

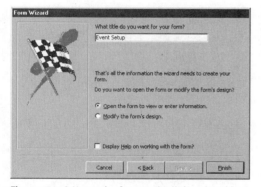

Figure 32.18 Name the form and tell the wizard how you want the form to be opened.

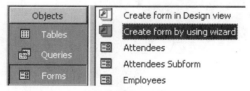

Figure 32.19 The Create Form selections on the Forms tab.

9. In the next page of the Form Wizard, choose a form style and then click Next.

You can click each button and inspect the sample in the dialog box (**Figure 32.17**).

10. In the last page of the Form Wizard, enter a name for the form and then choose whether to open the form showing the table's data or open the form in Design view so that you can modify the form's design (**Figure 32.18**).

11. Click Finish.

The form is automatically saved.

✔ Tip

■ You can also start the Form Wizard by double-clicking Create Form by using wizard at the top of the Forms list (**Figure 32.19**).

USING THE FORM WIZARD

Opening the Form in Design View

To modify a form, you must open it in Design view or, if it is already open, switch to Design view.

To open the form in Design view:

◆ On the Forms tab of the Database window, choose a form and click the Design button (**Figure 32.20**).

or

If you are currently using the form to enter or edit data, click the View button on the Access toolbar and choose Design View from the drop-down menu (**Figure 32.21**).

or

From the View menu, choose Design View (**Figure 32.22**).

Figure 32.20 With the form selected, click the Design button.

Figure 32.21 Click the View button and choose Design View if the form is already open.

Figure 32.22 Choose Design View from the View menu.

Figure 32.23 The form in Design view.

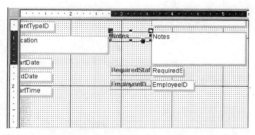

Figure 32.24 Drag the selected control to reposition it in Design view.

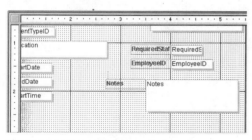

Figure 32.25 Repositioned control.

Moving a Control

You can move a control on a form and you can move the control and its label separately.

To move a control and its label:

1. With the form open in Design view (**Figure 32.23**), position the mouse pointer anywhere on the control.

2. Hold down the mouse button and drag the control to its new position (**Figure 32.24**).

3. Release the mouse button.

   The control is repositioned (**Figure 32.25**).

4. Click the Save button, or press Ctrl+S, or choose Save from the File menu to save changes to the form design.

Sizing a Control and Moving Labels Independently

You can change the size of a control on a form. You can also move labels and fields independently.

To size a control:

1. Drag one of the size handles on the control (**Figures 32.26** and **32.27**).

2. Save the changes to the form design.

✔ Tips

■ Hold down the Shift key as you select several controls or drag a selection box around the controls to select them. You can then move the selected controls simultaneously, as a group.

■ The length of a text field remains the same even if you change the size of the text box for the field.

To move labels and fields independently:

1. Drag the move handle for a label to move the label independently of the field (**Figure 32.28**).

2. Save the changes to the form design.

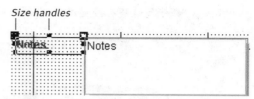

Size handles

Figure 32.26 Size handles for label.

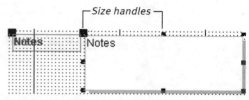

Size handles

Figure 32.27 Size handles for field.

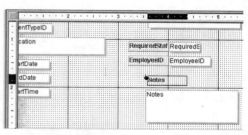

Figure 32.28 Label and field moved independently.

SIZING AND MOVING

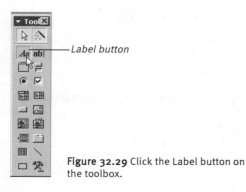

Figure 32.29 Click the Label button on the toolbox.

—Label button

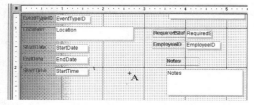

Figure 32.30 Click the form and begin typing the label.

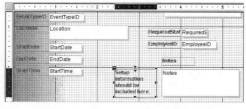

Figure 32.31 Size and move the label by dragging its handles.

Adding Labels

Each field on a new form has a label, but you can add labels to the form to provide special instructions to the person using the form. For example, you can enter a label for a group of fields that reads "Complete only if you are a nonresident."

To add a label:

1. With the form open in Design view, make sure the toolbox is visible. If it's not visible, click the Toolbox button on the Access toolbar.

2. Click the Label button on the toolbox (**Figure 32.29**).

3. Click the form at the location for the new label (**Figure 32.30**).

4. Type the label text.

5. Use the move and size handles to position the label (**Figure 32.31**).

6. Save the changes to the form design.

Formatting Labels

You can give a label any appearance you want by changing its formatting.

Figure 32.32 Formatting buttons on the Formatting toolbar.

To format a label:

1. With the form open in Design view, select the label.

2. Click the text formatting buttons on the Formatting toolbar (**Figure 32.32**).

3. Save the changes to the form design.

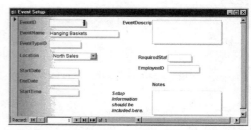

Figure 32.33 The formatted label in Form view.

✔ Tips

■ To view the label on the completed form, switch to Form view by clicking the Form View button on the Access toolbar (**Figure 32.33**).

■ To edit a label, click the label and then click again to position an insertion point in the label. Then edit the label text.

■ To add a control, drag it from the field list and place it on the form.

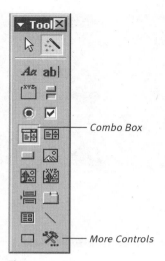

Combo Box

More Controls

Figure 32.34
Click the Combo Box
button on the toolbox.

Figure 32.35 Choose how you want the combo box
to get its values.

Adding a Combo Box

A combo box is an especially useful control
for a form. It provides a drop-down list of
alternatives or allows users to type any other
entry. The Combo Box Wizard guides you
through the steps for adding a combo box.

Combo boxes are only one type of control
in the toolbox. Other controls also provide
wizards that help you create the control.

To add a combo box:

1. With the form open in Design view, click
the Combo Box button in the toolbox
(**Figure 32.34**).

2. With the mouse pointer, drag out a
rectangle on the form that will contain
the combo box.

3. In the first page of the Combo Box
Wizard, select the I want the combo box
to look up the values in a table or query
option and click Next if you'd like the user
to select a record from a particular table
(**Figure 32.35**). The wizard then guides
you through the steps required to select
the table and set the size of the column(s).

   or

   Select the I will type in the values that I
   want option and click Next to enter a list
   of alternatives. Then, in the next page,
   select the number of columns of options
   to enter and type the alternative options
   in the columns, pressing Enter after each.
   Then click Next.

   or

   Select the Find a record on my form based
   on the value I selected in my combo box
   option and click Next. The wizard takes
   you through the necessary steps.

   (continued)

ADDING A COMBO BOX

4. In the next page of the wizard, choose a field name from the drop-down list next to the Store that value in this field label and click Next (**Figure 32.36**).

5. In the last page of the wizard, supply a label for the combo box and click Finish.

The combo box appears (**Figure 32.37**).

6. Save the changes to the form design.

✔ Tip

■ If the Combo Box Wizard does not appear when you add a combo box, click the Controls Wizards button on the toolbox and then click the Combo Box button in the toolbox.

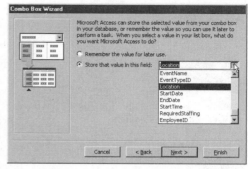

Figure 32.36 Choose whether the value is stored or remembered.

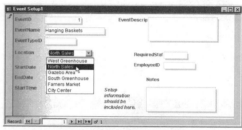

Figure 32.37 The combo box in Form view.

Properties button

Figure 32.38 Click the Properties button on the Form Design toolbar.

Figure 32.39 Choose Properties from the View menu.

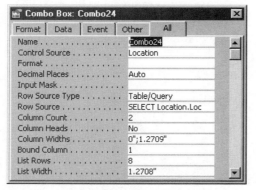

Figure 32.40 The Combo Box dialog box displays properties for the selected element.

Setting the Form and Control Properties

The properties of a form, a section, or a control are the settings that govern its appearance and behavior. In the Properties window, you can change these settings.

To set the form and control properties:

1. With the form open in Design view, click the Properties button on the Access toolbar (**Figure 32.38**).

   or

   Choose Properties from the View menu (**Figure 32.39**).

2. Click the section, control, or label whose properties you want to inspect.

3. Make changes to any of the properties (**Figure 32.40**).

4. Close the Properties window.

5. Save the changes to the form design.

✔ Tips

- You can also double-click any control to change its properties.

- When you open the Properties window, you may need to drag it to the side to see the fields on the form.

- If a control is "unbound," you must bind it to a field in the table. Enter the name of the field in the Control Source box in the Properties window.

FORM/CONTROL PROPERTIES

339

WORKING WITH RECORDS

Sort buttons   Filter buttons   Find button

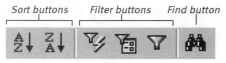

Figure 33.1 The Sort, Filter, and Find buttons.

Events : Table

		Event ID	Event Name	Event Type ID	Start Date
▶	+	1	Starting Begonias	demonstration	2/22/99
	+	3	New Veg Varieties for 1999	lecture	4/12/99
	+	6	Hanging Baskets	demonstration	5/22/99
	+	7	Hanging Baskets	demonstration	6/5/99
	+	8	Choosing Rhododendrons	lecture	5/10/99
	+	9	Benefits of Double Digging	lecture	6/14/99
	+	10	Landscaping on Slopes	workshop	6/19/99
	+	11	Landscaping on Slopes	workshop	6/18/99

Figure 33.2 A table in the database.

Events : Table

		Event ID	Event Name	Event Type ID	Start Date
▶	+	1	Starting Begonias	demonstration	2/22/99
	+	3	New Veg Varieties for 1999	lecture	4/12/99
	+	8	Choosing Rhododendrons	lecture	5/10/99
	+	6	Hanging Baskets	demonstration	5/22/99
	+	7	Hanging Baskets	demonstration	6/5/99
	+	9	Benefits of Double Digging	lecture	6/14/99
	+	11	Landscaping on Slopes	workshop	6/18/99
	+	10	Landscaping on Slopes	workshop	6/19/99

Figure 33.3 The table sorted by Start Date.

Events : Table

		Event ID	Event Name	Event Type ID
▶	+	1	Starting Begonias	demonstration
	+	6	Hanging Baskets	demonstration
	+	7	Hanging Baskets	demonstration

Figure 33.4 The table filtered to show only demonstration events.

As you'll see in the next chapter, you can locate information and extract it from the database using queries, but you can also sort records in a table, filter records to show only those that match certain criteria, and find items in a database using simple toolbar buttons (**Figure 33.1**).

Figure 33.2 shows a database table. This table can be sorted by the entries in any column (**Figure 33.3**), and it can be filtered to show only entries that have certain entries in a field (**Figure 33.4**).

Finding a Match in a Form or a Table

You can use the Find command to search a form or a table.

To find a match:

1. Open the form or table that includes the field containing the data you want to find.

2. Click the field (**Figure 33.5**).

3. Click the Find button on the Access toolbar (**Figure 33.6**).

   or

   Press Ctrl+F.

   or

   From the Edit menu, choose Find.

4. In the Find and Replace dialog box, type the entry you're looking for in the Find What text box (**Figure 33.7**).

5. Choose an option from the Look In pull-down list to look only in the current field or in the whole table.

6. Choose an option from the Match pull-down list to further define the search (whole field, any part of field, or start of field).

7. Click More to choose other options (search direction and matching case).

8. Click the Find Next button to find the first match (**Figure 33.8**).

9. Click the Find Next button again if the first match is not the one you're looking for.

10. Click Cancel to close the Find dialog box.

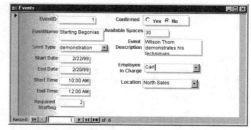

Figure 33.5 Click a field.

Find button

Figure 33.6 Click the Find button.

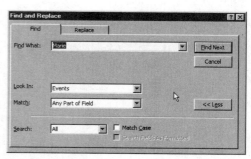

Figure 33.7 Type a word in the Find and Replace dialog box.

Figure 33.8 The record shows the first instance of the word.

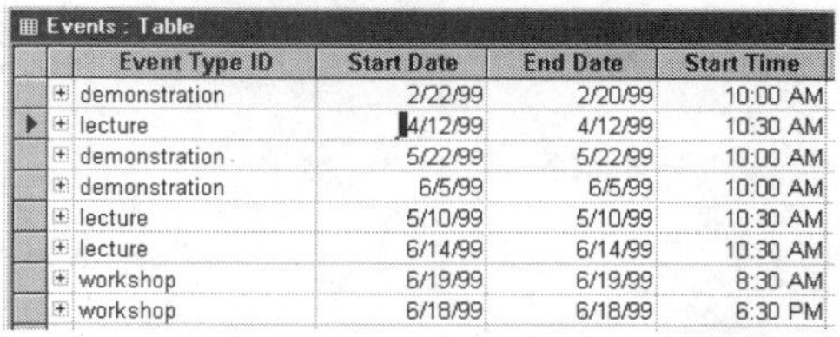

Figure 33.9 Click in a field to select the Sort field.

Sort Ascending

Sort Descending

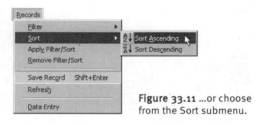

Figure 33.10 Click a Sort button to sort the table or form...

Figure 33.11 ...or choose from the Sort submenu.

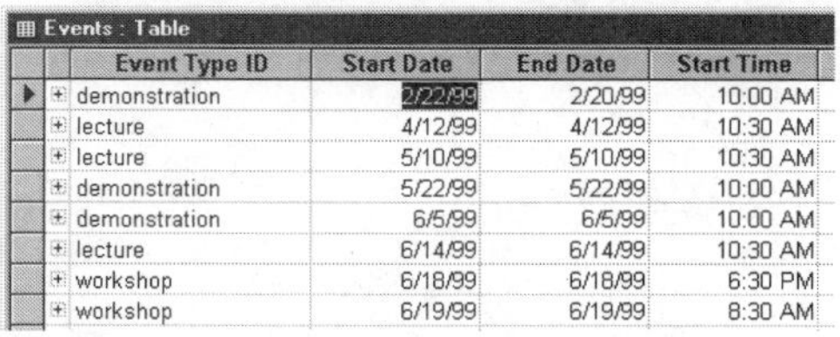

Figure 33.12 The table sorted by Start Date.

Sorting Records

You can sort records in a form or a table by any field, and you can specify whether the order of the records should be ascending (a–z, 1–9) or descending (z–a, 9–1).

To sort records:

1. In a form or in a table, click the field (in any record) on which you want to sort the data (**Figure 33.9**).

2. Click the Sort Ascending or Sort Descending button on the Access toolbar (**Figure 33.10**).

   or

   From the Records menu, choose Sort, and then choose Sort Ascending or Sort Descending from the Sort submenu (**Figure 33.11**).

   The table is sorted (**Figure 33.12**).

✔ Tip

- You can sort a subset of data after you've used a filter to display only the subset (all events of a certain type, for example).

SORTING RECORDS

Creating a Filter

A filter displays only certain records from a table according to the criteria you set. For example, you can use a filter to display only employees who live in Chicago.

To create a filter by selecting the criterion:

1. While viewing a form or table, click a field to use its contents as the criterion for the filter (**Figure 33.13**).

2. Click the Filter By Selection button on the Access toolbar (**Figure 33.14**).

   or

   From the Records menu, choose Filter, and then choose Filter By Selection from the Filter submenu (**Figure 33.15**).

   The records are filtered and the Apply Filter button is replaced by the Remove Filter button.

✔ Tips

■ After you apply a filter, the Apply Filter button becomes the Remove Filter button. Click it to view all the records again.

■ If you want the filter to select all records that do not contain the entry in the field you've clicked, choose Filter Excluding Selection from the Filter submenu.

Figure 33.13 Select a value in a field to filter by that value.

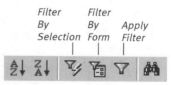

Figure 33.14 Click the Filter By Selection button...

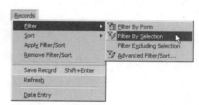

Figure 33.15 ...or choose Filter By Selection from the Filter submenu.

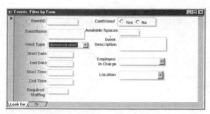

Figure 33.16 Select a value on the Look For tab for a form.

Figure 33.17 Select a value on the Look For tab for a table.

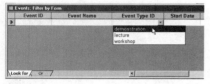

Figure 33.18 Select a value on the first Or tab for a form.

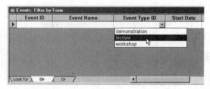

Figure 33.19 Select a value on the first Or tab for a table.

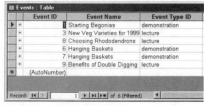

Figure 33.20 The records are filtered to include only two event types.

To create a filter using a form:

1. While viewing a form or table, click the Filter By Form button on the Access toolbar.

   or

   From the Records menu, choose Filter, and then choose Filter By Form from the Filter submenu.

2. In the Filter window, type the criterion you want to use to filter the data in the appropriate field or choose an item from the drop-down list in the field (**Figures 33.16** and **33.17**).

3. Continue to type entries or select from lists in other fields, if necessary.

4. Click the Or tab at the bottom of the window to add another item in one of the fields (**Figures 33.18** and **33.19**).

5. Click the Apply Filter button to close the Filter window and apply the filter (**Figure 33.20**).

✔ Tips

- To once again view all records, click the Remove Filter button.

- If you want to sort the data that is displayed, click in the field that contains the data you want to sort the list on, and then click the Sort Ascending or Sort Descending buttons on the toolbar.

- After you view the filtered data, you can click one of the Filter buttons again, modify or refine the filter, and then click the Apply Filter button to further filter the records.

- You can save a filter as a query so that you can use it again later. Choose Save As Query from the File menu and name the query.

CREATING A FILTER

Adding an Expression to a Filter

If you simply type text or a number in a cell and click Apply Filter, Access attempts to match the entry you've typed. You can also use an expression in a criterion to have Access match a range of values. You can use "or," "not," or "in" as part of the expression to further refine the acceptable values. **Table 33.1** displays examples of criteria you can use.

To create a filter that uses an expression:

1. While viewing a form or table, choose Filter from the Records menu, and then choose Advanced Filter/Sort from the Filter submenu.

2. Use expressions listed in **Table 33.1** to add criteria to the filter (**Figure 33.21**).

3. Click the Apply Filter button to close the Filter window and apply the filter. (**Figure 33.22**)

✔ Tips

- To once again view all the records, click the Remove Filter button.

- You can type criteria in the Criteria cells of two fields to have the filter match only those records that match both criteria.

- After you enter the criteria, Access adds whatever special punctuation it needs. For example, *In(TX, FL)* becomes *In("TX","FL")*.

- To get help while adding criteria, you can right-click in the criteria cell and choose Build from the shortcut menu to open the Expression Builder dialog box.

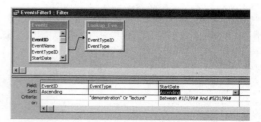

Figure 33.21 Apply a filter using an expression.

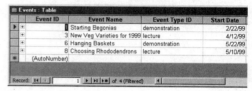

Figure 33.22 The records further filtered to include only events between two dates.

Table 33.1

Useful Criteria	
CRITERION	**RESULT**
<100	Numbers less than 100
>200	Numbers greater than 200
<=75	Numbers less than or equal to 75
Between 1/1/99 and 2/28/99	Any date in January or February of 1999
2/*/99	Any date in February 1999
France or Spain	Either "France" or "Spain"
Not 20	All records that do not have a value of 20 in the field
In(TX,FL)	Only those records that have TX or FL in the field

USING
QUERIES

Start Date	Event Name	Event Type	SetupRequirements
4/12/99	New Veg Varieties for 199	lecture	chairs in rows, coffee at bac
5/10/99	Choosing Rhododendrons	lecture	chairs in rows, coffee at bac
6/14/99	Benefits of Double Digging	lecture	chairs in rows, coffee at bac
2/22/99	Starting Begonias	demonstration	table at front, chairs in rows
5/22/99	Hanging Baskets	demonstration	table at front, chairs in rows
6/5/99	Hanging Baskets	demonstration	table at front, chairs in rows
6/19/99	Landscaping on Slopes	workshop	worktables, chairs, coffee at
6/18/99	Landscaping on Slopes	workshop	worktables, chairs, coffee at

Figure 34.1 A query result in a datasheet.

Figure 34.2 A list of queries on the Queries tab.

When you run a query, you are asking the database for specific information that you'd like to view and/or edit. The query is the question. Access responds by showing the data you've asked for in a datasheet (**Figure 34.1**), where you can view, sort, or filter the data. If you edit the data in the datasheet, the table on which it is based will also be modified. Each query you create can be saved so that you can reuse the query.

Although the most common type of query is a select query, which displays the results of the query in a datasheet, you can also use action queries, which enable you to make changes to the records of many tables at once, and crosstab queries, which display different views of summarized values.

Access provides query wizards that help you through the design of more complex queries, but simple queries are easy to create without the help of a wizard. All available queries are shown on the Queries tab (**Figure 34.2**).

Creating and Running a Select Query

You can design a simple select query or use the query wizard to help you design a query and then add criteria.

To start a query:

1. In the Database window, click the Queries tab.

2. Click the New button on the Database window toolbar (**Figure 34.3**).

3. In the New Query dialog box, select Design View (**Figure 34.4**).

4. Click OK.

5. In the Show Table dialog box that opens, select the tables you want included in your query, clicking Add after each (**Figure 34.5**).

6. After you have added all the tables you want included, click Close.

7. Select a field from the pull-down menu in a Field cell in the query design grid, the lower half of the Select Query dialog box (**Figure 34.6**).

   or

   Double-click a field in the field box in the upper portion of the Select Query dialog box to add it to the query design grid.

   or

   Click and drag a field in the table box to a column in the query design grid.

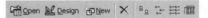

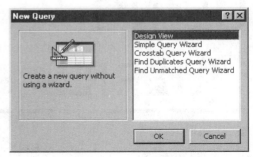

Figure 34.3 Click the New button.

Figure 34.4 Select Design View and click OK.

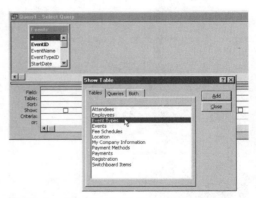

Figure 34.5 Select tables in the Show Table dialog box.

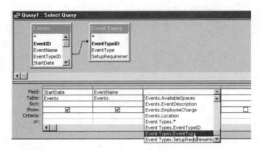

Figure 34.6 Select a field from the pull-down menu.

Run button

Figure 34.7 Click the Run button on the Access toolbar...

Figure 34.8 ...or choose Run from the Query menu.

Figure 34.9 The query result.

✔ Tips

■ The Show check boxes in the grid should be checked for all the fields that you want displayed in the resulting datasheet.

■ To sort the records in the resulting datasheet, click the Sort cell for the field that you want to sort and then select Ascending or Descending from the drop-down list.

To run the query:

◆ Click the Run button on the Access toolbar (**Figure 34.7**).

or

Choose Run from the Query menu (**Figure 34.8**).

Access displays the results of the query in a datasheet (**Figure 34.9**).

✔ Tips

■ Click the Design View button to return to designing the query.

■ If no queries are open, on the Queries tab of the Database window, double-click a query to run it.

RUNNING A SELECT QUERY

Saving a Query and Printing the Results

You can save a query design and open it in Design view later to refine or change the criteria. You can also print the results of a query to obtain a result on paper.

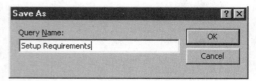

Figure 34.10 Type a name for the new query.

To save the query:

1. While the Query window is open, click the Save button.

    or

    Press Ctrl+S.

    or

    From the File menu, choose Save.

2. In the Save As dialog box, enter a name for the query (**Figure 34.10**).

3. Click OK.

    The new query now appears on the Queries tab (**Figure 34.11**).

Figure 34.11 The query appears on the Queries tab.

✔ Tip

■ To save a query as a form that you can use for data entry or as a report that you can print, or to save it with a new name, select the query on the Queries tab and then choose Save As from the File menu.

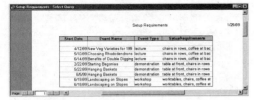

Figure 34.12 Choose Print from the File menu.

Figure 34.13 The query results in Print Preview.

To print the results of a query:

1. While the resulting datasheet is open, click the Print button on the Access toolbar.

   or

   Press Ctrl+P.

   or

   From the File menu, choose Print (**Figure 34.12**).

2. Click OK in the Print dialog box.

✔ Tips

- You can choose Print Preview from the File menu to see how the query datasheet will look when it's printed (**Figure 34.13**) and then choose Page Setup from the File menu to adjust the settings.

- To print a query without opening it, select the query on the Queries tab and then choose Print from the File menu.

Starting a Query Using the Simple Query Wizard

You can use the Simple Query Wizard to help you design a simple query.

To start a query using the Simple Query Wizard:

1. In the Database window, click the Queries tab.

2. Click the New button on the Database window toolbar.

3. In the New Query dialog box, select Simple Query Wizard (**Figure 34.14**).

4. Click OK.

5. On the first page of the Simple Query Wizard, select first one table, adding the fields you want to include, and then select additional tables and add the fields you need (**Figure 34.15**).

6. When you have finished adding tables and their fields, click Next.

7. On the next page, select Details or Summary and click Next.

8. On the last page of the Simple Query Wizard, type a name for this query or accept the default name that Access has assigned, choose whether to open the query or modify its design, and click Finish.

   The query appears in Design view (**Figure 34.16**).

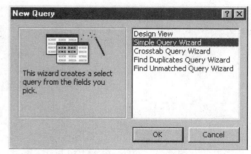

Figure 34.14 Select Simple Query Wizard and click OK.

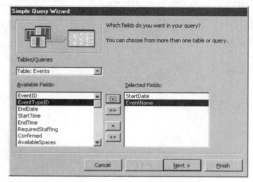

Figure 34.15 Select tables and add fields in the Simple Query Wizard dialog box.

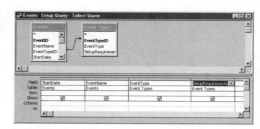

Figure 34.16 The query in Design view.

Figure 34.17 Choose Build from the shortcut menu...

Build button

Figure 34.18 ...or click the Build button on the Access toolbar.

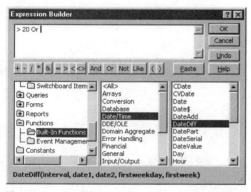

Figure 34.19 Build the expression in the Expression Builder dialog box.

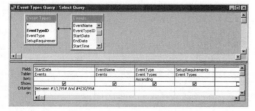

Figure 34.20 The query in Design view.

Adding Criteria to a Query

As you design a query, you can add criteria to make the query more specific.

To add criteria:

1. On the Queries tab of the Database window, select a query and click the Design button.

   or

   Click the Design view button if the query is open.

2. In the Criteria cell for a field in the query design grid, enter the number or text to match.

   or

   Enter an expression to match a range of values.

3. For help in constructing an expression, right-click in the Criteria cell for a field and choose Build from the shortcut menu (**Figure 34.17**).

   or

   Click in the Criteria cell for a field and click the Build button on the Access toolbar (**Figure 34.18**).

4. In the Expression Builder dialog box, you can type in the box at the top, click buttons to add the common operators, and click the Paste button to add items from the submenus in the bottom section (**Figure 34.19**).

5. Click OK when you have finished building the expression.

6. Click the Run button to view the results.

7. Click the Design view button to return to designing the query (**Figure 34.20**).

8. Save the query design.

ADDING CRITERIA TO A QUERY

Calculating Totals in a Query

When some of the data in the query datasheet is numeric, you might want to tally the information in some way. You can easily sum and average the numbers in a query datasheet or determine the minimum and maximum values.

To calculate totals:

1. On the Queries tab of the Database window, select a query and click the Design button.

   or

   If the query is open, click the Design View button.

2. Click the Totals button (**Figure 34.21**).

   or

   From the View menu, choose Totals (**Figure 34.22**).

   A Total row appears in the query design grid.

3. To group the data by the entries in a particular field, choose Group By from the drop-down list in the Total cell for that field.

4. Select an option from the drop-down list in each Total cell of each field in the query window design grid (**Figure 34.23**).

5. Run the query.

6. Save the query.

✔ Tip

■ The Total cell of each field must contain an entry. If you don't want to total a field, don't include the field in the query.

Totals button

Figure 34.21 Click the Totals button on the toolbar...

Figure 34.22 ...or choose Totals from the View menu.

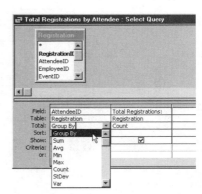

Figure 34.23 Select a method from the Totals drop-down list.

CALCULATING TOTALS

Figure 34.24 Select Find Duplicates Query Wizard and click OK.

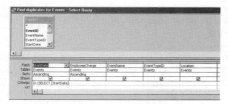

Figure 34.25 The query finds duplicates for employee in charge for each date.

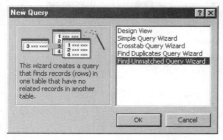

Figure 34.26 Select Find Unmatched Query Wizard and click OK.

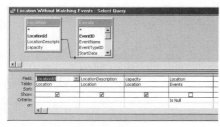

Figure 34.27 The query finds unassigned locations.

Finding Duplicate or Unmatched Records

Access provides two wizards that help you find duplicate field values in a table and find records in one table with no related records in another table.

To find duplicate records:

1. Click the New button on the Queries tab of the Database window toolbar.

2. In the New Query dialog box, select Find Duplicates Query Wizard (**Figure 34.24**).

3. Click OK.

4. Follow the wizard steps to select the table, choose the fields that might contain duplicate information, and select the other fields you want to display.

5. On the last page, type a name for the query or accept the default name and click Finish.

6. Run the query (**Figure 34.25**).

To find unmatched records:

1. Click the New button on the Queries tab of the Database window toolbar.

2. In the New Query dialog box, select Find Unmatched Query Wizard (**Figure 34.26**).

3. Click OK.

4. Follow the wizard steps to select the first table, select the table with the related records, choose the field in each record containing the same information, and select the fields you want to display.

5. On the last page, type a name for the query or accept the default name and click Finish.

6. Run the query (**Figure 34.27**).

Updating Table Records Using an Update Query

Four kinds of action queries will be covered on the next few pages: update, delete, append, and make-table. The first of these, the update query, makes changes to all records in the selected fields of one or more tables. You can create a new update query or you can adapt an existing select query.

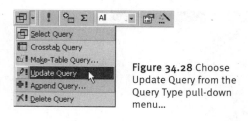

Figure 34.28 Choose Update Query from the Query Type pull-down menu...

To start an update query:

1. Create a query containing the records you want to update in one or more tables, and select the fields you want to use for the criteria.

2. With the query open in Design view, choose Update Query from the Query Type pull-down menu (**Figure 34.28**).

   or

   Choose Update Query from the Query menu (**Figure 34.29**).

3. Type information in the Criteria cells, if necessary.

4. Type an expression or a value in the Update To cell in the query design grid (**Figure 34.30**).

5. Click the Datasheet view button to see the fields that will be updated.

6. Click the Design View button to return to Design view.

7. Run the query.

   Values will be changed in the tables.

Figure 34.29 ...or choose Update Query from the Query menu.

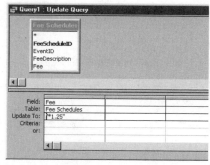

Figure 34.30 The query increases all fees by 25 percent.

✔ Tip

- You cannot undo the update action, but you can stop the query while it is running by pressing Ctrl+Break.

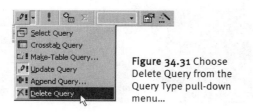

Figure 34.31 Choose Delete Query from the Query Type pull-down menu...

Figure 34.32 ...or choose Delete Query from the Query menu.

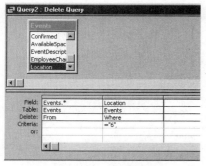

Figure 34.33 The query deletes records that contain a Location of 6.

Deleting Table Records Using a Delete Query

A delete query is an action query that deletes records in the selected table.

To start a delete query:

1. Create a query containing the records you want to delete.

2. With the query open in Design view, choose Delete Query from the Query Type pull-down menu (**Figure 34.31**).

   or

   Choose Delete Query from the Query menu (**Figure 34.32**).

3. Specify all (*) for each table from which you want records deleted (From) and then specify the field and the criteria for deletion (Where) (**Figure 34.33**).

   In the figure, the query deletes records that contain a location of 6.

4. Click the Datasheet view button to see the records that will be deleted.

5. Click the Design View button to return to Design view.

6. Run the query.

   The records will be deleted from the table or tables.

✔ Tips

- To check on relationships between tables, choose Join Properties from the View menu and use the Join Properties dialog box to review and add relationships.

- You cannot undo the delete action, but you can stop the query while it is running by pressing Ctrl+Break.

USING A DELETE QUERY

Appending Table Records Using an Append Query

An append query appends a group of records in one table to another table.

To start an append query:

1. Create a new query, selecting the table containing the records you want to append to another table.

2. With the query open in Design view, choose Append Query from the Query Type pull-down menu (**Figure 34.34**).

   or

   Choose Append Query from the Query menu (**Figure 34.35**).

3. In the Append dialog box, select the table to which the records will be added. You can specify a table in another database (**Figure 34.36**).

4. Click OK.

5. Select the fields to be added, adding criteria where necessary (**Figure 34.37**).

6. Click the Datasheet View button to view the records that will be appended.

7. Click the Design View button to return to Design view.

8. Run the query.

   The records will be appended to the second table.

✔ Tip

■ You cannot undo the append action, but you can stop the query while it is running by pressing Ctrl+Break.

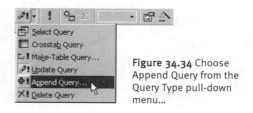

Figure 34.34 Choose Append Query from the Query Type pull-down menu...

Figure 34.35 ...or choose Append Query from the Query menu.

Figure 34.36 Choose the table you want to receive the appended records.

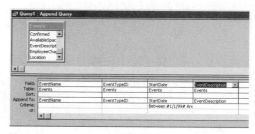

Figure 34.37 The query appends records between two dates.

Figure 34.38 Choose Make-Table Query from the Query Type pull-down menu...

Figure 34.39 ...or choose Make-Table Query from the Query menu.

Figure 34.40 Type a name for the new table in the Make Table dialog box.

Creating a Table of Query Results Using a Make-Table Query

A make-table query creates a table containing the query results.

To start a make-table query:

1. Create a new query, selecting the fields from one or more tables, and adding criteria as required.

   or

   Open an existing query.

2. With the query open in Design view, choose Make-Table Query from the Query Type pull-down menu (**Figure 34.38**).

   or

   Choose Make-Table Query from the Query menu (**Figure 34.39**).

3. Type a name for the new table in the Make Table dialog box (**Figure 34.40**).

4. Click OK.

5. Click the Datasheet View button to view the records that will be included in the new table.

6. Click the Design View button to return to Design view.

7. Run the query.

   The new table is created.

✔ Tip

■ You cannot undo the make-table action, but you can stop the query while it is running by pressing Ctrl+Break. You can also delete the new table from the database.

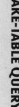

Creating a Crosstab Query

A crosstab query presents the information in spreadsheet-type format; you can select the fields to use for rows and the field to use for the columns.

Starting a crosstab query:

1. In the Database window, click the Queries tab.

2. Click the New button on the toolbar.

3. In the New Query dialog box, select Crosstab Query Wizard (**Figure 34.41**).

4. Click OK.

5. Follow the wizard steps, clicking Next on each page. Select the table or query containing the records, up to three fields for the row headings, a field for the column headings, and a calculation to include.

6. On the last page, type a name for the query or accept the default name and click Finish.

7. Run the query.

✔ Tip

■ If you haven't specified fields correctly and you receive an error message, you can use the wizard to begin again or you can work with the query in Design view (**Figure 34.42**).

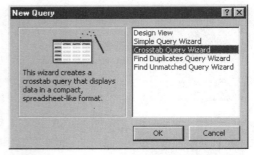

Figure 34.41 Select Crosstab Query Wizard and click OK.

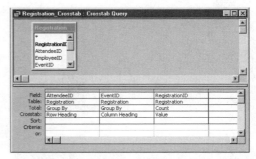

Figure 34.42 The crosstab query in Design view.

CREATING
A REPORT

Figure 35.1 A report in Print Preview.

A report (**Figure 35.1**) presents your data in a printed format, using a query or a table as its source. You can format the report in a number of predefined ways, or you can create and save a custom format.

Access provides report wizards to help you group and categorize your information; you can also make changes to any report in Design view.

Viewing and Printing a Report

Each time you open a report to view or print it, the report reflects any changes made to the table or query on which it is based.

To view a report:

1. Click the Reports tab in the Database window (**Figure 35.2**).

2. Select a report and then click Preview to view a preview of the printed report (**Figures 35.3** and **35.4**).

✔ Tips

- Click the Page buttons at the bottom of the print preview window to move from page to page of the report.

- To close the report, click the Close button on the Access toolbar (**Figure 35.5**).

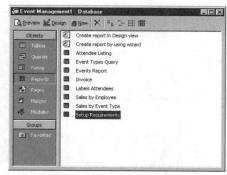

Figure 35.2 The Reports tab in the Database window.

Figure 35.3 Click Preview to view the report.

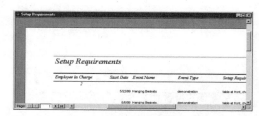

Figure 35.4 The report in Print Preview.

Figure 35.5 Click the Close button to close the report.

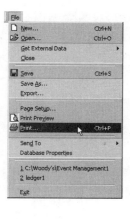

Figure 35.6 Choose Print from the File menu.

To print a report:

◆ With the report open in Print Preview, click the Print button on the Access toolbar.

or

Press Ctrl+P.

or

From the File menu, choose Print (**Figure 35.6**).

✔ Tips

■ You can also print a report by selecting the report on the Reports tab and clicking the Print button or choosing Print from the File menu.

■ To distribute a report electronically and to allow someone to view it using the Snapshot Viewer instead of Access, choose Export from the File menu and create a snapshot of the report. The Snapshot Viewer is installed automatically the first time you create a report snapshot. The program can also be downloaded from the Microsoft Access Developer's Web site.

VIEWING/PRINTING A REPORT

Starting a Report Using an AutoReport

The quickest way to create a report is to use one of the AutoReports. You can then revise your report in Design view.

To create a columnar report:

1. On the Reports tab of the Database window, click the New button (**Figure 35.7**).

2. In the New Report dialog box, select AutoReport: Columnar and select a table or query on which to base the report (**Figure 35.8**).

3. Click OK.

   The report is displayed in Print Preview (**Figure 35.9**).

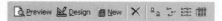

Figure 35.7 Click the New button on the Database toolbar.

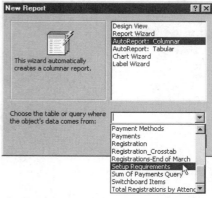

Figure 35.8 Select a table or query in the New Report dialog box.

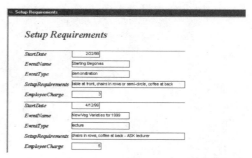

Figure 35.9 A columnar report in Print Preview.

USING AN AUTOREPORT

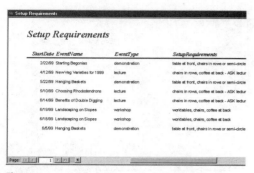

Figure 35.10 A tabular report in Print Preview.

Figure 35.11 Type a name in the Save As dialog box.

To create a tabular report:

1. On the Reports tab of the Database window, click the New button.

2. In the New Report dialog box, select AutoReport: Tabular and select a table or query on which to base the report.

3. Click OK.

   The report is displayed in Print Preview (**Figure 35.10**).

To save the report:

1. From the File menu, choose Save.

   or

   Press Ctrl+S.

2. In the Save As dialog box, enter a name for the report (**Figure 35.11**).

3. Click OK.

✔ Tip

■ It's easiest to base your report on a query that contains only the fields you want in your report.

Starting a Report Using the Report Wizard

Although you can start a new report in Design view, it is easier to begin the report using the Report Wizard and then revise it in Design view.

To start a new report using the Report Wizard:

1. On the Reports tab of the Database window, click the New button.

2. In the New Report dialog box, select Report Wizard (**Figure 35.12**).

3. Click OK.

4. On the first page of the Report Wizard, select the table or query on which the report will be based, select the fields to display, and click Next (**Figure 35.13**).

5. Select grouping options, and click Next (**Figure 35.14**).

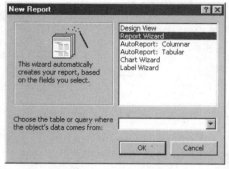

Figure 35.12 Select Report Wizard in the New Report dialog box.

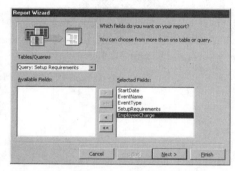

Figure 35.13 Select the fields for the report.

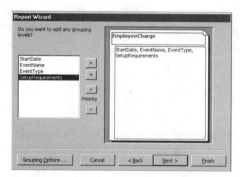

Figure 35.14 Specify the grouping for the report.

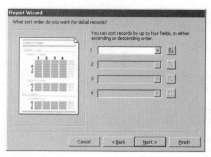

Figure 35.15 Specify the sort orders.

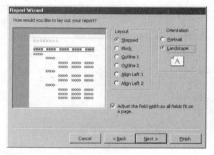

Figure 35.16 Choose a layout option.

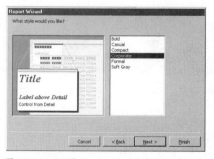

Figure 35.17 Choose a report style.

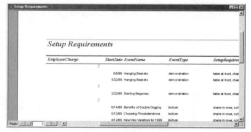

Figure 35.18 The finished report.

6. Select sort orders, if required, and click Next (**Figure 35.15**).

7. Select a layout, and click Next (**Figure 35.16**).

8. Select a style, and click Next (**Figure 35.17**).

9. On the last page of the Report Wizard, type a name for this report or accept the default, choose whether you want to view the report or modify the design, and click Finish.

The finished report appears in Print Preview (**Figure 35.18**).

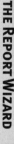

Revising a Report in Design View

In Design view, you can view the contents of each section of a report. The Report Header and Footer sections appear at the beginning and end of the report. The Page Header and Footer sections appear on each page. Other sections repeat as necessary during the report. Each section contains controls that act just like the controls you use when designing a form.

To revise a report in Design view:

1. On the Reports tab of the Database window, select a report and click Design (**Figure 35.19**).

   or

   If the report is already open in Print Preview, click the Design button on the Access toolbar (**Figure 35.20**).

2. In Design view, move or resize the controls as needed (**Figure 35.21**).

3. Double-click any section heading or control to change its properties.

4. To add a field to the report, drag the field from the field list to a report section.

5. Use the tools in the toolbox to add or modify controls, just as you do when designing a form.

✔ Tip

- To view the result of your revisions, choose Layout Preview from the View pull-down menu (**Figure 35.22**). Layout Preview displays the layout without showing all the records. Press Esc to return to the report in Design view.

Figure 35.19 Click the Design button.

Design button

Figure 35.20 Click the Design button on the Access toolbar.

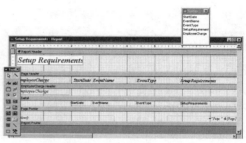

Figure 35.21 The report in Design view.

Figure 35.22 Choose Layout Preview to view the changed layout.

Sorting and
Grouping button

Figure 35.23 Click the Sorting and
Grouping button.

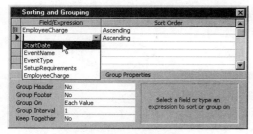

Figure 35.24 Select fields in the Sorting and
Grouping dialog box.

Sorting and Grouping Records in a Report

A report can group together similar records (for example, all the employees that have the same department in the Dept field), and it can also sort the entries within groups.

To sort and group records:

1. With the report open in Design view, click the Sorting and Grouping button on the Access toolbar (**Figure 35.23**).

2. In the Sorting and Grouping dialog box, use the drop-down menu to select the field you want to group on (**Figure 35.24**).

   or

   Drag a field from the field list.

3. Select the sorting method for the grouping.

4. If you want, select a second field to group on, within the first grouping .

5. Click a new row to save your changes.

6. Close the dialog box.

Choosing an AutoFormat for the Report

Rather than create your own format for a report, you can use one of the AutoFormats supplied with Access for a professional-looking design.

To choose an AutoFormat:

1. With the report open in Design view, click the AutoFormat button on the Access toolbar (**Figure 35.25**).

2. In the AutoFormat dialog box, select a new format. You can apply all or only some attributes (**Figure 35.26**).

3. Click OK.

✔ Tips

- You can customize an AutoFormat or add your own formatting as an AutoFormat. Click Customize in the AutoFormat dialog box to display the Customize AutoFormat dialog box (**Figure 35.27**).

- Be sure to save the report after you have revised it.

AutoFormat button

Figure 35.25 Click the AutoFormat button.

Figure 35.26 Select a different format.

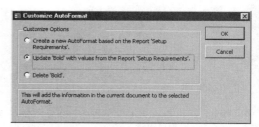

Figure 35.27 Use the Customize AutoFormat dialog box to make format changes.

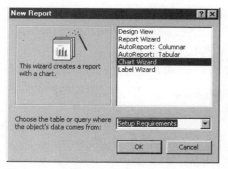

Figure 35.28 Choose Chart Wizard and select a table or query on which to base the chart.

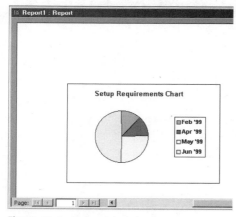

Figure 35.29 A completed chart.

Creating Charts and Labels

You can create a report in chart format, which represents numeric information graphically, and you can also create a report that prints labels that can be used for sending a mailing to a mailing list.

To create a chart:

1. On the Reports tab of the Database window, click the New button.

2. In the New Report dialog box, select Chart Wizard and select a table or query on which to base the report (**Figure 35.28**).

3. Click OK.

4. Follow the steps in the Chart Wizard, clicking Next after each step. Select up to six fields to include, select a chart type, and then plan a layout.

5. On the last page of the Report Wizard, type a name for this report or accept the default, choose whether to display a legend, choose whether you want to view the chart or modify the design, and click Finish.

If you've chosen to view the chart, it appears on the screen (**Figure 35.29**).

To create labels:

1. On the Reports tab of the Database window, click the New button.

2. In the New Report dialog box, select Label Wizard and select a table or query on which to base the report.

3. Click OK.

4. Follow the steps in the Label Wizard dialog box, clicking Next after each step. Select a label size and type, select the font and color for text, add fields to construct the label (**Figure 35.30**), and select a field on which to sort the labels.

5. On the last page of the Label Wizard, type a name for the report or accept the default, choose whether you want to view the report or modify the design, and click Finish.

   If you've chosen the view the report, it appears on the screen (**Figure 35.31**).

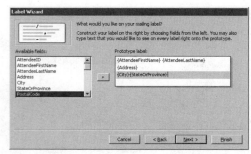

Figure 35.30 Construct the label in the Label Wizard dialog box.

Figure 35.31 The completed label report.

ACCESS AND THE WEB

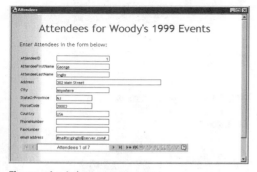

Figure 36.1 A data access page.

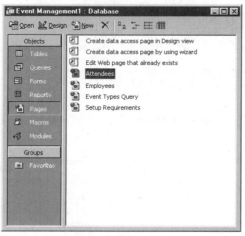

Figure 36.2 The Pages tab in the Database window.

In Access, you can create data access pages (**Figure 36.1**), which are Web pages that allow authorized individuals to view and work with a database. Although data access pages are saved separately from the database, they are connected directly to it. Data access pages are listed on the Pages tab of the Database window (**Figure 36.2**).

You can use a data access page the way you would a report, to display grouped information and summaries and to organize the data to analyze it. You can also use a data access page the way you would a form, to allow others to view, edit, and add records, either using a Web browser or via Page View in Access.

You can use an existing Web page as a base or begin with a new Web page, designing the page the same way you design a form or report.

You can also add hyperlinks to forms and data access pages and add hyperlink fields to tables.

Creating and Saving a Data Access Page

You can start a data access page in Design view.

To create a data access page:

1. In the Database window, click the Pages tab.

2. Click the New button on the Database window toolbar (**Figure 36.3**).

3. In the New Data Access Page dialog box, select Design View and select a table or query on which to base the page (**Figure 36.4**).

4. Click OK.

5. In the Field List dialog box, select individual fields or the table itself and click Add to Page (**Figure 36.5**).

   If you select the table itself, you can add it as individual controls or as a Pivot-Table list.

6. Use the toolbox to add elements to your page (**Figure 36.6**).

✔ Tip

■ You can also begin with an existing Web page and then add the data access controls and save the page as a data access page. Select Existing Web Page in the New Data Access Page dialog box.

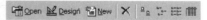

Figure 36.3 Click the New button to start a new page.

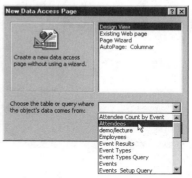

Figure 36.4 Choose a table or query as the data source.

Figure 36.5 Add fields as individual controls or as a PivotTable list.

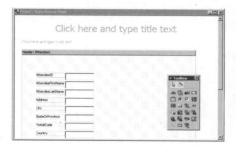

Figure 36.6 Add elements to the new page by clicking icons in the toolbox.

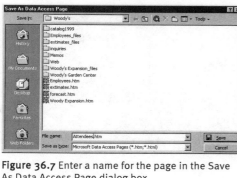

Figure 36.7 Enter a name for the page in the Save As Data Access Page dialog box.

To save the data access page:

1. From the File menu, choose Save.

   or

   Press Ctrl+S.

2. In the Save As Data Access Page dialog box, enter a name for the page, changing the location if necessary (**Figure 36.7**).

3. Click Save.

✔ Tips

- If your database has been set up to be accessible through a browser and you have Internet Explorer 5 installed, you can preview your page. Choose Web Page Preview from the File menu.

- If you move the data access page and its accompanying folder, you need to help Access find them again by specifying a new path.

SAVING A DATA ACCESS PAGE

Starting a Data Access Page Using the Page Wizard

The Page Wizard leads you through the steps for designing a page.

To start a data access page using the Page Wizard:

1. On the Pages tab of the Database window, click the New button.

2. In the New Data Access Page dialog box, select Page Wizard (**Figure 36.8**).

3. Click OK.

4. On the first page of the Page Wizard, select the table or query on which the report will be based, select the fields to display, and click Next (**Figure 36.9**).

5. Select grouping options if you want this page to be read-only, and click Next (**Figure 36.10**).

6. Select sort orders, if required, and click Next (**Figure 36.11**).

Figure 36.8 Choose Page Wizard and click OK.

Figure 36.9 Select the fields from the table or query.

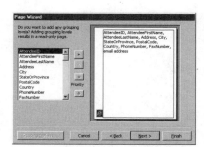

Figure 36.10 Add grouping levels if this page will not be used for data entry.

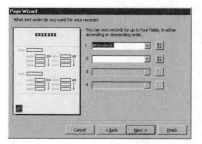

Figure 36.11 Select sort orders.

Figure 36.12 Give the page a title or accept the default.

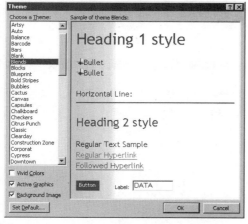

Figure 36.13 Choose a theme for the new page.

Figure 36.14 The new page in Design view with the Field List dialog box open.

7. On the last page of the Page Wizard, type a name for the report or accept the default, choose whether you want to view the report or modify the design, check the Theme check box if you want to apply a theme immediately, and click Finish (**Figure 36.12**).

The new data access page is displayed with the default theme. If you chose to apply a theme now in the last page of the Page Wizard, the Theme dialog box is open (**Figure 36.13**).

8. Select a theme and save the new design.

The design appears on the new page (**Figure 36.14**).

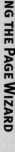

Creating a Data Access Page Using an AutoPage

An easy way to begin a data access page is to select the AutoPage: Columnar option and then revise the design in Design view.

To create a data access page using an AutoPage:

1. On the Pages tab of the Database window, click the New button.

2. In the New Data Access Page dialog box, select AutoPage: Columnar and select a table or query on which to base the page (**Figure 36.15**).

3. Click OK.

   The new data access page is displayed with the default theme (**Figure 36.16**).

4. To save your data access page with the default name, click the Save button or choose Save from the File menu.

   or

   To save the page with a different name, choose Save As from the File menu and specify a new name.

✔ Tip

■ To change the default theme, choose Theme from the Format menu, select a new style in the Theme dialog box and click Set Default.

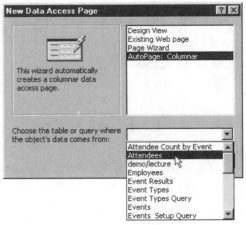

Figure 36.15 Choose a table or query on which to base the page.

Figure 36.16 An AutoPage: Columnar page in Page view.

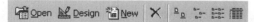

Figure 36.17 Click the Design button to open a page in Design view.

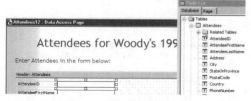

Figure 36.18 The control handles are visible if the control is selected.

Figure 36.19 Click a toolbox tool to add a control.

Revising the Page in Design View

As with all other objects in Access, you can revise the design of your data access page.

To revise a data access page in Design view:

1. On the Pages tab of the Database window, select a page and click Design.

   or

   If the page is open in Page view, click the Design button on the Access toolbar (**Figure 36.17**).

2. In Design view, move or resize the controls as needed.

3. Double-click any control to change its properties (**Figure 36.18**).

4. To add a field to the page, drag the field from the Field List dialog box to a page section or click the Add to Page button in the Field List dialog box.

5. Use the toolbox to add or modify controls, just as you do when designing a form (**Figure 36.19**).

6. Click Save to save the changes you've made to the design.

✔ Tip

■ Right-click in any field to view special options on a shortcut menu.

REVISING THE PAGE

Changing the Theme in Design View

Changing the theme of a data access page gives it a whole new look.

To change the theme:

1. With the page open in Design view, choose Theme from the Format menu (**Figure 36.20**).

2. Select a new theme (**Figure 36.21**).

3. Click OK.

4. Click Save to save design changes.

✔ Tip

■ You can also change the background by choosing Background from the Format menu and then selecting a new color or adding a picture (**Figure 36.22**).

Figure 36.20 Choose Theme from the Format menu.

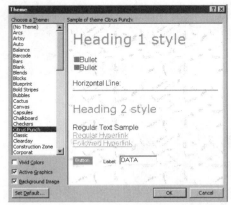

Figure 36.21 Choose a new theme for the page.

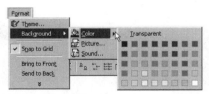

Figure 36.22 Click a different background color.

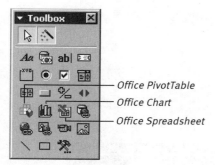

Office PivotTable
Office Chart
Office Spreadsheet

Figure 36.23 Click the Office Chart button on the toolbox.

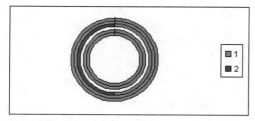

Figure 36.24 The finished chart.

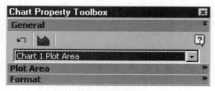

Figure 36.25 The Chart Property Toolbox.

Inserting a Chart in a Data Access Page

You can add a chart to a data access page.

To add a chart:

1. With the page open in Design view, click the Office Chart button on the toolbox (**Figure 36.23**). The Microsoft Office Chart Wizard opens.

2. Drag the chart cursor to where you want the chart to appear.

3. Follow the steps in the Microsoft Office Chart Wizard, clicking Next at each step, to select a chart type, table, or query as a data source and to choose an organization option.

4. On the final page of the wizard, select series and values for the chart, and click Finish.

   The chart is displayed on the page (**Figure 36.24**).

5. To change the design or any of the chart elements, right-click the chart and choose Property Toolbox from the shortcut menu. Make changes in the Chart Property Toolbox (**Figure 36.25**).

Inserting a PivotTable in a Data Access Page

You can add a PivotTable to a data access page. Users can then reorganize and summarize the data in their Web browser and move columns to rows or rows to columns.

To add a PivotTable:

1. With the page open in Design view, click the Office PivotTable button on the toolbox.

2. Drag the PivotTable cursor to where you want the PivotTable to appear.

   The blank PivotTable appears on the page (**Figure 36.26**).

3. Right-click the PivotTable and choose Property Toolbox from the shortcut menu to open the PivotTable Property Toolbox dialog box (**Figure 36.27**).

4. Use the Field List dialog box and the PivotTable Property Toolbox to design the PivotTable.

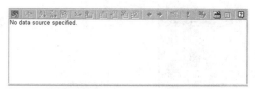

Figure 36.26 The blank PivotTable.

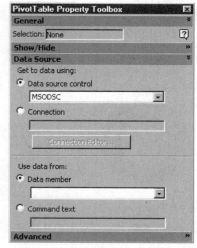

Figure 36.27 The PivotTable Property Toolbox.

Figure 36.28 The blank spreadsheet.

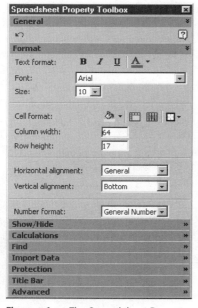

Figure 36.29 The Spreadsheet Property Toolbox.

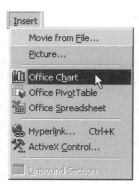

Figure 36.30
Choose Office Chart,
Office PivotTable, or
Office Spreadsheet
from the Insert
menu.

Inserting a Spreadsheet in a Data Access Page

A spreadsheet on a data access page is similar to an Excel spreadsheet. You can add data and perform calculations.

To add a spreadsheet:

1. With the page open in Design view, click the Office Spreadsheet button on the toolbox.

2. Drag the spreadsheet cursor to where you want the spreadsheet to appear.

    The spreadsheet appears on the page (**Figure 36.28**).

3. Add data to your spreadsheet.

4. To add formatting and to change the design, right-click the spreadsheet and choose Property Toolbox from the shortcut menu to open the Spreadsheet Property Toolbox (**Figure 36.29**).

✔ Tip

- You can also choose Office Chart, Office PivotTable, or Office Spreadsheet from the Insert menu (**Figure 36.30**).

INSERTING A SPREADSHEET

Adding a Hyperlink Field

A hyperlink is specially marked text or a graphic that you click to go to a file or an HTML page on the Web or on an intranet, or to send an e-mail message. You can specify a hyperlink data type field in a table so that whatever is entered in that field becomes a hyperlink. You can then make that field available on a form.

To add a hyperlink field to a table:

1. With the table open in Design view, add a new row, with a hyperlink data type (**Figure 36.31**).

2. Save the change to the design.

To add a control to a form:

1. With the form open in Design view, add the control to the form by dragging it from the field list (**Figure 36.32**).

2. Save the change to the design.

3. Click the Datasheet button to view the change in the form (**Figure 36.33**).

4. Save the change to the design.

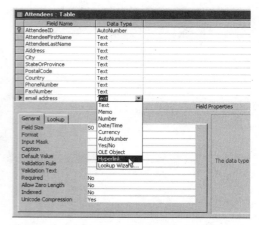

Figure 36.31 Add a hyperlink field to the table.

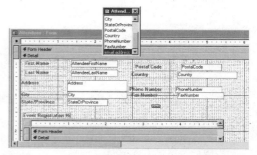

Figure 36.32 Add the hyperlink control to the form.

Figure 36.33 The new control in Datasheet view.

Insert Hyperlink button

Figure 36.34 Click the Insert Hyperlink button to add a link.

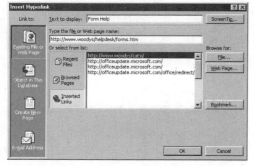

Figure 36.35 Type the destination link or browse for the destination.

Figure 36.36 The link in place on a form.

Adding a Hyperlink

You can add a hyperlink to a data access page and to a form if it will be viewed on screen or in a browser.

You can also add a hyperlink to a report if you plan to publish the report in Word.

To add a hyperlink:

1. With the form or data access page open in Design view, click the Insert Hyperlink button on the Access toolbar (**Figure 36.34**).

   or

   Press Ctrl+K.

2. Type the text to display as the hyperlink, or accept the default name.

To link to another file:

1. In the Insert Hyperlink dialog box, type the file or the Web page name (**Figure 36.35**).

   or

   Select from recent files, pages, and links.

   or

   Click the File button to navigate to the file you want in the Link to File dialog box.

   or

   Click the Web Page button to navigate to the Web page you want in the browser window. (You must be connected to the Web to use this method.)

2. Click OK.

   The control, with the text colored and underlined, appears on the page or form.

3. Position the control (**Figure 36.36**).

ADDING A HYPERLINK

To link to another page in the database:

1. If the link is being inserted in a data access page, in the Insert Hyperlink dialog box, click Page In This Database in the Link To sidebar buttons.

2. Select a page as the destination (**Figure 36.37**).

3. Click OK.

   The control, with the text colored and underlined, appears on the page.

4. Position the control on the page.

To link to another object in the database:

1. If the link is being inserted in a form or a report, in the Insert Hyperlink dialog box, click Object In This Database in the Link To sidebar buttons.

2. Click the Object expansion box to select an object as the destination (**Figure 36.38**).

3. Click OK.

   The control, with the text colored and underlined, appears in the upper left corner of the form.

4. Position the control on the form.

✔ Tip

- To edit or remove a hyperlink, right-click the link in Design view, and choose Hyperlink from the shortcut menu (**Figure 36.39**).

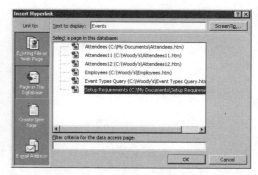

Figure 36.37 Select another page in this database.

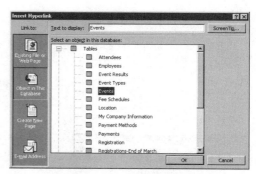

Figure 36.38 Select another object in this database.

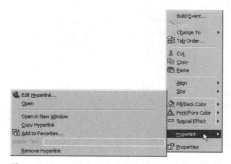

Figure 36.39 Right-click the link to edit or remove the hyperlink.

ADDING A HYPERLINK

Part 6
Microsoft Outlook

Part 6
Microsoft Outlook

INTRODUCING

OUTLOOK 2000

37

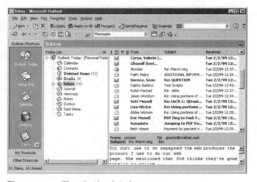

Figure 37.1 The Outlook Inbox.

Figure 37.2 Microsoft Outlook Today.

Outlook 2000 (**Figure 37.1**) is the electronic mail, scheduling, and contact management system within the Microsoft Office suite. Using Outlook 2000, you can easily organize and prioritize tasks and appointments and send and receive e-mail messages. You can create any number of folders for storing your messages, and you can flag messages and contacts for follow-up activities.

Outlook's Find capability lets you narrow your search for text in e-mail messages, the calendar, contacts, tasks, notes, and journal lists.

With the Outlook Today feature (**Figure 37.2**), you see at a glance your schedule, a list of tasks, and the number of messages waiting to be read.

The Steps to an Outlook Management System

Setting up Outlook

You can set up Outlook to open with Outlook Today, which lets you view at a glance tasks, appointments, and the number of new messages in your Inbox. You can also set up Outlook to show your Inbox instead and to send and receive message at certain intervals.

Organizing incoming messages

You can organize your Inbox, creating folders that best suit your needs, and then use the Rules Wizard to direct messages to the folders, where you can sort them and read them.

Setting up your outgoing messages

You can choose Outlook or Word as your e-mail text editor, and you can select different e-mail formats (HTML, Plain Text, or Outlook Rich Text). You can also create different signatures to use for different circumstances, and, if you use HTML format, add stationery backgrounds to your messages.

Building a contacts list

Outlook has built in, easy ways to create and organize a list of the people you deal with. You can use this contacts list to perform a mail merge and to produce an e-mail address book, task assignments, and invitations to meetings. You can use journal entries for each contact to record the results of telephone conversations and meetings, and you can flag the contact name for follow-up activities.

Assigning tasks

Use the tasks list to give assignments to yourself and others, and use Outlook for accepting and sending updates about assignments others have given to you. You can change priority and status of a task as the due date approaches.

Scheduling appointments

Outlook offers you a number of ways to view the calendar as you enter your appointments and meetings. You can set a recurrence interval and the reminder time for each event. When you set up a meeting, Outlook helps you coordinate acceptance and schedule conflicts.

Tracking activities

Notes and journal entries help you track your daily activities, with an archiving system built in. You can also use Outlook to record the time you spend using other Office 2000 application files.

Figure 37.3
Choose Microsoft
Outlook from the
Programs
submenu.

Figure 37.4 Outlook Today shows your schedule, a list of tasks, and the number of messages waiting to be read.

Figure 37.5 The Inbox window.

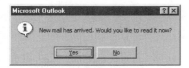

Figure 37.6 Outlook notifies you that new mail has arrived.

Starting Outlook

You start Outlook the same way you start every application in the Microsoft Office suite.

To start Outlook:

1. From the Start menu, choose Programs, and then choose Microsoft Outlook (**Figure 37.3**).

   Outlook begins with the Outlook Today or the Inbox (**Figures 37.4** and **37.5**).

2. If Outlook has collected your messages on startup, click Yes to start reading your messages or No to read them later (**Figure 37.6**).

✔ Tips

- If Microsoft Outlook is already started, click its icon on the Taskbar to restore the window.

- If your Startup folder contains a shortcut to Outlook, Outlook starts when the computer starts.

STARTING OUTLOOK

The Outlook Inbox Window

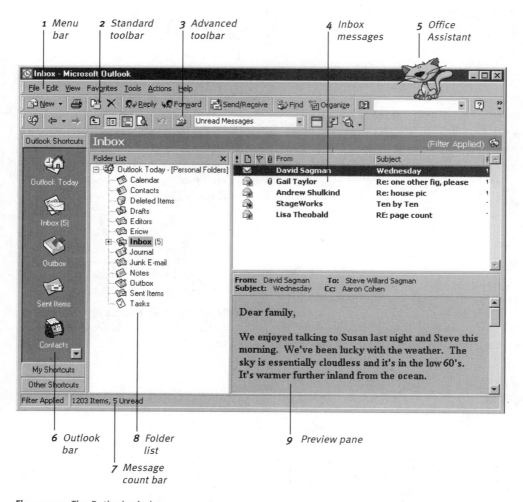

1 Menu bar   2 Standard toolbar   3 Advanced toolbar   4 Inbox messages   5 Office Assistant

6 Outlook bar   8 Folder list   9 Preview pane   7 Message count bar

Figure 37.7 The Outlook window.

Key to the Inbox Window

1 Menu bar

Click any name on the menu bar to pull down a menu.

2 Standard toolbar

Toolbar with buttons for the most frequently needed commands. Outlook provides the buttons appropriate for the current folder.

3 Advanced toolbar

An additional set of buttons appropriate for the folder.

4 Inbox messages

Shows the current Inbox messages.

5 Office Assistant

Online help utility.

6 Outlook bar

Displays shortcuts to the major areas of Outlook. You can add your own shortcuts.

7 Message count bar

Shows number of messages in folder, total and unread.

8 Folder list

Lists current folders. You can change folders by clicking on a folder or click the expansion box to view subfolders. Can be open or hidden.

9 Preview pane

Shows the first few lines of the highlighted message. Size is adjustable.

THE INBOX WINDOW

Connecting to the Internet

Depending on your setup, Outlook will either connect to the Internet immediately to collect your messages or you will have to log on.

To set up your mail delivery:

1. From the Tools menu, choose Options (**Figure 37.8**).

2. On the Mail Delivery tab of the Options dialog box, check both Mail account options to have your messages sent immediately on connection and to have your messages checked for at regular intervals (**Figure 37.9**).

3. Specify the interval in minutes between checks for messages.

4. In the Dial-up options section, turn on the appropriate options if you want Outlook to hang up after it sends and receives e-mail or if you want Outlook to automatically dial to check for new messages.

5. Click OK.

✔ Tip

■ To change account information or to add an account, choose Accounts from the Tools menu, and then click the Mail tab in the Internet Accounts dialog box. Click Add and then choose Mail from the submenu. (**Figure 37.10**).

Figure 37.8 Choose Options from the Tools menu.

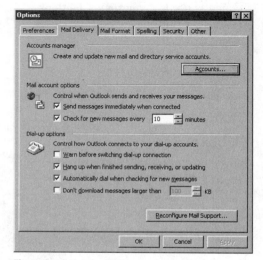

Figure 37.9 Set the Mail account and Dial-up options.

Figure 37.10 Click Mail on the Add submenu to add an account.

Figure 37.11 Click Outlook Today on the Outlook toolbar to display Outlook Today.

Customize Outlook Today

Figure 37.12 Click Customize Outlook Today to change the settings.

Figure 37.13 Check the Startup box to have Outlook Today displayed at startup.

Using Outlook Today

Outlook Today shows today's date, your calendar, a task list, and the number of messages in your mailboxes. You can set Outlook Today as your opening Outlook window.

To display Outlook Today:

◆ Click the Outlook Today button on the Outlook bar (**Figure 37.11**).

To make Outlook Today your opening window:

1. In the Outlook Today display, click Customize Outlook Today (**Figure 37.12**).

2. In the Customize Outlook Today window, check the Startup box (**Figure 37.13**).

3. Change other options to the settings you want.

4. Click Save Changes to save your changes and return to Outlook Today.

   or

   Click Cancel to return without making changes.

   The next time you start Outlook, Outlook Today will appear as the opening window.

✔ Tip

■ To change the look of the Outlook Today page, you can choose a style when you customize Outlook Today by clicking Customize Outlook Today.

READING
MESSAGES

Figure 38.1 Outlook opens the message in a new window.

Depending on your setup, when Outlook starts it will collect your messages automatically or you will need to start the process yourself. Once the new messages are in your Inbox, you can open them (**Figure 38.1**), move them, delete them, and organize them into folders.

Collecting Messages

You can set Outlook to automatically check for messages at intervals, or you can have Outlook check for messages whenever you want.

To check for messages:

1. In the Inbox window or the Outlook Today window, click the Send/Receive button on the Standard toolbar (**Figure 38.2**).

2. If your connection is not automatic, click Connect in the Dial-up Connection dialog box (**Figure 38.3**).

   Outlook reports its progress in the lower right corner of the window (**Figure 38.4**).

3. When messages arrive, Outlook asks whether you want to start reading them. Click Yes in the Microsoft Outlook dialog box to starting reading messages, or click No to read them later (**Figure 38.5**).

✔ Tip

■ Outlook sends any messages waiting in the Outbox folder when you check for incoming messages.

Figure 38.2 Click the Send/Receive button on the Standard toolbar.

Figure 38.3 Click Connect to connect to the Internet.

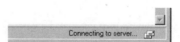

Figure 38.4 Outlook displays the current status in the lower right corner.

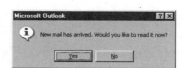

Figure 38.5 Click Yes to read the first new message.

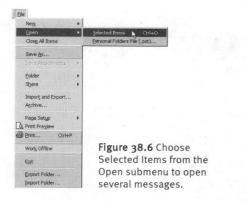

Figure 38.6 Choose Selected Items from the Open submenu to open several messages.

Figure 38.7 Each message opens in a separate window.

Reading a Message

The list of messages in the Inbox includes symbols next to each message to help you decide whether to open a message for reading. **Table 38.1** shows these symbols and their meanings.

To read a message:

◆ Double-click a message in the Inbox list.

or

Select the messages to open and press Ctrl+O.

or

Select the messages to open and, from the File menu, choose Open. Then choose Selected Items from the submenu (**Figure 38.6**).

Each message opens in a separate window (**Figure 38.7**).

Table 38.1

Mailbox Symbols	
SYMBOL	**MEANING**
✉	Unread message
! ✉	High importance
↓ ✉	Low importance
✉	Message that has been read
✉ 📎	Message with attachment
✉	Message that has been forwarded
✉	Message that has been replied to
✉	Meeting for which response is requested
✉ ⚑	Follow-up flag

(Side tab: READING A MESSAGE)

Closing a Message

After you've read a message, you can close it and then go on taking care of other tasks.

To close a message:

◆ Press Esc.

or

Click the Close button in the message window (**Figure 38.8**).

or

From the File menu, choose Close.

or

Click the Next Item or Previous Item button on the Standard toolbar to read the next or previous message (**Figure 38.9**).

✔ Tips

■ If you select more than one message to open, Outlook opens each message in a separate window.

■ The sort arrow on a column name button at the top of the list of messages in the Inbox window indicates that the list is sorted on that column. The direction of the arrow indicates the sort order by date or alphabetically. Click a column name to sort on that column, and click it a second time to reverse the sort order (**Figure 38.10**).

Close button

Figure 38.8 Click the Close button to close the message window.

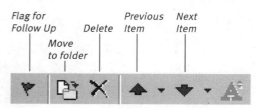

Figure 38.9 Click the Next Item or Previous Item button on the Standard toolbar.

Sort arrow

Figure 38.10 The Sort arrow in the Received column.

CLOSING A MESSAGE

Click the arrow next to the window title

Figure 38.11 Click the Inbox arrow to see the folder list.

Close button

Figure 38.12 Close the folder list by clicking the close button.

Viewing the Folder List

Outlook comes with several folders installed, and you can add folders to organize and store messages. The Inbox (incoming messages), Outbox (messages waiting to be mailed), Sent Items (messages already sent), and Drafts (messages still being composed) folders are created automatically.

To view the folder list:

1. Click the down arrow to the right of the window title (**Figure 38.11**).

2. Click the pushpin icon if you want to keep the folder list open.

✔ Tips

- Click a folder to view its contents in the right pane.

- If you clicked the pushpin to keep the folder list open, you can click the close button at the upper right corner of the list to close it (**Figure 38.12**).

VIEWING THE FOLDER LIST

Replying to a Message

You can reply to a message immediately, or you can close a message if you want to disregard it or deal with it later.

To reply to a message:

1. With a message selected in the Inbox window or with the message open, click the Reply button on the Standard toolbar (**Figure 38.13**).

   The reply has the sender in the To box and the original subject in the Subject box preceded by *RE:*.

2. In the text area, type your reply. The reply appears above the original message (**Figure 38.14**).

To send the reply:

◆ Click Send on the Standard toolbar (**Figure 38.15**).

   Outlook places the reply in the Outbox folder, ready to be sent the next time you check for new messages.

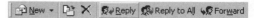

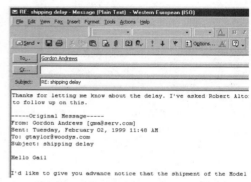

Figure 38.13 Click the Reply button on the Standard toolbar.

Figure 38.14 Type a reply above the original message.

Figure 38.15 Click Send to move the reply to the Outbox.

Figure 38.16 From the File menu, choose Save to save and work on a reply later.

To save a reply to be completed later:

1. Click Save on the Standard toolbar.

   or

   From the File menu, choose Save (**Figure 38.16**).

2. Close the window.

   Outlook places the reply in the Drafts folder. You can open it there to continue working on it.

✔ Tips

- To reply to all recipients, click the Reply to All button on the Standard toolbar.

- You can still edit a message that is waiting in the Outbox. Just double-click the message, make your changes, and then click Send again.

REPLYING TO A MESSAGE

Forwarding a Message

Forwarding a message enables you to send a copy of a message to another recipient. Before you send the message, you can also add your own comments to it.

To forward a message:

1. With a message selected in the Inbox window or with the message open, click the Forward button on the Standard toolbar (**Figure 38.17**).

   The new message shows the original subject in the Subject box preceded by *FW:* .

2. Type the recipient's e-mail address in the To box (**Figure 38.18**).

   or

   To select an address from the Address Book, click the To button, select one or more names in the Select Names dialog box, click the to button in the dialog box, and click OK (**Figure 38.19**).

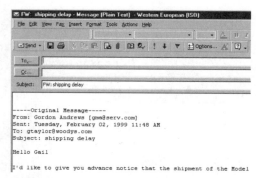

Figure 38.17 Click the Forward button on the Standard toolbar.

Figure 38.18 Type an e-mail address in the To box...

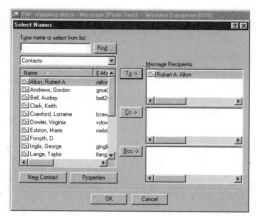

Figure 38.19 ...or select names in the Select Names dialog box, click To, and click OK.

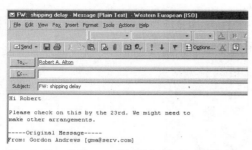

Figure 38.20 Type a message above the original message.

Figure 38.21 Click Send to move the message to the Outbox.

3. Type any comments you want to add in the space above the message (**Figure 38.20**).

4. Click Send on the Standard toolbar to move the message to the Outbox folder (**Figure 38.21**).

✔ Tips

■ If a message has files attached, the files are forwarded as well.

■ Be sure to consider whether the original creator of the message would want the message forwarded to others.

FORWARDING A MESSAGE

Printing a Message

You can print a selected message, regardless of whether it's open. Outlook also enables you to customize the appearance of your message printouts.

To print a message:

1. With the message open or selected, choose Print from the File menu (**Figure 38.22**).

   or

   Press Ctrl+P.

2. In the Print dialog box, choose a style and set the options you want (**Figure 38.23**).

3. To change a style, double-click it, make changes in the Page Setup dialog box, and click OK (**Figure 38.24**).

4. Click OK to begin printing.

✔ Tips

- To print an open message using all the default options, click the Print button on the Standard toolbar (**Figure 38.25**).

- To create a new style, click the Define Styles button in the Print dialog box and then copy and edit an existing style.

Figure 38.22 Choose Print from the File menu.

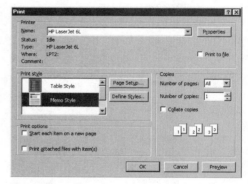

Figure 38.23 Choose a style in the Print dialog box.

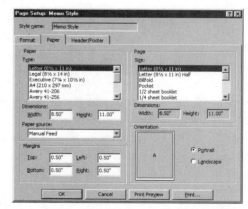

Figure 38.24 Use the Page Setup dialog box to change width or height.

Print button

Figure 38.25 To print an open message, click the Print button on the Standard toolbar.

PRINTING A MESSAGE

Figure 38.26
Choose a view
from the Current
View submenu.

Figure 38.27 The Messages with AutoPreview view.

Figure 38.28 The By Follow-up Flag view.

Figure 38.29 Choose from
the Current View pull-
down menu on the
Advanced toolbar.

Figure 38.30
Choose Customize
Current View from
the Current View
submenu to make
changes to a view.

Changing a View

Outlook lets you view the contents of a
message folder in a number of ways.

To change the view:

◆ From the View menu, choose Current
View, and then choose a view from the
submenu (**Figure 38.26**).

The view of the current folder is changed
(**Figures 38.27** and **38.28**).

✔ Tips

■ If the Advanced toolbar is open, you can
click the AutoPreview button or use the
Current View pull-down list to select
another view (**Figure 38.29**). To open the
Advanced toolbar, choose Toolbars from
the View menu and then click Advanced
on the Toolbars submenu.

■ To customize a view, choose Customize
Current View from the Current View
submenu (**Figure 38.30**) and click a
button in the View Summary dialog box.

CHANGING A VIEW

Finding Text in a Message

You can search messages for specific text, and you can specify the fields to be searched.

To find text:

1. From the Tools menu, choose Find.

   or

   Click the Find button on the Standard toolbar (**Figure 38.31**).

2. In the Find Items pane that opens in the message window, type the word or words you're searching for (**Figure 38.32**).

3. If you want to search all the text in the message, not just the message subjects, click Search All Text in the Message.

4. Click Find Now.

   Outlook lists the messages containing the search item.

✔ Tips

- Click Advanced Find and use the Advanced Find dialog box to further refine your search (**Figure 38.33**).

- Click the close button to close the Find Items pane.

- To find messages that are related to the selected message, you can also choose Find All from the Actions menu and choose Related Messages from the submenu (**Figure 38.34**).

Figure 38.31 Click the Find button on the Standard toolbar.

Figure 38.32 Enter the search word in the Look for text box.

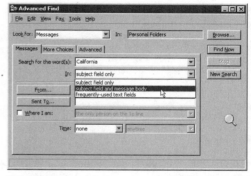

Figure 38.33 Use the Advanced Find dialog box to refine the search.

Figure 38.34 Choose Related Messages from the Find All submenu.

Delete

Figure 38.35 Click the Delete button on the toolbar in the message window.

Delete

Figure 38.36 Select messages in the list and click the Delete button on the Standard toolbar.

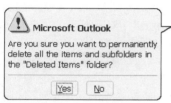

⚠ **Microsoft Outlook**

Are you sure you want to permanently delete all the items and subfolders in the "Deleted Items" folder?

[Yes]   No

Figure 38.37 Outlook asks for confirmation before it permanently deletes items in the Deleted Items folder.

Deleting a Message

You can delete a single message or several messages at one time.

To delete an open message:

◆ Click the Delete button on the toolbar in the message window (**Figure 38.35**).

or

Press Ctrl+D.

The message is moved to the Deleted Items folder.

To delete a message or messages in the list:

1. Click the message to be deleted.

or

To select a series of messages, click the first message, press Shift, and then click the last message.

or

Click the first message and press Ctrl while you click other messages.

2. Click the Delete button on the Standard toolbar (**Figure 38.36**).

or

Press Ctrl+D.

The selected messages are moved to the Deleted Items folder.

✔ Tip

■ When you quit Outlook, a message box appears and asks whether you want to empty the Deleted Items folder (**Figure 38.37**).

DELETING A MESSAGE

SENDING

MESSAGES

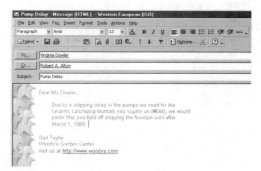

Figure 39.1. An Outlook message with a design provided by stationery.

Outlook gives you a great deal of freedom in the design of your outgoing messages. You can use stationery to give your e-mail a distinctive look (**Figure 39.1**), and you can include automatic signatures, which provide a tag line of your choosing (such as your address or a favorite quote) at the end of the message. You can also set flags to call attention to important messages and to request follow-up actions such as asking the recipient to reply to the message before a certain date.

If you want to send files, such as documents or pictures, you can attach them to e-mail messages, too.

Setting Mail Format Options

You can use the mail format options to specify the appearance of your outgoing messages. You can override these default settings for individual messages.

To set mail format options:

1. From the Tools menu, choose Options (**Figure 39.2**).

2. On the Mail Format tab of the Options dialog box, choose a format from the Send in this Message Format drop-down list (**Figure 39.3**).

   Choose HTML to send the message in the format used for Web pages, which allows text formatting. Most popular mail programs can display HTML e-mail messages.

   Choose Microsoft Outlook Rich Text if you know that your recipient uses Outlook too. This setting allows you to use boldfacing and other formatting in the message.

3. Check the Use Microsoft Word to edit e-mail messages option if you want to be able to use all of Word's features, such as the thesaurus, when you create e-mail messages.

4. Click OK when you have finished.

Figure 39.2 Choose Options from the Tools menu.

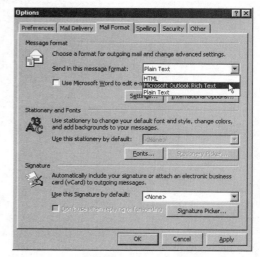

Figure 39.3 Choose a format and set the applicable options.

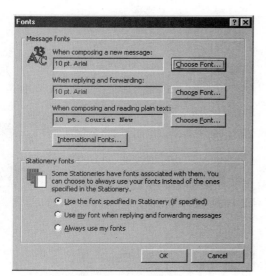

Figure 39.4 For Plain Text and Microsoft Outlook Rich Text, you can change font settings.

To choose default fonts:

1. On the Mail Format tab of the Options dialog box, choose the Plain Text or Microsoft Outlook Rich Text format option.

2. Click the Fonts button.

3. In the Fonts dialog box, choose the default fonts for messages you type (**Figure 39.4**).

4. Click OK to return to the Options dialog box.

5. Click OK when you have finished setting options.

✔ Tips

- If you choose HTML or Microsoft Outlook Rich Text as the mail format, a formatting toolbar appears in a new message window. You can use the buttons on this toolbar to set text formatting for the message text.

- In the Fonts dialog box, you can indicate when you want your default fonts to override stationery fonts.

CREATING STATIONERY

Creating Stationery

For e-mail in HTML format, you can choose predesigned stationery, which includes a background; graphical elements such as bullets, pictures, and horizontal lines; text fonts; and colors that blend with the background design.

If Word is specified as your e-mail editor and HTML is the selected format, the first time you create a new message you can choose a theme.

To choose default Outlook stationery:

1. From the Tools menu, choose Options.

2. On the Mail Format tab of the Options dialog box, choose HTML as the format.

3. Click the Stationery Picker button.

4. In the Stationery Picker dialog box, choose a stationery design (**Figure 39.5**).

5. Click OK to return to the Options dialog box.

6. Click OK when you have finished setting options.

To create default Word stationery:

1. From Word's Format menu, choose Theme.

2. In the Theme dialog box, choose a theme for your messages (**Figure 39.6**).

3. Click OK.

✔ Tip

■ If you don't need to preview the stationery, you can choose stationery in the Options dialog box from the Stationery Picker drop-down list (**Figure 39.7**).

Figure 39.5 With HTML, you can choose a stationery design.

Figure 39.6 In the Theme dialog box, choose a theme.

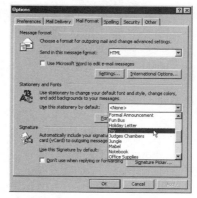

Figure 39.7 Select from the Stationery drop-down list.

Figure 39.8 Enter a name for the new signature.

Figure 39.9 Type the signature text.

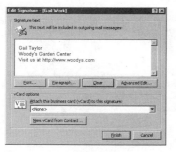

Figure 39.10 Select the signature.

Figure 39.11 Click the Signature button on the Standard toolbar to add a signature.

Creating a Signature

You can have Outlook add a signature, a special tag line, to each message you send.

To create a default signature:

1. From the Tools menu, choose Options.

2. On the Mail Format tab of the Options dialog box, click the Signature Picker button.

3. Click the New button in the Signature dialog box.

4. In the Create New Signature dialog box, enter a name for the new signature and click Next (**Figure 39.8**).

5. In the Edit Signature dialog box, type the signature that will appear at the end of your messages if this signature is selected (**Figure 39.9**).

6. Click Finish.

7. In the Signature dialog box, select the new signature and click OK to return to the Mail Format tab of the Options dialog box.

8. On the Mail Format tab, make sure the new signature is selected.

9. Check the Don't use when replying or forwarding check box if that's what you want (**Figure 39.10**).

10. Click OK when you have finished.

✔ Tip

- If you plan to change signatures often, select <None> as the default setting on the Mail Format tab. You can then add a signature to an open message by clicking the Signature button on the Standard toolbar (**Figure 39.11**).

Starting and Addressing a Message

You can start a message from any Outlook e-mail folder, address the message to as many recipients as you want, and send copies to anyone who might want to be informed. You can also send a blind copy (hidden from other recipients) to someone.

To start a message:

1. In the Inbox or Outlook Today window (or any other e-mail folder), click the New button on the Standard toolbar (**Figure 39.12**).

   or

   Press Ctrl+N.

2. If your e-mail editor is not Word, choose whether you want Word to be the default editor (**Figure 39.13**). (You can also check the Please do not show me this dialog again check box.)

   A message window with the default format opens (**Figure 39.14**).

To type addresses:

◆ In the To box, type a single e-mail address.

   or

   Type several addresses, separating them by commas or semicolons.

To use the Address Book:

1. Click the To or the Cc button to choose from the Address Book.

2. Choose a name in the Select Names dialog box and click the To, Cc, or Bcc button to add the name (**Figure 39.15**).

3. When you have finished adding names, click OK to return to the new message.

Figure 39.12 Click the New button to begin a new message.

Figure 39.13 Outlook invites you to use Word as your e-mail editor.

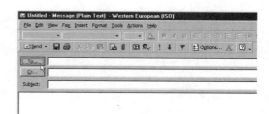

Figure 39.14 A blank message.

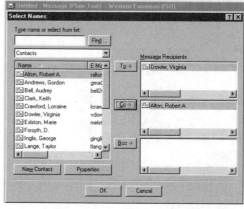

Figure 39.15 Select names in the Select Names dialog box.

Address Check
Book Name

Figure 39.16 Click the Check Name button on the Standard toolbar to verify a name.

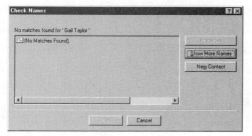

Figure 39.17 Outlook looks in the Address Book for a matching name.

Figure 39.18 Choose Bcc Field from the View menu to see the BCC field.

Figure 39.19 Type the name you want to find in the Find People dialog box.

✔ Tips

- If you want others to receive a copy of this message, you can add e-mail addresses in the Cc box as well.

- To verify that you've typed an e-mail address properly, click the Check Name button on the Standard toolbar (**Figure 39.16**). Outlook checks the address against the Address Book and warns you if no match is found (**Figure 39.17**).

- If you want to display the Bcc field, choose Bcc Field from the View menu (**Figure 39.18**).

- For help finding a name, click the Find button in the Select Names dialog box to open the Find People dialog box (**Figure 39.19**).

- To open the Address Book quickly, click the Address Book button on the Standard toolbar.

STARTING/ADDRESSING

Entering and Formatting the Text

After your message has been addressed, you can type a subject in the Subject box and add your text. The default editor is Outlook's own, but you can also choose to create the text for the message in Word so you can use Word's more advanced text features, such as the thesaurus.

To enter the text:

1. Type a one-line subject in the Subject box.

2. Press Tab to move the cursor to the message area.

3. Type the body of the message (**Figure 39.20**).

To change the format using the Outlook editor:

1. To change from Plain Text format, select the text and choose Microsoft Office Rich Text or HTML from the Format menu (**Figure 39.21**).

   The body of the message is changed to the new format.

2. With Rich Text, use the Formatting toolbar to add formatting (**Figure 39.22**).

   or

   With HTML, you can choose from among the standard HTML styles in addition to using the Formatting toolbar buttons (**Figure 39.23**).

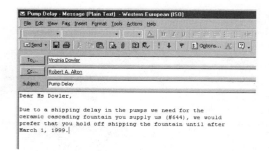

Figure 39.20 A message in Plain Text format.

Figure 39.21 Choose a format from the Format menu.

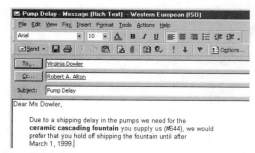

Figure 39.22 A message in Microsoft Outlook Rich Text format.

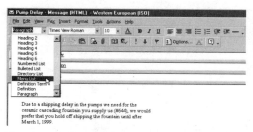

Figure 39.23 You can choose HTML styles and click buttons on the Formatting toolbar.

ENTERING/FORMATTING TEXT

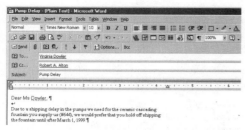

Figure 39.24 The message with Word as the editor.

✔ Tips

■ You can paste text into the body of your message from other applications as well. If you are using the Outlook editor, the pasted text receives the default formatting. If you are using Word, the graphical elements and formatting from Word are retained when you paste the text.

■ If your default format is not HTML, your message won't automatically use the stationery you've selected.

■ If you are using the Word editor, Word's menus and toolbars are available (**Figure 39.24**).

ENTERING/FORMATTING TEXT

Starting a Message Using a Different Format or Program

Outlook allows to you ignore the default mail format settings and start a new message using any of the available formats. It also lets you launch other Office 2000 programs to create messages.

To start using a different format:

◆ From the Actions menu, choose New Mail Message Using and choose a format from the submenu (**Figure 39.25**).

The new message opens in the chosen format (**Figure 39.26**).

To start using a different program:

1. From the Actions menu, choose New Mail Message Using, choose Microsoft Office from the submenu, and then choose an option (**Figure 39.27**).

    The Microsoft program you've chosen opens (**Figure 39.28**).

2. When you have finished using the program to create a message, click the program's Send button.

3. Save the work in the program if you want.

4. Close the program.

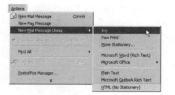

Figure 39.25 Choose a format from the New Mail Message Using submenu.

Figure 39.26 A new message in HTML format.

Figure 39.27 Choose an application from the Microsoft Office submenu.

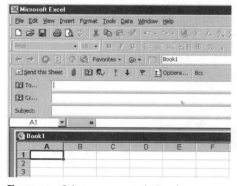

Figure 39.28 A new message in Excel.

Figure 39.29 Click the Options button on the message toolbar.

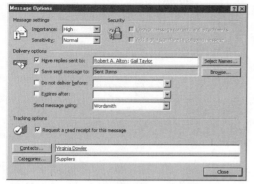

Figure 39.30 Set options in the Message Options dialog box.

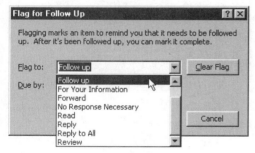

Figure 39.31 Choose a Flag to option.

Figure 39.32 Choose a Due by date.

Setting Message Options

Before you send a message, you can indicate its importance and sensitivity, and you can specify options for delivery and tracking. You can also flag a message for follow-up.

To set message options:

1. From the View menu in any open message, choose Options.

   or

   Click the Options button on the toolbar in a message (**Figure 39.29**).

2. In the Message Options dialog box, set the importance as Low, Normal, or High and the sensitivity as Normal, Personal, Private, or Confidential (**Figure 39.30**).

3. Set the delivery options as needed.

4. Request a receipt if you want to know that a message was read.

5. Click Close when you have finished.

To flag a message for follow-up:

1. Click the Flag for Follow Up button on the Standard toolbar.

2. In the Flag for Follow Up dialog box, select an action from the Flag to pull-down list (**Figure 39.31**).

3. Select a Due by date if you want (**Figure 39.32**).

4. Close the dialog box. A flag appears to the left of the header.

✔ Tip

■ You can set the importance of a message by clicking the Importance: High or Importance: Low button on the Standard toolbar.

Attaching a File or an Item to a Message

You can attach files to your message, and you also attach or include as text the items in your Outlook folders.

To attach a file:

1. From the Insert menu, choose File (**Figure 39.33**).

   or

   Click the Insert File button on the Standard toolbar (**Figure 39.34**).

2. In the Insert File dialog box, select the file you want to attach and click Insert (**Figure 39.35**).

   The file icon appears at the bottom of the message (**Figure 39.36**). The recipient can view the attachment by double-clicking its icon.

Figure 39.33 Choose File from the Insert menu...

Insert File button

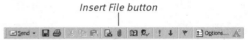

Figure 39.34 ...or click the Insert File button on the Standard toolbar.

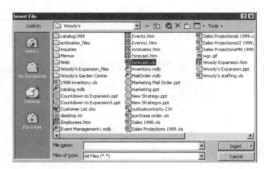

Figure 39.35 Choose a file to insert.

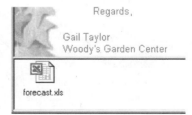

Figure 39.36 A file icon appears in your message.

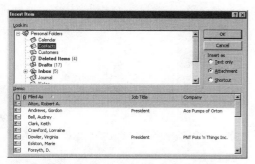

Figure 39.37 Choose an Outlook folder and then choose an item.

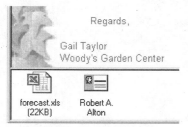

Figure 39.38 An item icon appears in your message.

To attach an Outlook item:

1. From the Insert menu, choose Item.

2. In the Insert Item dialog box, choose an Outlook folder and then choose an item (**Figure 39.37**).

3. Choose whether to insert the item as text, as an attachment, or as a shortcut.

4. Click OK.

If you choose to insert the item as an attachment, an item icon appears at the bottom of the message. The recipient can view the attachment by clicking the icon (**Figure 39.38**) or save the attachment.

✔ Tip

■ You can also attach a file or an item to a reply or a forwarded message.

ATTACHING A FILE/ITEM

Inserting an Object in a Message

Although you can't insert objects in a plain text message using Outlook as the editor, you can insert objects in messages in other formats using the Outlook editor. If you use Word as your editor, you have all the Word Insert methods available.

To insert an object in a Microsoft Outlook Rich Text format message:

1. From the Insert menu, choose Object (**Figure 39.39**).

2. In the Insert Object dialog box, select Create New or Create from File (**Figure 39.40**).

   You can link to a file or display it as an icon in addition to inserting it.

3. If you select Create from File, click the Browse button to locate the file.

4. In the Browse dialog box, select a file to insert and click OK (**Figure 39.41**).

   The object is inserted (**Figure 39.42**).

Figure 39.39. For Microsoft Outlook Rich Text, choose Object from the Insert menu.

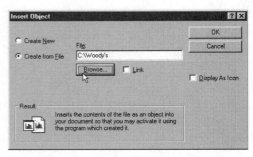

Figure 39.40 Choose an existing file or create a new one.

Figure 39.41 Browse for the file to insert.

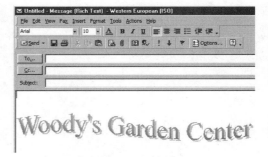

Figure 39.42 A bitmap file is inserted.

Figure 39.43 For HTML format, choose Picture from the Insert menu.

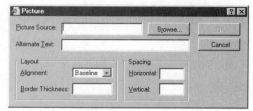

Figure 39.44 Enter settings in the Picture dialog box and browse for the picture.

To insert a picture in an HTML format message:

1. From the Insert menu, choose Picture (**Figure 39.43**).

2. In the Picture dialog box, click Browse to locate a picture for display by a browser (.GIF or .JPG file format) (**Figure 39.44**).

3. Add alternative text and set layout and spacing options if necessary.

4. Click OK.

INSERTING A PICTURE

425

Saving and Sending the Message

When you send a message, the message is automatically placed in your Outbox. If Outlook is not set to send messages immediately, the message is not actually sent until you choose Send/Receive or until Outlook next checks for new mail according to its schedule. You can also save a message for further editing later.

To save a message to complete later:

1. Click Save on the Standard toolbar (**Figure 39.45**).

or

From the File menu, choose Save (**Figure 39.46**).

2. Close the window.

Outlook places the message in the Drafts folder. You can open it there to continue working on it.

To send a message:

◆ Click Send on the Standard toolbar.

Outlook places the message in the Outbox folder, ready for the next Send/Receive.

✔ Tips

■ When you open a message in the Drafts folder or the Outbox folder to edit it, Outlook alerts you that the message has not yet been sent (**Figure 39.47**).

■ You can still edit a message in the Outbox by double-clicking it. After you've made changes, click Send again.

Save

Figure 39.45 Click the Save button on the Standard toolbar...

Figure 39.46 ...or choose Save from the File menu.

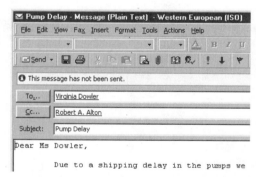

Figure 39.47 Outlook alerts you that the message has not yet been sent.

MANAGING YOUR MAILBOX

Figure 40.1 Organizing the Inbox using folders.

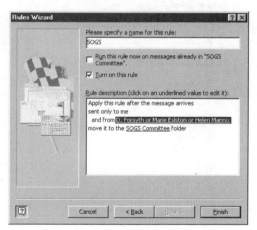

Figure 40.2 Creating a rule using the Rules Wizard.

Outlook provides you with several ways to manage the contents of your Inbox and other mailbox folders. You can create folders and rules to direct and filter incoming messages and to color-code them. An Organize page lets you organize, filter, and move messages quickly and easily (**Figure 40.1**). For help setting up rules, you can turn to the Rules Wizard (**Figure 40.2**). You can even have Outlook delete junk e-mail before you see it.

Moving a Message to a Folder

When you receive messages that you want to keep, it's good practice to file them in a folder named in a way that will help you locate them later.

To move a message to a folder:

1. With the message open or selected in a mailbox pane, click the Move to Folder button (**Figures 40.3** and **40.4**).

2. Select from the menu of folders that opens.

   or

   Select Move to Folder from the menu, and in the Move Items dialog box, select a folder and click OK (**Figure 40.5**).

✔ Tips

- You can select several messages in a mailbox and move them all at once. To select a range of messages, select the first message, hold down the Shift key, and select the last message in the range. To select multiple messages that are not in sequence, hold down the Ctrl key while you click each messages.

- To move a message and establish a rule at the same time, click Organize on the Standard toolbar.

- You can also drag one or more messages from the mailbox pane to the Outlook bar or the Folder list.

Move to Folder button

Figure 40.3 With a message open, click the Move to Folder button on the Standard toolbar.

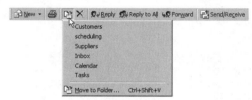

Figure 40.4 With a message selected in the list, click the Move to Folder button.

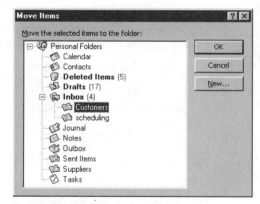

Figure 40.5 The Move Items dialog box.

Figure 40.6 Choose Folder from the New pull-down menu.

Figure 40.7 Select a folder type.

Figure 40.8 Select a place for the new folder.

Figure 40.9 Click Yes if you want to add a shortcut to this folder on the Outlook bar.

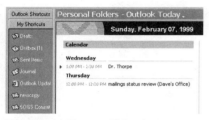

Figure 40.10 The new folder shortcut on the Outlook bar.

Creating a Folder

You can create folders as needed for organizing your messages. You can also create folders to hold appointment, contact, note, and task items.

To create a folder:

1. Click the arrow next to the New button and, from the New pull-down menu, choose Folder (**Figure 40.6**).

   or

   Click the Organize button on the Standard toolbar and then click New Folder in the Organize pane.

2. In the Create New Folder dialog box, name the folder and choose the folder type from the Folder Contains pull-down list (**Figure 40.7**).

3. Select a folder in which to place the new folder. To place the folder at the same level as the other folders, select Personal Folders (**Figure 40.8**).

4. Click OK.

5. Click Yes or No as appropriate if Outlook asks whether you want to create a shortcut for this folder (**Figure 40.9**).

   The folder appears in the Folder list.

   If you choose to add a shortcut, the folder will be listed in My Shortcuts on the Outlook bar (**Figure 40.10**).

✔ Tip

■ You can also create a new folder by clicking the New button in the Move Items dialog box or by clicking the Organize button on the Standard toolbar.

Organizing Messages

Outlook provides a quick way to organize the items in any folder. In the Organize pane, you can set rules, create folders, and change the view of the contents of the current folder.

Figure 40.11 Click the Organize button on the Standard toolbar.

Figure 40.12 Select a folder from the pull-down list.

To use the Organize pane:

1. With a message selected in a mailbox folder (the default is the top message), click the Organize button on the Standard toolbar (**Figure 40.11**).

   or

   From the Tools menu, choose Organize.

   In the Organize pane that opens above your messages, Outlook suggests a move to a folder and a rule for future messages from the same source.

2. To close the Organize pane, click the Close button in the upper right corner.

To move a message:

1. On the Using Folders tab of the Organize pane, accept the suggestion or select another folder from the pull-down list (**Figure 40.12**).

2. Click the Move button.

   Outlook displays a suggested move and rule for the next message.

✔ Tips

- Click the New Folder button to create a new folder, and then select the new folder from the list and click Move.

- You can select several messages in a mailbox and move them all at once.

ORGANIZING MESSAGES

Figure 40.13 Create a color rule.

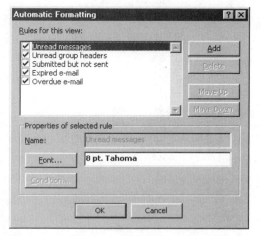

Figure 40.14 Use the Automatic Formatting dialog box to change the formatting for types of messages.

Figure 40.15 Choose colors for junk mail messages.

To organize messages using colors:

1. On the Using Colors tab of the Organize page, accept the suggested rule or use the drop-down lists to create the color rule you want for this and subsequent messages from the same source (**Figure 40.13**).

2. Click the Automatic Formatting button to make further changes to the formatting and the rule (**Figure 40.14**).

3. Click OK to return to the Using Colors tab.

4. Click the Apply Color button to apply the rule.

   Outlook applies the color to those messages in this folder.

5. Click another message in the folder to apply another color rule.

To organize junk e-mail:

1. On the Junk E-mail tab of the Organize page, accept the suggested rule or use the drop-down lists to create the rule you want for this and subsequent junk messages (**Figure 40.15**).

2. Click the Turn On button to apply the rules.

ORGANIZING MESSAGES

Creating a Message Rule

Rules can determine what happens to incoming and outgoing messages.

To create the conditions for a rule:

1. In the Outlook Today window or any mailbox window, click the Rules Wizard button on the Advanced toolbar (**Figure 40.16**).

   or

   From the Tools menu, choose Rules Wizard.

   or

   Click Rules Wizard on the Organize page.

2. Click the New button on the first page of the Rules Wizard.

3. Select the type of rule you want to apply and click Next (**Figure 40.17**).

4. Select the conditions you want to apply and, in the description in the Rule Description area, click People or Distribution List (**Figure 40.18**).

5. In the Rule Address dialog box, select from the contacts list and click OK (**Figure 40.19**).

Rules Wizard button

Figure 40.16 Click the Rules Wizard button.

Figure 40.17 Choose a type of rule.

Figure 40.18 Select the conditions and click to add people.

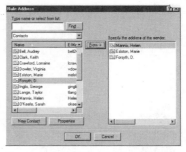

Figure 40.19 Make selections in the Rule Address dialog box.

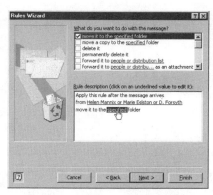

Figure 40.20 Select an action to be taken if the conditions are met.

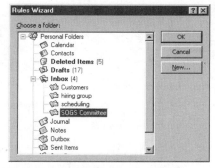

Figure 40.21 Select a destination folder.

Figure 40.22 Name the rule and click Finish.

To create the action for a rule:

1. In the Rules Wizard dialog box, select an action to be taken if the conditions are met and click Specified (**Figure 40.20**).

2. Select the destination folder and click OK (**Figure 40.21**).

3. Add any exceptions, if necessary, and click Next.

4. Specify a name for the rule and click Finish (**Figure 40.22**).

✔ Tip

■ You can edit the rule at any time by double-clicking it in the opening page of the Rules Wizard dialog box.

Moving or Deleting a Folder

You can move a folder in the Folder list, and you can delete a folder and its contents.

To move a folder:

◆ Drag a folder to another folder (**Figure 40.23**).

To delete a folder:

1. Select the folder in the Folder list, and click the Delete button on the Standard toolbar (**Figures 40.24** and **40.25**).

   or

   Press Ctrl+D.

   or

   From the Edit menu, choose Delete.

2. Click Yes to delete or No to cancel the deletion when Outlook asks you for confirmation (**Figure 40.26**).

   The contents are moved to the Deleted Items folder.

✔ Tip

■ At any time, you can open the Deleted Items folder and delete the items within it or right-click the folder in the Folder list and choose Empty "Deleted Items" Folder from the shortcut menu.

Figure 40.23 Drag a folder to move it to a new location.

Figure 40.24 Choose a folder to delete.

Delete button

Figure 40.25 Click the Delete button on the Standard toolbar.

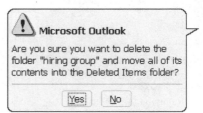

Figure 40.26 Outlook asks whether you really want to do this.

KEEPING A CONTACTS LIST

Figure 41.1 The Contacts list.

When you use the Address Book to address a message, Outlook displays the contacts list. You can use the contacts list to maintain not only the e-mail addresses of friends and associates, but also their phone numbers, addresses, Web page addresses, nicknames, birthdays, and much more (**Figure 41.1**).

You can view the contacts list by clicking Contacts on the Outlook bar or by clicking the Contacts folder in the Folder list (**Figure 41.2**).

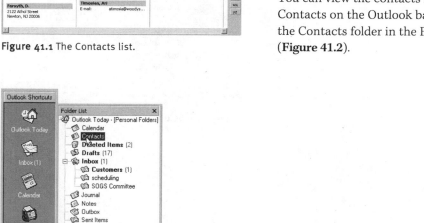

Figure 41.2 Click Contacts in the Folder list or on the Outlook bar.

Setting Contact Options

You can set options for how the names in your contacts list will be sorted and stored.

To set contact options:

1. From the Tools menu, choose Options.

2. On the Preferences tab of the Options dialog box, click the Contact Options button (**Figure 41.3**).

3. In the Contact Options dialog box, choose the name and the filing order from the pull-down lists (**Figure 41.4**).

4. Click OK to return to the Options dialog box.

5. Click OK when you have finished.

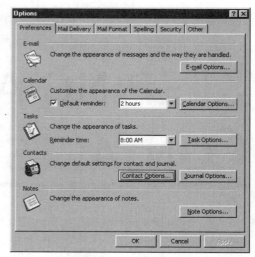

Figure 41.3 Click the Contact Options button in the Options dialog box.

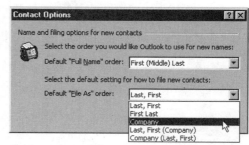

Figure 41.4 Select a File As order.

Figure 41.5 Click the New button to add a contact.

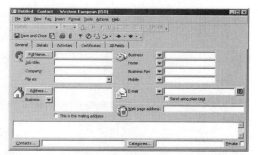

Figure 41.6 Fill in the contact information you need.

Save and Close button

Figure 41.7 Click the Save and Close button when you have finished.

Adding a Contact

You can build your contacts list by entering information about each contact.

To add a contact:

1. Click the New button on the Standard toolbar (**Figure 41.5**).

   or

   Press Ctrl+N.

   or

   Choose New from the File menu and choose Contact from the submenu.

2. In the blank Contact dialog box, fill in as many fields as you want for this type of contact (**Figure 41.6**).

3. When you have finished adding information, click the Save and Close button (**Figure 41.7**).

✔ Tips

- The File As box is filled in for you according to the contact options you set earlier.

- You can add up to three addresses for each contact.

- Double-click the contact in the contacts list to edit it at any time.

Adding a Contact from an E-mail Message

You can add contacts from among your e-mail correspondents quickly and easily. You can fill in other information later if you want to.

To add a contact from an e-mail message:

1. With the message open, right-click the name you want to add to your contacts list in the From, To, or Cc lines above the message text.

2. Choose Add to Contacts from the shortcut menu (**Figure 41.8**).

   In the new Contact dialog box, the name and e-mail address are already filled in (**Figure 41.9**). You can add further information now or later.

3. Click the Save and Close button.

Figure 41.8 Right-click the name, and choose Add to Contacts from the shortcut menu.

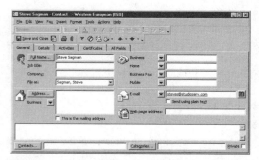

Figure 41.9 Outlook fills in the name and e-mail address.

Figure 41.10 Click a contact in the Contacts list.

Delete button

Figure 41.11 Click the Delete button...

Figure 41.12 ...or choose Delete from the Edit menu.

Deleting a Contact

It's important to keep your contacts list current, so you should delete obsolete entries.

To delete a contact or contacts from the list:

1. Click the contact to be deleted (**Figure 41.10**).

   or

   Click the first contact, press Shift, and click the last contact in a sequence.

   or

   Click the first contact, and press Ctrl while you click other contacts.

2. Click the Delete button on the Standard toolbar (**Figure 41.11**).

   or

   Press Ctrl+D.

   or

   From the Edit menu, choose Delete (**Figure 41.12**).

   The selected contacts are moved to the Deleted Items folder.

✔ Tips

- If you make a mistake, you can drag an item from the Deleted Items folder back to the Contacts folder.

- When you quit Outlook, the default action is to empty the deleted items.

- At any time, you can open the Deleted Items folder and delete the items within it or right-click the folder in the list and choose Empty "Deleted Items" Folder from the shortcut menu.

DELETING A CONTACT

SCHEDULING
TASKS AND MEETINGS

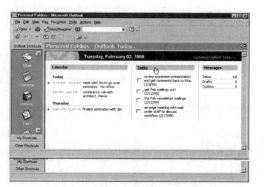

Figure 42.1 The Calendar and Tasks lists in Outlook Today.

In addition to displaying the number of messages waiting to be read, Outlook Today lists the tasks you've assigned to yourself and others and the tasks that others have assigned to you (**Figure 42.1**). A task can be any job or errand that you want to track to its completion.

The day's, week's, or month's appointments, meetings, and events are displayed both in Outlook Today and in the Calendar.

To view your to-do items and schedule in greater detail and to schedule tasks and meetings, you can switch to the Tasks or Calendar window by clicking Tasks or Calendar on the Outlook bar or Folder list.

Looking at Tasks

The tasks list is available on the Outlook bar and in the Folder list.

To view the tasks list:

◆ Click Tasks on the Outlook bar.

or

Click the Tasks folder in the Folder list (**Figure 42.2**).

The tasks list lists the tasks that have been assigned (**Figure 42.3**). The symbols preceding the task names indicate the type of task. See **Table 42.1** for a description of these task symbols.

To view task details:

◆ Select the task in the tasks list, and then double-click it (**Figure 42.4**).

or

Press Ctrl+O.

or

From the File menu, choose Open and then choose Selected Items from the submenu.

✔ Tip

■ You can also double-click a task in Outlook Today or in the Calendar window to view details.

Figure 42.2 Click Tasks in the Folder list or on the Outlook bar.

Figure 42.3 The tasks are listed in the Tasks window.

Figure 42.4 When you double-click a task, you view its details.

Table 42.1

Task Symbols	
SYMBOL	**MEANING**
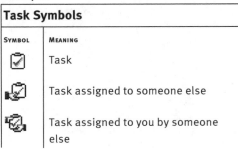	Task
	Task assigned to someone else
	Task assigned to you by someone else

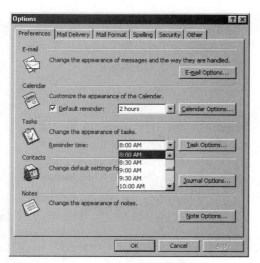

Figure 42.5 Change the default reminder time in the Options dialog box.

Figure 42.6 Change the color coding in the Task Options dialog box.

Setting Task Options

You can set a reminder time and color coding for the tasks in your list.

To set task options:

1. From the Tools menu, choose Options.

2. On the Preferences tab of the Options dialog box, use the Reminder Time pull-down list to change the reminder time (**Figure 42.5**).

3. Click the Task Options button to change the color coding for tasks.

4. In the Task Options dialog box, choose a color for overdue tasks and a color for completed tasks (**Figure 42.6**).

5. Click OK to return to the Options dialog box.

6. Click OK when you have finished setting options.

SETTING TASK OPTIONS

Adding a Task

To add an entry to Outlook's task list, you add a task.

To add a task:

1. In the Tasks window, click the top line of the list (**Figure 42.7**).

   or

   Click the New button on the Standard toolbar (**Figure 42.8**).

   or

   Press Ctrl+N.

2. In the blank Tasks dialog box, fill in as many fields as you need for this task (**Figure 42.9**).

3. When you have finished adding information, click the Save and Close button.

✔ Tips

- Click the Recurrence button if this is a recurring task, and select the recurrence pattern in the Task Recurrence dialog box (**Figure 42.10**).

- To add a task quickly, you can simply type the task in the Click here to add a new task line and use the pull-down calendar to add a due date (**Figure 42.11**).

- You can add a task in any window by choosing Task from the New pull-down menu.

Figure 42.7 Add a new task in the top line of the list.

Figure 42.8 Click the New button to add a task.

Figure 42.9 Fill in the fields for this new task and click Save and Close.

Figure 42.10 Set the recurrence pattern in the Task Recurrence dialog box.

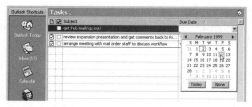

Figure 42.11 Type a new task and set the due date.

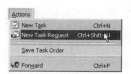

Figure 42.12 Choose New Task Request from the Actions menu.

Figure 42.13 From the New submenu, choose Task Request.

Figure 42.14 The dialog box now contains a box for the assignee.

Figure 42.15 You can also click the Assign Task button in the Task dialog box.

Assigning a Task

You can also create a task and assign it to someone else.

To assign a task:

1. From the Actions menu, choose New Task Request (**Figure 42.12**).

   or

   From the File menu, choose New, and then choose Task Request from the submenu (**Figure 42.13**).

   The Task dialog box now includes an assignment box (**Figure 42.14**).

2. In the Tasks dialog box, fill in as many fields as you need for this task.

3. Type an e-mail address in the To box or click the To button to select a name from the Address Book.

4. When you have finished adding information, click the Send button.

   The request is sent to your Outbox.

✔ Tips

- The task assignment appears in your list but it is up to the person to whom you've assigned the task to report progress on the task.

- When you open a task, you can click the Assign Task button to change a task to a task request (**Figure 42.15**).

ASSIGNING A TASK

Changing the Status of a Task

All tasks begin with the status Not Started. As you progress with a task, you can update the status for the task until you reach Completed.

To change the status of a task:

1. Double-click the task to view the task details.

2. In the Task dialog box, use the pull-down list to change the status (**Figure 42.16**).

3. Select a % Complete setting if you want (**Figure 42.17**).

4. Click the Send Status Report button if you want to send an e-mail message with information about your progress on the task (**Figure 42.18**).

   Outlook displays a message containing details about the task.

5. Add an address and comments and send the message.

6. When you have finished, click the Save and Close button.

✔ Tips

- If a task was assigned to you by someone else, Outlook sends a status report automatically to the person who assigned the task when you change the status.

- In views that show the task status, you can quickly change the status by using the Status drop-down list (**Figure 42.19**).

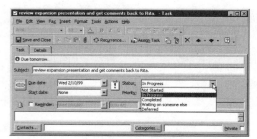

Figure 42.16 Select a status from the pull-down list in the Task dialog box.

Figure 42.17 Change the % Complete.

Send Status Report button

Figure 42.18 Click the Send Status Report button to complete and send a report.

Figure 42.19 You can also change a task's status in the list.

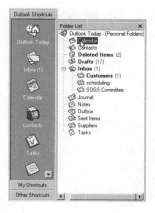

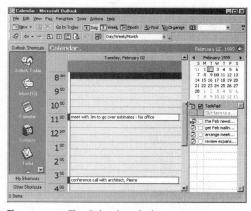

Figure 42.20 Click Calendar in the Folders list or on the Outlook bar.

Figure 42.21 The Calendar window.

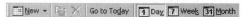

Figure 42.22 Click Day, Week, or Month on the Standard toolbar...

Figure 42.23 ...or choose from the View menu.

Viewing the Calendar

The calendar is available from the Outlook bar and from the Folder list.

To view the Calendar:

◆ Click Calendar on the Outlook bar.

or

Click the Calendar folder in the Folder list (**Figure 42.20**).

The calendar appears in the view in which it was last displayed (**Figure 42.21**).

To change the number of days displayed:

◆ Click the Day, Week, or Month button on the Standard toolbar (**Figure 42.22**).

or

From the View menu, choose Day, Work Week, Week, or Month (**Figure 42.23**).

VIEWING THE CALENDAR

Setting Calendar Options

You can set a reminder time and color coding for the events in your calendar.

To set calendar options:

1. From the Tools menu, choose Options.

2. On the Preferences tab of the Options dialog box, set a default reminder time for calendar events (**Figure 42.24**).

3. Click the Calendar Options button.

4. In the Calendar Options dialog box, set the days in the work week (**Figure 42.25**).

5. Click the Time Zone, Add Holidays, and Resource Scheduling buttons to adjust those settings, if necessary, clicking OK to return to the Calendar Options dialog box.

6. If you want, click the Free/Busy Options button to share your calendar with others and, in the Free/Busy Options dialog box, set the publishing options and click OK (**Figure 42.26**).

7. Click OK to return to the Options dialog box.

8. Click OK when you have finished setting options.

✔ Tip

■ If your network server has FrontPage server extensions installed, you can publish your free/busy information on a corporate intranet. Enter the URLs in the Free/Busy Options dialog box and click OK to use the Microsoft Web Publishing Wizard.

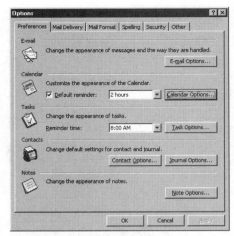

Figure 42.24 Change the default reminder time in the Options dialog box.

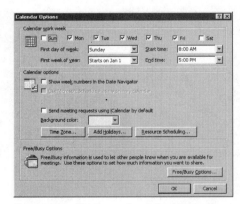

Figure 42.25 Set the work week and calendar appearance.

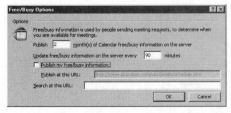

Figure 42.26 Share free/busy information using the Free/Busy Options dialog box.

Figure 42.27 Type an item in the calendar.

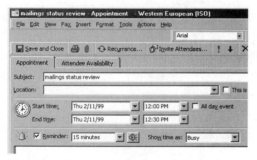

Figure 42.28 Use the Appointment dialog box to add details.

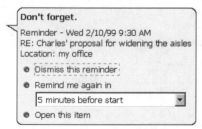

Figure 42.29 Outlook reminds you at the time you specified.

Adding an Item to the Calendar

The quickest way to add an item to the calendar is to simply select the day and hour and type the entry. You can also use the Appointment dialog box.

To enter an appointment:

1. Select the day and the time in the calendar.

2. Type a short description of the appointment into the text box that appears and then press Enter (**Figure 42.27**).

3. Drag the border of the appointment box to block off the time required.

To fill out the Appointment form:

1. Select the day and the time by moving though the calendar.

2. Double-click the time that the appointment should begin.

3. In the Appointment dialog box, fill in the Subject and change the End Time, if necessary (**Figure 42.28**).

4. If you want to receive a reminder, check the Reminder button.

5. Type a time or use the pull-down list to specify how soon before the meeting to make the reminder.

6. Click Save and Close.

   At the time for the appointment, Outlook will open a reminder (**Figure 42.29**).

✔ Tip

■ To edit an appointment, double-click the entry in the Calendar window.

Creating a Recurring Appointment

A recurring appointment can be a meeting that is scheduled daily, a reminder to yourself to complete a monthly report, or even an annual event such as a birthday.

To create a recurring appointment:

1. If the appointment is not already open, double-click it in the calendar to open it.

2. On the Appointment tab of the Appointment dialog box, click the Recurrence button on the Standard toolbar (**Figure 42.30**).

3. In the Appointment Recurrence dialog box, specify the recurrence pattern (**Figure 42.31**).

4. Click OK to return to the Appointment dialog box.

5. Fill in the details you need.

6. Click Save and Close.

✔ Tip

■ When you double-click a recurring appointment in the calendar, Outlook asks whether you want to open this occurrence or the series of appointments (**Figure 42.32**).

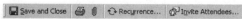

Figure 42.30 Click the Recurrence button on the Standard toolbar.

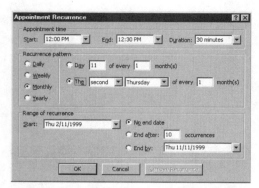

Figure 42.31 Set the recurrence pattern in the Appointment Recurrence dialog box.

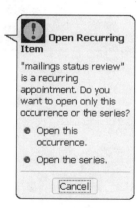

Figure 42.32 You can view this occurrence or the series.

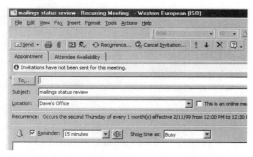

Figure 42.33 Invite the attendees by adding their names in the To box.

Figure 42.34 Use the Attendee Availability tab to find a meeting time.

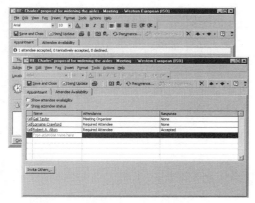

Figure 42.35 Outlook shows the status in the Meeting dialog box.

Inviting Attendees to a Meeting

You can also create a meeting to which other attendees are invited.

To invite attendees:

1. If the appointment is not already open, double-click it in the calendar.

2. On the Appointment tab of the Appointment dialog box, fill in the meeting particulars, typing a location or selecting from the pull-down list.

3. Click the Invite Attendees button on the Standard toolbar.

4. In the To text box, type e-mail addresses for invitees (**Figure 42.33**).

   or

   Click the To button to select from the Address Book, and click OK when you have finished adding names.

5. To check on attendee availability, click the Attendee Availability tab.

6. On the Attendee Availability tab, if your group is set up to share free/busy information, Outlook collects calendar information and displays it. Find a suitable meeting time by dragging the meeting block in the calendar (**Figure 42.34**).

7. Click Send.

   Outlook sends invitations to the people you specified.

✔ Tip

- When attendees respond to the request, the Attendee Availability tab displays their responses (**Figure 42.35**).

Adding an All-Day Event

An all-day event appears as a banner at the top of the day, leaving you free to schedule meetings and appointments.

To add an all-day event:

1. If the appointment is not already open, double-click it in the calendar.

2. On the Appointment tab of the Appointment dialog box, check the All Day Event button (**Figure 42.36**).

3. Fill in other pertinent information.

4. Select the number of days for the event.

5. Choose how you want the event time to be displayed: Free, Tentative, Busy, Out of Office.

6. Click Save and Close.

   Outlook displays a banner for the event in the calendar (**Figure 42.37**).

✔ Tips

■ To delete a calendar entry or task, select the entry or task and click the Delete button on the Standard toolbar.

■ If you delete an upcoming meeting, Outlook asks whether to inform the other attendees.

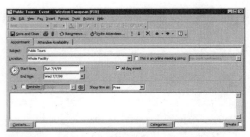

Figure 42.36 Check the All Day Event box and select the days.

Figure 42.37 Outlook displays a banner for the event.

INDEX

INDEX

INDEX

INDEX